# Table of Contents

# List of Figures and Tables

# Preface

There are many good texts on the administration of the public library. Most are designed to give the student or beginning administrator insight into the work and problems that a practicing director is likely to experience. However, this preparation often places the library in the abstract, as a physical entity with a well-established role in the community, a governance soundly prepared to take positions on budget and planning, and a staff well trained to undertake its prescribed tasks.

My first job in a public library was as a director. Little that I had learned in graduate school could be applied to cope with a leaky roof, bad plumbing, a meager budget and a host of other problems that were of far greater priority than the development of a book selection policy, implementation of a program budget and design of a new organization chart, as I had been instructed.

It wasn't that my instructors were unqualified or that the texts were out of date or their authors out of touch with reality. Years later I could return to my lecture notes, and to my texts, and find the background I needed to aid in critical decisions. Experience prepares us for understanding the theory we are presented in the classroom. Unfortunately, the classroom precedes the experience for too many administrators.

## PURPOSE OF THIS BOOK

The intent of this book is to discuss the fundamentals of public library administration, leavened with what I have gained from experience. It will not present a caretaker's approach. As figures given in Chapter 1 will show, the majority of public libraries in the United States—from the very smallest rural library to the great urban institutions with millions of volumes and hundreds staff of members—are relatively poor. It is my assumption that the professionals who will be preparing to direct these institutions in the future do not need a handbook on maintaining the status quo. They do need insight into the available alternatives by which they can compete for more adequate support, develop more effective staff, take advantage of new technology, communicate more effectively with their communities and expand their usefulness to their clientele.

This book, then, is for those who are interested in changing the public library, in developing its value and importance in the nation. It is for those who may be willing to take some risks. It is my hope that some of the information contained in this volume can reduce those risks, but many of the options discussed are certain to be controversial.

## FOCUS OF THIS BOOK

It is generally recommended that an author restrict his or her subject to allow greater focus. Based on my experience, I believe that the same principles of management can be applied whether a library is large or small. If a library is inadequately financed—whether it serves 25,000 people or 500,000—its administrator must correct that through improved communication, better planning and identification of alternative financial sources.

However, the very small library, serving a population of 5,000 or fewer, does have severe restrictions. Some small communities are able to support libraries through high taxes or other resources and offer truly excellent levels of service. Regrettably, they are in the minority. The best recourse for the small public library is cooperation with other libraries. While this book has some sections on cooperative approaches, that is not its primary emphasis.

The large metropolitan library also represents an unusual case and merits an individual approach for management and development. The recent studies undertaken by Lowell Martin on the Atlanta, Philadelphia and San Francisco public libraries reveal some common features, but also indicate many individual differences. History, local governmental policies and practices, financial conditions, demographic trends and a host of other factors dictate the need for more individualized solutions.

# MANAGING THE PUBLIC LIBRARY

Donald J. Sager

Knowledge Industry Publications, Inc.
White Plains, NY and London

*Professional Librarian Series*
Managing the Public Library

**Library of Congress Cataloging in Publication Data**


Sager, Donald J., 1938 -
   Managing the public library.

   Bibliography: p.
   Includes index.
   1. Public libraries—Administration. I. Title.
Z678.S228   1984      027.4      84-9675
ISBN 0-86729-097-8
ISBN 0-86729-096-X (pbk.)

In short, this book should be most useful to the administrator of a public library serving a population of more than 5,000 and less than 500,000. There are certainly differences in personnel administration between Kingston, NY, and Columbus, OH, but they are minor when these libraries are compared with the Chicago Public Library and its employment procedures.

## STRUCTURE OF THIS BOOK

This book is divided into 11 chapters. Major emphasis has been placed on finance, personnel management and organization, and the adoption of new technology, since I believe that these areas represent the greatest concern for the administrator today and into the foreseeable future.

### History and Philosophy

Chapter 1 focuses on the historical and philosophical foundations of the library and presents a picture of what the institution is today. There are commonalities among all sizes of public libraries, and some characteristic differences. These, as well as demographics and the range of services, usage and staffing, are covered.

### Governance

While there is no uniform type of governance for public libraries, the most common forms, including municipal, county, regional, school district, association and special library districts, are covered in Chapter 2. The chapter looks at the role of the library board of trustees, the most common policy-making body for public libraries. A major emphasis is procedures the administrator can use in working with the board, since this is the primary path for implementing change in the institution. An administrator must also understand how to work effectively with elected officials and the role of the library in the political process.

### Finance

Most libraries rely on the property tax for much of their financial support. There are a variety of other sources as well, and the administrator should have an understanding of basic taxation, public finance, grantsmanship, investment practice and entrepreneurship. These are covered in Chapter 3. Separate sections of this chapter discuss budgeting and the different types of budgets in common use today, operating and capital improvement budgets, the management of endowments and restricted funds, grantsmanship, and the steps that have to be considered when retrenchment must occur.

### Planning

Planning is being given heavy emphasis in the profession thanks largely to the efforts of the Public Library Association. One of the major responsibilities of library administration and governance is planning and evaluation of progress toward relevant goals. Chapter 4 is devoted to the planning process; data gathering techniques; participatory models appropriate for planning; the definition of goals, objectives and strategies; prioritization; implementation and evaluation. The chapter also considers some of the reasons many library administrators are reluctant to invest enough time to develop a sound plan.

### Personnel

The most important resource in any public library is its personnel. Recruiting, retaining and developing staff are fundamental responsibilities of library leadership. Other concerns are motivating personnel and removing those who are incompetent or ineffective. No single style or method is appropriate, but there are some techniques and policies which have proven to be particularly effective in public library settings. These are covered in Chapter 5. Personnel policies, recruitment and retention, affirmative action and fair labor standards, evaluation, and motivation techniques are discussed in some detail.

### Organization

Certain functions are common in almost every public library, regardless of its size and staff. Chapter 6 presents an overview of circulation, adult reference services, juvenile and young adult services, technical services, extension services and audiovisual units. The role and staffing of these units can vary widely, depending upon the goals and priorities of the library.

Chapter 6 also looks at basic administration and organizational alternatives. Traditionally, libraries have followed the pattern of local government and private business in using a hierarchical organization. Other options are also considered. The philosophies underlying service to different groups are discussed, with an emphasis on meeting needs in the community. Organization of the administrative section of the library is also covered, and the changes new technologies are bringing to many of the library's functions are considered.

## Automation

The impact of automation is given greater attention as the subject of Chapter 7. Because libraries are relatively labor intensive, computerization offers good potential for improved use of tax funds, more effective use of personnel and better control of resources. Beyond this, automation holds the promise of vastly improving the quality of library service and offering far greater access to the resources held by other institutions. Automation is changing traditional services, such as circulation and acquisitions. It is also creating new services, including online database searching and the provision of public access microcomputers.

Some of the considerations involved in planning and implementing automation are considered in this chapter. Computerization is certainly not an end in itself, and careful planning and justification are essential. Estimation of cost, financing alternatives, selection of automated systems, conversion and training personnel for effective use of automation are included.

## Public Relations

Because a number of recent outstanding books on public relations for libraries are available, this subject is not treated at length in this book. However, I am very much aware of the importance of effective communications for the success of this institution. Surveys of public library users and nonusers reveal that the typical citizen knows relatively little about the resources and services the institution can provide. This may result in part from public prejudice against the use of tax funds to support public relations activities but also from the library's lack of knowledge regarding marketing research, the use of volunteers and effective programming.

Chapter 8 considers the role of public relations and marketing research and the role of the administrator, the board and the staff in the public information program of the library. Topics include marketing basics, community relations, effective use of the media, the role of graphic design, programs and exhibits, the role of volunteers and the function of Friends organizations.

## Construction, Design and Maintenance

The perfect library remains to be constructed, and libraries vary with the varied needs of the community, collection, staff and administrator. Still, there are some practices and standards that merit consideration in planning for the more perfect public library. In Chapter 9, I discuss public library design in historical perspective and the planning of public library facilities, including the planning team.

The different factors in designing the single or central library and the branch or regional library are considered in terms of space estimates and public and staff areas. Other topics include interior design and finishes, lighting, communications, development of specifications and contracts, maintenance and custodial services, and finally a section on insurance.

## Cooperation

Although this book will not emphasize interlibrary cooperation, Chapter 10 does address the subject, because of its importance both now and in the future. No library, regardless of its size and level of financial support, can afford to satisfy all the needs of its clientele. This is particularly true of the public library.

The chapter defines interlibrary cooperation and discusses library federations, cooperative systems and trends in multitype cooperation. Cooperation does cost money. It often results in delays and sometimes in a loss of autonomy. Nonetheless, there may also be substantial savings, particularly in the use of new technology.

## The Future

Finally, Chapter 11 focuses on renewal and future growth of the public library. No text concerning the public library should end without a summary of both the challenges and the potential that face staff, governance and administration in the future. The chapter also discusses some of the frustrations and demands that are unique to the public library and that can lead to stagnation and deterioration of service.

Suggestions for keeping the institution and its staff and governance responsive and evolving are given. Chapter topics include staff development and training, participation and exchange, self-evaluation, the use of innovation, assessment of community change, the impact of local, state and federal governments upon the local library, and finally a section on the importance of leadership.

This book is largely built on my 20 years of experience in library management, and I owe the staff, boards, public officials and general public of the communities I have served a debt of gratitude for the support and opportunities they have given me.

Considerable credit is due Adrienne Hickey, Senior Editor of Knowledge Industry Publications, for her assistance in developing the manuscript from its original outline and for her cogent suggestions at critical points in its completion. Ellen Smith, Assistant Editor, deserves high praise for making this manuscript infinitely more readable and for her keen insight and talent in converting what I wrote into what I really meant.

*Donald J. Sager*
*April 1984*

# 1

# What Is the Public Library?

Libraries have existed as long as people have valued the preservation of written knowledge. Until the Renaissance, however, libraries usually belonged to private individuals, monasteries or universities, and access to collections was limited.

## THE FIRST PUBLIC LIBRARIES

America is often credited with originating the concept of the public library, but in fact Europe had public libraries before the New World was discovered. If we define a public library as one that is publicly owned, we would have to include the national libraries, such as France's Bibliotheque Nationale, founded in 1480. Libraries at state-supported universities could also be considered "public." Both national and university libraries were open to qualified scholars with references. At a time when literacy was the exception rather than the rule, this was probably sufficient.

Many cities also established local libraries. Lyons created its library in 1530, and Aix-la-Chapelle in 1556.[1] The French Revolution and the Napoleonic era also furthered the creation of public libraries, in France and other European nations. Shortly after the revolution began, all religious libraries were declared national property, and their collections were confiscated. The same fate befell books belonging to the nobility and their supporters.

Millions of volumes were collected and distributed to various cities. Although hundreds of thousands were also lost or damaged in the process, a large portion of the more valuable titles ended up in the Bibliotheque Nationale. Unfortunately, most of these collections in France and elsewhere in Europe languished for lack of use. The educated were still limited in number.

## Colonial Libraries

Libraries in colonial America were also limited in number. Where they existed at all, most belonged to ministers or governmental leaders, who had both the education and the need for a collection of books. The majority of the early settlers were too occupied with carving a new nation out of the raw wilderness to have time for libraries.

There was also a small number of university libraries in the colonies. However, these collections were not intended for the public, and the emphasis was heavily on custodial care, not on promoting circulation or use. A classic story involving an early librarian at Harvard illustrates this concern for preservation. A professor met the librarian crossing the Yard one evening and asked how the library was doing. The librarian responded that it was in good condition: All the books but one were in their places, and he was on his way to retrieve that one now.

The first known attempt to establish a public library in the colonies came in 1656 when Captain Robert Keayne, a Boston merchant, donated his book collection to the city, on the condition that the community construct a suitable facility for it.[2] Boston constructed a building with a separate room for the library, but records indicate that the collection was poorly used and that little effort was made to keep the collection current and growing. The library was lost when the building burned in 1747. New Haven benefitted from a similar bequest by Governor Eaton in 1659. Unfortunately, the collection consisted of less than 100 volumes and was so poorly used that the city subsequently sold the collection.

These are but two of many reports of public libraries being established through the generosity of some visionary citizen. None of these early libraries had the benefit of continuing, permanent tax support. All relied on the benevolence of early donors, and their life seemed to depend on the degree of endowment given to support the collection and on the successful management of the endowment by its trustees.

The first recorded effort to establish and maintain a public library in America using governmental funds occurred in 1697, at the port of Annapolis, MD, when Governor Nicholson proposed that the king allocate part of the money granted to the colony for arms and ammunition to establish a free public library.[3] Such a service was created in the State House, where it continued until 1704, when the collection burned—a common fate for many of the early collections.

## Subscription Libraries

Tax-supported public libraries did not rapidly increase in numbers. Instead, the 18th century witnessed the growth of the subscription library. Groups of individuals would pool their assets to create a basic collection of books and then maintain the collection with a regular subscription fee. This type of library had its origins in England and Scotland, but Benjamin Franklin is often credited with transplanting the idea to Philadelphia in 1731.[4] He formed the Philadelphia Library Company with 50 of his friends. Each contributed two pounds and then paid ten shillings annually for dues. Before the end of the Revolutionary War, more than 50 subscription libraries existed in New England. Their numbers increased rapidly in the early 19th century, as educational levels rose and printing became more commonplace.

Subscription libraries took many forms—as social libraries, lyceum libraries, mercantile or mechanic's libraries, YMCA libraries and workers' libraries. There could be several libraries in a community, and some might specialize in certain subjects, such as fiction or business. They ranged in size from a few hundred to more than 100,000 volumes, depending upon the number of subscribers and the fee. Subscription fees may seem relatively small in retrospect, but in their time they could still represent a barrier to joining. For example, the Mercantile Library Association of Baltimore, founded in 1839, had a collection of more than 31,000 volumes by 1875, when the annual membership cost was $5.[5] In 1875 the sum of 5¢ would pay for a very good meal.

## TAX-SUPPORTED LIBRARIES

The concept of a general library accessible to the public without charge and supported by local or state taxes did not develop until the latter half of the 19th century. It appeared first in the New England states, where the library tradition was strong and educational levels were high. Peterborough, NH, is generally credited with being the first community to establish a permanent public library supported by public funds.[6] In 1833 the community's town meeting decided to use the State Literary Fund, generally used for public schools, to purchase books for a local library. Supplemented with donations, the books were housed in the general store that also served as the community's post office. The storekeeper/postmaster took on triple duty as the first librarian.

In 1849 New Hampshire passed a law permitting the levy of local taxes to support public libraries.[7] Massachusetts followed suit in 1851, as did Maine in 1854. Not until after the Civil War did other states begin to follow this lead.

## Municipal Libraries

Establishment of the Boston Public Library in 1854 really laid the foundation for the American public library movement.[8] The library was founded through a combination of local gifts and approval of local tax support—and after many years of discussions. It benefitted from many rich bequests, such as Edward Everett's collection of American documents, the Bowditch library of mathematics and science, and the George Ticknor library of Spanish history and literature. The city also had the foresight to recruit Charles Coffin Jewett from the Smithsonian Institution library as its first librarian.

Through the latter half of the 19th century, many major cities followed Boston's example. After many years of operating a variety of public reference libraries, city officials in New York combined all their libraries in 1895 to form the New York Public Library.[9] The Brooklyn Public Library was formed in a similar fashion in 1897. In 1896 the New Orleans Public Library was founded. The Los Angeles Public Library came into being in 1889 as a municipal agency, although it still charged subscription fees to its users. Many subscription libraries were gradually converted to tax-supported institutions through subsidies granted by local officials. To this day, there are some "association" libraries, which are governed by a privately elected board but are largely supported by direct grants from the local government.

## School-based Libraries

A number of public libraries had their origins in public school systems. Maintenance of a public library was considered in some cities to be the logical extension of the public school system, and school district libraries still exist in both large and small cities throughout the United States. The St. Louis Public Library began in this way, and the Kansas City (MO) Public Library continues to function as a department of the local school system, with the librarian reporting to the Board of Education.

### The Philanthropy of Andrew Carnegie

The greatest impetus to the American public library movement came from the philanthropy of Andrew Carnegie, the Scottish immigrant who founded what became U.S. Steel Corp. and became one of the richest men in the world. In 1881 Carnegie made the first of several gifts to Pittsburgh, for the purpose of constructing a free public library. From that point until his death in 1919, he donated $56,162,622 for the construction of 2509 library buildings throughout the English-speaking world.[10] More than $40 million alone was given to communities in the U.S. for the construction of 1679 public library buildings in 1412 communities.

A critical part of his philanthropy, however, was the requirement that local communities receiving grants for construction must then contribute 10% of the construction cost annually for the operation of the library and the maintenance of the collection. While some communities later reneged on this pledge, the majority committed themselves to the support of their local library on a permanent basis.

### THE GROWTH OF PUBLIC LIBRARIES

The growth of the American public library can be documented in several landmark reports. *Public Libraries in the United States of America*, prepared by the U.S. Bureau of Education in 1876, estimated that, when this nation was founded in 1776, there were only 29 public libraries with total holdings of 45,623 volumes[11]. As we have noted, these were not truly public in our sense of the word. By 1876 the number had increased to 3682 libraries, possessing more than 12 million volumes.[12] Even those figures were misleading, for the government's statistics were based upon a definition of public libraries as those "open to the public without charge or for a nominal fee only."

The most accurate source of information today on the status of public libraries is the *Library General Information Survey: Public*

*Libraries*,[13] or LIBGIS III, which was conducted by the National Center for Educational Statistics (NCES), a federal agency. Several surveys have been conducted by NCES during the past decade; LIBGIS III estimates that there were 8456 public libraries in the U.S. in the fiscal year 1977-78. *The American Library Directory*, 36th edition (1983) lists 8822 public libraries,[14] while the *Survey of State Library Agencies, 1977* reports 10,134 public libraries.[15] The number and types of libraries in the U.S. today will be discussed later in this chapter.

Whatever the exact numbers, clearly the public library movement survived the Great Depression and changing needs, and has evolved into a stable institution, making a continuing contribution to the local community.

## PHILOSOPHY OF SERVICE

As this brief historical perspective suggests, those active in establishing the early public libraries had only a general idea of the role that instition should play. Libraries were established to provide as many citizens as possible with reading material appropriate for either their education or their entertainment. Even Andrew Carnegie never spelled out a purpose for the thousands of libraries his grants constructed throughout the world, other than to function as public libraries. Yet as time has passed and the demand for public funds has increased, there has been greater need for the public library to define its purpose and role in the community.

### Statements of Purpose

During the past several years, chiefly because of the Public Library Association's encouragement of long-range planning, hundreds of libraries have examined their function and role, and have adopted statements of purpose. Examination of these statements reveals many common features.

First, most public libraries are committed to serving all of the people in the area that is taxed for their support. Second, most believe they should provide materials for loan, furnish information on matters pertinent to their clientele, and conduct programs of an educational, cultural or informational nature for the benefit of the public. Some also add a recreational function, in providing materials of quality for the enjoyment or enrichment of their patrons. In addition, many public libraries note that the resources they offer should be in a variety of formats appropriate for the community.

**Public Library Association Principles**

In 1982 the Public Library Association adopted a statement of principles it recommended as a basis for local libraries. The document reviews the function of maintaining free access to resources, considers the varying clientele that should be served, discusses the variety of resources and services that should be provided in modern society, and identifies that primary role of maintaining a free and informed democratic society. An excerpt from the document summarizes this role:

> Without regard to race, citizenship, age, education level, economic status, or any other qualification or condition, public libraries freely offer access to their collections and services to all members of the community. The ideas and information available through public libraries range the entire spectrum of knowledge and opinions. The uses made of the ideas and information are as varied as the individuals who seek them. Only the public library offers that unique opportunity for each person by providing an open and non-judgmental environment in which the individual and his interests are brought together with the universe of ideas and information. No other institution provides this service for the American people.[16]

**Local Differences**

Despite this recommendation and the many common features that exist among public libraries, there is also a host of differences. Not every community may feel a commitment to *extend* service to everyone, believing rather that emphasis should be placed upon those who already regularly use the collection and services. While every community may support in principle the concept of free access to a balanced collection of literature, some may hesitate to grant unrestricted access to all age groups or to literature that some members of the community find controversial. Some libraries allow the use of their meeting facilities by all groups, while others would not permit religious groups or those presenting only one point of view on public issues.

Public libraries are still local entities, creations of a community and its citizens, reflecting local customs and the heritage of the region and state, influenced by issues unknown at the national level. The local library has always been fiercely autonomous, often to the frustration of those hoping to encourage more interlibrary cooperation. But in that insularity are pride and a determination to have the public library reflect the character of the community. As long as both the minority and the majority can contribute to the definition of the role of the public library, there need be no alarm about the absence of a uniform purpose for the public library.

Chapter 4 will discuss the steps an administrator can take in developing a statement of purpose for the library. This process should be based on a solid understanding of the community and of current trends in library and information science, as well as in the city and state.

## NUMBER AND TYPE OF LIBRARIES

As previously noted in this chapter, there are differing estimates of the number of public libraries in the United States, but the most complete source of information is the LIBGIS III survey. As noted, the survey was conducted in the fiscal year 1977-78, and data were first released in 1982. The statistics are based upon a complete survey of all public libraries serving 100,000 or more people (334) and of 1117 randomly selected libraries serving different size populations, which formed a basis for statistical projections about all public libraries. No survey has been conducted since that is as comprehensive and as statistically sound.

Table 1.1 shows the types and total number of library outlets reported by the survey. Comparison with the previous LIBGIS survey of public libraries, conducted four years earlier, indicates some growth in the number of central and branch libraries, but the total number of library outlets, particularly bookmobile stops, decreased.[17]

There are many different ways to categorize public libraries— by size, budget, staffing, etc.—but NCES used population served, which usually conforms to the population being taxed for supporting the library. NCES defined six categories, which are indicated in Table 1.2. Although the public library has often been considered primarily an urban institution, Table 1.2 shows that the greatest numbers of public libraries are in the smaller villages and towns of the U.S. Of course, larger city libraries may have numerous outlets

**Table 1.1: Public Library Outlets, 1977-78**

| Type of Outlet | Number |
|---|---|
| Central or single unit | 8,456 |
| Branches | 6,527 |
| Bookmobile stops | 49,343 |
| Deposit collections | 6,630 |
| Total | 70,956 |

Source: National Center for Educational Statistics, *Preliminary Report, Library General Information Survey, LIBGIS III: Public Libraries, 1977-78* (Washington, DC: NCES, 1982).

in the form of branches, bookmobile stops and deposit collections, but even when those outlets are tabulated, the smaller and medium-sized city libraries remain in the majority.

The branch or neighborhood library is the most common public library facility other than the central library itself. There is no clear relationship between the population served and the number of branches, but Table 1.2 also indicates the range found by the survey. Bookmobiles can be considered an alternative to branch libraries, particularly for those libraries serving large geographical areas. The bulk of bookmobile stops are provided by libraries that serve between 10,000 and 250,000 people.

**Table 1.2: Libraries by Population Served, 1977-78**

| Population Served | Number of Library Systems | Number of Library Outlets | Number of Branches per Library System Median | Mean |
|---|---|---|---|---|
| 500,000 or more | 54 | 6,149 | 22 | 28 |
| 250,000-499,999 | 61 | 4,663 | 11 | 12 |
| 100,000-249,999 | 219 | 13,310 | 5 | 6 |
| 50,000-99,999 | 444 | 14,525 | 1 | 2 |
| 10,000-49,000 | 2,176 | 23,100 | — | 1 |
| Under 10,000 | 5,502 | 9,209 | — | — |

Source: LIBGIS III.

For purposes of comparison, this book will designate libraries serving more than 500,000 people as major urban libraries; those serving 100,000 to 499,999 people (combining two LIBGIS categories) as urban libraries; those serving 10,000 to 99,999 people (also combining two LIBGIS categories) as medium-sized city libraries; and those serving fewer than 10,000 people as small community libraries. This typology may not apply everywhere, for some rural systems encompass several counties without a single medium-sized or urban community, yet still serve comparatively large populations.

## EXTENDING SERVICE

Since the implementation of the federal Library Services and Construction Act in 1964, most state library agencies have made a strong effort to extend library service to as much of the population as possible, either through the creation of new libraries in areas previously unserved or through extension of existing library service boundaries, funding of reciprocal agreements or similar contractual approaches. Current estimates, based on the 1980 Census, are that existing public libraries serve all but 6,433,633 Americans—that is, all but 2.8% of the population.[18]

The actual number of unserved persons may be much greater, however, because of varying state policies. Some states, for example, may support regional libraries that theoretically serve large geographic areas, but that, in reality, do not provide convenient access for large portions of the populace.

## FINANCIAL RESOURCES

Levels of financial support among public libraries also vary considerably. A large urban library may actually seem poor, despite its large tax base, when its budget is compared on a per capita basis to that of a suburban library.

### Revenues

Total revenues for all public libraries in the U.S. in the 1977-78 fiscal year were more than $1.5 billion. This figure is not very impressive when one considers that Americans spent $5.5 billion for toys during that same fiscal year.[19] Furthermore, almost one-third of the total revenue was received by the 54 libraries serving major urban areas. The largest category of libraries, those 5502 serving small communities, received only 7.9% of the revenues, or approximately $124 million.

The primary source of this revenue was local property taxes, which accounted for almost 75% of the total. State funds represented only 6.6% of income, and federal funds accounted for almost 8%. Fees, fines, contractual services and donations provided the balance of more than 10%. Generally, the larger the library, the more likely it was to receive a higher percentage of its income from state and federal sources and from other nontax sources, such as grants, donations and endowments.

## Per Capita Expenditures

The most common measure of relative poverty or adequacy of support among public libraries is per capita income, the total revenues of the institution divided by the population to be served. In 1977-78, the average per capita support for libraries was $7.30.

LIBGIS III does not provide data on per capita revenues for the different categories of libraries, but it does report per capita expenditures by categories. Among the major urban libraries, more than half exceeded the average per capita level of support. Only a third of the urban and medium-sized city libraries were as fortunate. Among public libraries serving smaller communities, less than 25% spent above average levels. Over 7% of those small community libraries had expenditures of less than $1 per capita, and almost 30% spent less than $3 per capita. By way of contrast, 5.6% of the major urban libraries reported expenditures exceeding $15 per capita.

## Allocation of Revenues

Another insight on the public library can be gained by examining how revenues are allocated. Table 1.3 summarizes the percentage of revenues allocated to different budget categories. Major urban and urban libraries tended to devote somewhat higher percentages of their budgets—up to 60% in some instances—to personnel and smaller percentages to the collection. Libraries serving small communities tended to devote less to personnel—as low as 50%—and more to materials.

Table 1.3: Revenue Allocation by Budget Category, 1977-78

| Budget Category | Percent of Revenues Allocated |
|---|---|
| Salaries | 57.9 |
| Materials | 15.7 |
| Maintenance and utilities | 11.7 |
| Binding | 0.4 |
| Equipment | 1.4 |
| Other (fringe benefits, interest, travel, etc.) | 12.7 |

Source: LIBGIS III.

## USAGE AND SERVICE

American public libraries loaned almost 1 billion items in 1977-78, and, despite gloomy forecasts to the contrary, this usage has continued to increase slowly since 1975. There is almost no difference in volume of usage between rural and urban library readership. Libraries serving major metropolitan areas account for 21% of circulation, but over 40% of all circulation is accounted for by those libraries serving areas with less than 50,000 population.

Circulation is only one measure of service. Another indicator is reference and directional service. NCES used statistics collected by participating libraries on their reference and directional questions during a typical week in the fall of 1978. Table 1.4 presents a breakdown of the questions asked by size of library. While the larger public libraries had relatively light circulation, they experienced a much heavier load of reference service, which reflects the nature of their collections and staffing.

## COLLECTIONS

LIBGIS III reported holdings of 439 million books in American public libraries in 1977-78. In addition, there were 6 million bound periodicals, almost a million current periodical subscriptions, more than 15 million units of microform, 9 million sound recordings, 430,000 films and 29 million other miscellaneous items. A majority of these materials are held by a comparatively small number of institutions. Forty-eight public libraries each hold more than 1

**Table 1.4: Reference and Directional Assistance (Weekly Figures), 1977-78**

| Population Served | Number of Libraries | Reference Questions Number | Reference Questions Percent | Directional Questions Number | Directional Questions Percent |
|---|---|---|---|---|---|
| 500,000 or more | 54 | 1,437,386 | 80.0 | 358,463 | 20.0 |
| 250,000-499,999 | 61 | 217,682 | 58.9 | 152,150 | 41.1 |
| 100,000-249,000 | 219 | 255,605 | 44.4 | 320,106 | 55.6 |
| 50,000-99,999 | 444 | 424,286 | 69.9 | 182,597 | 30.1 |
| 10,000-49,999 | 2,176 | 493,884 | 48.0 | 534,884 | 52.0 |
| under 10,000 | 5,502 | 221,528 | 50.1 | 220,431 | 49.9 |

Source: LIBGIS III.

million volumes. Libraries serving the major urban areas accounted for almost 25% of all the books held in American public libraries, and urban libraries in general accounted for almost 50%. The percentage of audiovisual materials and microform that is held in urban and suburban libraries is even greater, revealing the limited impact these newer media have had to date among smaller and rural libraries.

More than half of all American public libraries (4701) possessed fewer than 20,000 volumes. Although these small community libraries devote a greater percentage of their budgets to materials than do larger libraries, they do not have the resources to develop adequate collections. However, size of collection is no guarantee of quality, and other measurements provide some indication of the collection's currency and utility to the community. Among the evaluative methods recommended by the Public Library Association in its guide *Output Measures for Public Libraries*[20] is turnover, which is calculated by dividing circulation by the total book collection of an agency. Average collection turnover among American public libraries was 2.25 in 1977-78. Table 1.5 summarizes turnover in the different categories of libraries.

## STAFFING

It can safely be assumed that public libraries are not major employers. LIBGIS III reported that slightly less than 100,000 persons are employed in American public libraries. That represents a ratio of one library employee per 2306 persons in this nation. Of that number, almost 39,000 (about 41%) were classified as being professional, i.e., possessing a master's degree in library science

## Table 1.5: Collection Turnover, 1977-78

| Population Served | Number of Libraries | Turnover |
|---|---|---|
| 500,000 or more | 54 | 2.0 |
| 250,000-499,999 | 61 | 2.58 |
| 100,000-249,999 | 219 | 2.41 |
| 50,000-99,999 | 444 | 2.64 |
| 10,000-49,999 | 2,176 | 2.35 |
| Under 10,000 | 5,502 | 1.74 |

Source: LIBGIS III.

from an ALA-accredited institution. Slightly less than 52% were clerical or technical, and just under 7% were maintenance.

The urban and major urban libraries accounted for 45% of all professional employees. Thirty-nine percent of the available professional employees were employed in medium-sized cities, leaving only 16% of the remaining professional staff to serve in those 5502 libraries serving communities with population of 10,000 or less. These LIBGIS statistics may be somewhat misleading, since many personnel are considered professional in smaller libraries, because they have assumed professional responsibilities and roles even though they lack a professional degree.

## THE "TYPICAL" PUBLIC LIBRARY

These statistics give a general picture of American public libraries. Despite the many commonalities, it is difficult, if not impossible, to arrive at a description of a "typical" public library. However, using the categories defined earlier does allow us to draw profiles of typical public *libraries*, based on the size of the population served.

### The Small Community Library

The most common category is the public library serving a population of less than 10,000 persons; 64% fall into this group. They have a circulation of less than 30,000 annually, a collection of less than 40,000 books, an annual budget of less than $50,000, and three or fewer full-time-equivalent employees, one of whom is likely to have some advanced training. Four out of five of these small community libraries are located in rural areas.

## The Medium-sized City Library

Medium-sized city libraries, serving between 10,000 and 99,999 persons, are the next most common category. They represent the greatest degree of variation, perhaps because they include both suburban libraries, which are likely to have comparatively high levels of support, and poorer rural libraries. There are 2620 libraries in this category, representing 29% of all libraries and accounting for 37% of all revenues. Their budgets range from $50,000 to $1 million. Collections range from 20,000 to 300,000 volumes, and circulation falls between 100,000 and 300,000 per year. There are extremes in the levels of per capita support, from as little as $3 to above $15 per capita.

If we divide this category into those libraries serving 10,000 to 49,999 people and those serving 50,000 to 99,999 people, roughly half of the libraries in the first group would be located in rural areas and half in suburban areas. In the second group, libraries are almost equally divided among urban, rural and suburban communities.

## The Urban Library

There are 280 libraries that fall into the urban category, serving populations of between 100,000 and 499,999 people. They account for almost 47% of all library revenues, 21.6% of the collections, 23.5% of all staff and 23% of all circulation. Each is likely to have a well-developed branch system. Staff size averages more than 100 persons, and 40% are professional. Almost all these libraries have budgets exceeding $400,000, and collection size ranges from 100,000 volumes to more than 1 million. Circulation falls between 600,000 and more than 1 million. The vast majority of these libraries are in urban areas; some are suburban, and a very small number are rural regional systems.

## The Major Urban Library

Finally, there are those 54 major urban public libraries, serving more than 500,000 persons. Almost a third of all library revenues go to these institutions, which employ more than 30% of all library staff and which account for more than 20% of all circulation and 25% of all collections. Almost all have collections in excess of 1 million volumes. They maintain between 22 and 28 branches, on the average, and provide nearly half of all public library reference service in the United States. Staff size averages 450 persons.

## SUMMARY

Not until the middle of the 19th century did the concept of local tax support lead to the creation of permanent public libraries in major cities such as Boston. The philanthropy of Andrew Carnegie provided the major impetus for the American library movement, not only because of his contributions for construction but also because of his insistence upon a local commitment in tax funds to maintain the collection and facilities.

During the early years of public libraries, little thought was given to the role of the institution beyond the furnishing of books to satisfy the needs of the general public. As libraries have grown in service to the community and public needs have evolved, greater care has been taken to avoid duplicating services offered by other educational and social services agencies, to extend service to all in the community, and to provide resources and services that educate, inform and enrich. Nonetheless, there are still many local differences in attitude as to what the library should be in its own community.

The review of the most recent comprehensive statistics on the American public library offered here should aid in defining what that institution looks like today. A single "typical" public library cannot really be defined. Instead it is possible to define the public library through categories based on the size of population served: the major urban library, the urban library, the medium-sized city library and the small community library.

In sum, the public library is a complex organization with an evolving role in the community it serves but founded upon a rich tradition of service and a belief in the importance of providing balanced and current information to all.

## FOOTNOTES

1. Elmer Johnson, *A History of Libraries in the Western World*, 2nd edition (Metuchen, NJ: Scarecrow Press, Inc., 1970), p. 219.

2. *Ibid.*, p. 313.

3. David Ridgely, *Annals of Annapolis* (Baltimore: Cushing & Brother, 1841), p. 92.

4. U.S. Department of the Interior, Bureau of Education, *Public Libraries in the United States of America; Their History, Condition and Management: Special Report, Part I* (Washington, DC: Government Printing Office, 1876), p. 35.

5. *Ibid.*, p. 875.

6. Johnson, *History of Libraries*, p. 359.

7. *Ibid.*, p. 359.

8. *Ibid.*, p. 359.

9. *Ibid.*, p. 361.

10. George S. Bobinski, *Carnegie Libraries: Their History and Impact on American Public Library Development* (Chicago: American Library Association, 1969), p.5.

11. Bureau of Education, *Public Libraries*, p. iii.

12. *Ibid.*, p. iii.

13. National Center for Educational Statistics, *Preliminary Report. Library General Information Survey, LIBGIS III: Public Libraries, 1977-78* (Washington, DC: NCES, 1982).

14. *American Library Directory*, 36th edition. (New York: R.R. Bowker Co./Jacques Cattell Press, 1983), p. x.

15. Barratt Wilkins, *Survey of State Library Agencies, 1977* (Occasional Papers No. 142. Urbana, IL: University of Illinois Graduate School of Library Science, 1976), p. 36.

16. Public Library Association Principles Task Force, *The Public Library: Democracy's Resource* (Chicago: Public Library Association, 1983).

17. National Center for Educational Statistics. *Statistics of Public Libraries, 1974 (LIBGIS I)* (Washington, DC: Government Printing Office, 1978).

18. Donald J. Sager, *The American Public Library* (Columbus, OH: Online Computer Library Center, 1982), p. 5.

19. *Predicasts Basebook* (Cleveland: Predicasts, Inc., 1982), p. 678.

20. Douglas Zweizig and Eleanor Jo Rodger, *Output Measures for Public Libraries: A Manual of Standardized Procedures* (Chicago: American Library Association, 1982).

## SUGGESTIONS FOR FURTHER READING

*Fact Book of the American Public Library*, compiled by Herbert Goldhor. Occasional Papers No. 150. Urbana, IL: University of Illinois Graduate School of Library Science, 1981.

Marshall, John David, ed. *An American Library History Reader*. Hamden, CT: Shoe String Press, Inc., 1961.

Shera, Jesse H. *Foundations of the Public Library: The Origins of the Public Library Movement in New England, 1629-1855*. Chicago, IL: University of Chicago Press, 1949.

# 2

# Public Library Governance

The basis for all local public libraries is state legislation. Before a county, municipality, township, school district or any other local government entity can establish a library, levy taxes for its support, accept gifts or bequests toward its maintenance, hire staff, appoint a board or take any of the other steps associated with creation of a public library, enabling state legislation must exist.

Every public library administrator should become familiar with the powers and responsibilities granted to the local library by his or her state's statutes. Many state library agencies have prepared booklets containing these statutes along with attorney generals' opinions, regulations, calendars listing appropriate dates for submittal of budget requests to local authorities, information on applying for state and federal aid, and similar data essential to library administrators and trustees.

State law will normally define the types of public libraries that may exist, usually prescribed by the jurisdiction in which the institution may operate—municipal, county, regional, school district, township or special library districts; all of these will be described in this chapter. Public libraries may fall under the direct supervision of the elected officials of those jurisdictions, or they may function independently, with their own elected board of trustees. In general, the statutes will specify what officials are responsible for the library and what their powers are. Sometimes, statutes also define the powers and responsibilities of the library administrators; more commonly, these powers are delegated by the governing authorities of the library.

## ROLE OF THE STATE LIBRARY AGENCY

State library agencies are sometimes given certain responsibilities in conjunction with local libraries, such as administering state aid programs, setting standards, certifying administrators, sponsoring training programs or promoting interlibrary cooperation. Rarely, however, does their jurisdiction extend down to the point that they are given direct powers over local libraries. Legislators and local officials are generally very careful to maintain local control over agencies such as schools, libraries and similar services. In some states, other agencies, particularly those linked to state grant programs, may also exert indirect influence upon local libraries.

Every public library administrator should be aware of the responsibilities and authority granted the state library agency. State library agency policies relating to interlibrary loan, reciprocal borrowing, minimum standards for public service and similar programs can influence local policies and services. Generally, these policies are coupled with grants to aid the local library in meeting requirements or to offset any local expenses associated with their implementation.

## FEDERAL-STATE RELATIONSHIP

The federal role in local libraries is limited, because authority for the administration of any federal funds earmarked for public libraries has been delegated to state library agencies. The primary vehicle for federal support of public library service is the Library Services and Construction Act of 1964 (LSCA), which developed from earlier leglislation designed to extend public library service into rural areas previously unserved. LSCA extended assistance to all areas and has been amended to emphasize service to groups such as the economically disadvantaged, the handicapped and older persons.

To participate in LSCA programs, state library agencies must prepare a state plan of development, identifying goals, objectives, and strategies and priorities for implementation. Based upon its priorities, the state library agency can then use federal funds for

projects it develops, such as regional libraries, interlibrary cooperation, automation or reference support. Or it can encourage the
development of such projects by local libraries in the state and
award contracts for services to those libraries that will further its
state plan.

Many communities also receive substantial allocations through
the federal General Revenue Sharing Act, and originally library
services were a priority for these funds. However, the library
administrator and the library board of trustees must lobby directly
before the local government jurisdiction that receives the grants.
Funding from federal sources is discussed in greater detail in
Chapter 3.

## MUNICIPAL LIBRARIES

In a survey of 2478 cities, conducted in 1977 by the International
City Management Association, 891, or 49% of the total that
responded, indicated the local public library was a municipal
entity.[1] Probably the most common political jurisdiction is the city.
Smaller communities may have a village or town government.

### The Dual Nature of Municipal Libraries

In a municipal setting, the public library administrator usually
reports to a board of trustees who are appointed by the mayor and
approved by the city council. Thus the library may function as a
somewhat autonomous organization, because of the powers granted
to the library board, but it is also a department of city government.
That dual nature has both advantages and disadvantages. It
becomes particularly complicated during budgeting and when
contracting for services.

Many state laws grant authority to the local board to enter into
contracts and make purchases, as well as to hire and fire personnel.
Yet, as a department of city government, the library can also call
upon the purchasing and maintenance departments and the civil
service commission or city personnel department. In practice, many
municipal libraries are flexible in their relationship with local
government. If it is more economical or more expeditious  to
contract outside of city government, the library will do so. Or
tradition may dictate, for example, that the library's electrical work
will always be performed by the city electrical department.

Some cities do not directly charge a library for these services, and this will influence the decision. Increasingly, however, cities and villages are developing accounting systems that charge back the agency being served. Another factor an administrator must consider is whether the city accounting department also includes overhead expenses in charging for work or services. This could wipe out any benefits, such as volume discounts through the purchasing department.

Certain prerogatives are likely to be retained by the library board, particularly control over finances and over personnel. A city may, however, elect to exercise its control by its appointments to the board, in order to maintain its dominance in these areas. Sometimes state and local ordinances cloud the question of the board's authority. For example, state law may grant the library board authority over personnel, but it may also require that all municipal employees fall under a civil service or merit system and tie this in turn to a city personnel department.

An administrator in a municipal library soon learns that, despite the statutes, there is a great deal of flexibility. Effectiveness depends upon learning where it is necessary or expedient to use municipal or village services and when it would be advantageous to contract outside that system.

## Relationship with Local Officials

A general discussion on building rapport with public officials occurs later in this chapter, but some mention must be made here about relations with the mayor and city council. Most mayors and council members are extremely busy, no matter what size the city or village. Except in larger cities, mayors and council members usually have other full-time jobs, and they have commitments to their constituents. It is often difficult for them to keep current on all aspects of municipal government. Nonetheless, they do need to be kept informed on matters affecting their constituents.

In undertaking work in a council member's ward, for example— such as planning for a new branch, major changes in service or retrenchment—it is important to keep the appropriate council member informed. With this link, that individual is more likely to be committed to the library and will be in a position to respond to questions or complaints from constituents. However, maintaining such communications can become time-consuming.

For problems that affect library service in general, the library administrator should communicate with the mayor first. In a larger city, the mayor may not be directly available. In such cases, it is important that the aide who has been assigned as liaison can reach the mayor and can explain the nature of the problem. Because many states and local governments require public bodies to hold open meetings, it is rarely possible to discuss important issues and reach decisions with a library board privately, and then to discuss those issues with the mayor or a particular council member. However, it is always better if elected officials hear the bad news about a branch being closed in their wards from the library administration before they learn of it from media or their constituents.

**Understanding Local Politics**

To work effectively in a city or village, an administrator must always set up good communications or suffer the consequences when budget time rolls around. Establishing good communications requires an understanding of local political organization. If the administrator doesn't know the local political organization, then he or she had better find someone who does. Often, this is where the board can be of the greatest service to the library, in identifying which actions to avoid and who should be contacted prior to taking an action.

Most municipalities operate through a series of council committees, and often the library is assigned to one. While this committee rarely has significant power over the daily operations of the department, it does handle matters such as ordinances the library may request and approves appointments to the board. It may also have some role in the budget review process, although that is generally the prerogative of a finance committee. An effective library administrator must establish good communication with the chairperson of the committee to which the library is assigned and, if possible, with some of the more influential members. These individuals can function as important advocates for the library in council decisions, particularly if they are kept regularly informed of new programs and services as well as problems.

As a municipal department head, the library administrator must also understand the role of other departments and build rapport with them. Nothing could be worse—from the point of view of either taxpayers or another department head—than for the library to duplicate a service already being offered by another department or to assume the prerogatives of another department.

In summary, to be effective in a municipal library, the administrator must understand that form of government and become knowledgeable about the elected officials with whom he or she works.

## COUNTY LIBRARIES

There are many parallels between city and county government, and much of what was said in the preceding section applies to county libraries. The chairperson or president of the county board usually has many of the powers granted to the mayor, and the other members of that board have roles comparable to those of city council members. County government can be as complex as municipal government; it may be even more complex, depending upon the responsibilities given to the county by the state.

### Relationship with County Government

As between a municipality and its public library, lines of authority are often blurred between the county and a county library system. A library board may have the option of using county services or of contracting outside for certain services such as data processing or maintenance. While there are exceptions, county libraries located in metropolitan or suburban areas are not likely to be as closely tied to county government as are those in rural sections of the nation. County libraries tend to be larger than municipal libraries and may have broader taxing powers. Often they have the size and capacity to establish their own finance, personnel or printing functions and so do not rely upon the county for such services. The traditional emphasis of many counties upon bridge and road maintenance, welfare and health may also contribute to the autonomy that often exists in county library systems.

### Relationship with Other Local Governments

A complication for many county libraries is the existence of municipal libraries within the county, making jurisdiction an important issue. In those villages or cities where library service does not exist, the county librarian has the additional responsibility of building good rapport with local officials and keeping them aware of any important library activity, such as a planned branch.

Sometimes contractual services may be necessary between

local units of government and the county library. While it can happen that a municipal library will contract with surrounding communities or even with the county to provide a service, it is more customary for the county library to assume that role.

At one time, county libraries were widely promoted because they represented a larger unit of service and an alternative to the limited tax resources of town and village libraries. It was also believed that county library service would eliminate barriers and artificial boundaries to library use. More recently, however, the regional library has become the recommended entity, particularly for rural areas.

## REGIONAL LIBRARIES

The regional library owes its existence primarily to the Library Services and Construction Act. As previously noted, the origin of this federal legislation was a concern for extending library service into rural regions. Vast areas and relatively low tax bases made it extremely unlikely that rural villages or townships could afford to establish adequate public libraries. In some regions, even the county did not have sufficient population and tax base to support a library.

### Impact of Regional Libraries

Accordingly, many state library agencies and state library associations promoted passage of enabling legislation for the creation of public library systems that covered one or more counties. In some instances, regional libraries could be established in smaller jurisdictions, but the major impact was on the sparsely populated rural areas of the nation. LSCA grants were often used to provide an incentive for the establishment of regional libraries and to maintain them in their first years of operation, until they could demonstrate their effectiveness and obtain continuing local funding, generally from county grants.

The success of this effort soon became evident. The percentage of Americans unserved by public libraries dropped from more than 20% in 1950 to less than 3% in 1980.[2] While many regional libraries continue to depend on federal and state grants for their maintenance, many have made the full transition to local support.

### Relationship with County and State

Governance of regional libraries varies, but generally consists of a board with trustees appointed or elected by the participating counties. Their numbers are often proportionate to the population served. Links with elected county officials are not likely to be as close as would be the case with a county library and will vary depending upon the degree of support provided by the county. There may be a closer linkage with the state library agency because of its role in the origins and funding of the regional library.

Some state library agencies maintained regional libraries as branches of their library development work in the state, particularly if there was difficulty in gaining local leadership to create independent regional libraries. This happened infrequently, however, and it is now uncommon to find a state library agency providing local library service.

## SPECIAL LIBRARY DISTRICTS

A survey entitled *Public Employment in 1978*, prepared by the U.S. Bureau of the Census, reported that 52% of all public library employees worked for municipalities, and 25.5% were employed by county jurisdictions. The next largest group—8%—worked in special library districts.[3] This category also includes regional libraries, because they represent an unusual jurisdiction not confined to traditional entities such as the municipality, the county, the school district or the township.

### Why Special Districts?

Special districts evolved in metropolitan areas where bonding and legal requirements often led to the establishment of separate jurisdictions for water and waste treatment, health, parks and recreation, and similar services that were inadequately handled by townships, villages and other such smaller entities. Major projects often required larger tax bases, which led local units of government to sacrifice some of their autonomy to furnish these desirable services to their communities.

Special library districts are most common in suburban areas, where they may encompass parts of townships, villages or unincorporated areas of the county. They can include any unit of government in their jurisdiction, but almost always their creation is subject to referendum by those who would be included in the district and would subsequently be served and taxed by the district.

## Authority

Special library districts usually have elected boards of trustees, to ensure local control of the district. As a result, special library districts are given greater authority than other public libraries, including the right to levy taxes and issue bonds without review or approval by city councils or the county board. Special district taxes may, however, require referendums.

As a special district, the library assumes full responsibility for managing its operations, although it may elect to contract with local township or village authorities for certain services such as payroll or maintenance.

## Benefits

In some respects the special district represents a trend that runs counter to efforts made by the library profession to encourage larger units of service. However, although the special district tends to be small, it is a practical response to modern urban development, with its hodgepodge of suburbs, townships and unincorporated areas. Many of these smaller units lack the tax base to do more than handle public safety and public works. Residents may find themselves without library service, despite a comparatively high population density. For this reason, the special library district is a valuable means for extending library service, especially when there is no county library or when satisfactory contractual arrangements cannot be reached with libraries in adjoining cities and villages.

## OTHER FORMS OF GOVERNANCE

There are a few other types of public library, and it is quite possible that some new form of public library governance is currently being drafted in some state house. *Public Employment in 1978* identified 7.8% of public library employment in townships and 1% in school districts.[4] There are also association libraries, which remain in many states.

## Townships and School Districts

Traditionally, townships are governed by a group of trustees, often three in number, elected by the residents. Some states permit townships to establish public libraries and to appoint boards to administer them. These are customarily small libraries, most frequently in rural areas.

School district libraries conform to the service area of that district. The school board may directly function as the policy-making body for the public library system, as it does for the Kansas City (MO) Public Library. Or it may appoint a board of trustees to assume that role and grant the trustees full autonomy, as in the case of the Cleveland (OH) Public Library. State law determines which form governance will take.

School district libraries have their origins in the belief that the local board of education should assume responsibilities not only for the preparation of young people for their place in society, but also for the continuing education of the adult population. While many public school systems sponsor adult continuing education programs and many school district libraries remain as strong entities, the number of school district libraries is not likely to increase. Few school districts are anxious to assume additional responsibilities in these times, when so many school boards are embattled and must struggle to maintain present services.

## Association Libraries

In some communities, the collections of subscription and society libraries were absorbed by the public library when it came into existence. Some communities elected another course, finding it simpler to allocate an annual grant to the association library from the city or county budget, in return for public access to the collections and services. The governance of the association library then continued as before, electing its board and officers from among its membership. (Sometimes active membership declines, or the group may be transformed into a Friends organization; however, the association remains a legal entity.) Many states passed legislation permitting this method of supporting a public library, and many local officials found it expedient. In difficult times, it is easier to cut back on the appropriation than it would be if the library were a department of government.

The Youngstown and Mahoning County (OH) Public Library

is an example of an association library that has continued to this day. Because of Ohio's unique library financing method, the library has not had to rely on an annual appropriation from city and county. Instead, it may approach the voters directly for property taxes to supplement its other income. It is not likely that association libraries will increase in numbers in the future, although those that remain should continue to function effectively, unhampered by their unusual governance.

## CITY MANAGERS AND COUNTY ADMINISTRATORS

Many communities and counties have hired professionally trained administrators to manage their daily operations. This has been especially popular in medium-sized cities with a sufficient tax base and budget to warrant this step. Working with these executives is no different from working with elected officials—they, too, should be kept informed regarding the problems and activities of the library.

When the library does not have a board or the board is purely advisory, the library administrator is, in effect, a department head reporting to the executive or a top assistant and can be expected to function like any other department head. The mayor and the city council, or the county president and the county board, will continue to function, but their role will more likely focus upon policy and planning, with the executive assuming the operational responsibilities.

In theory, the library should benefit from the professional leadership provided by the executive and from the insulation from the traditional politics of city and county government. In practice, much will depend upon the authority granted the city or county manager, the leadership style that individual employs and the autonomy traditionally granted to the library. In addition, the amount of political contact is likely to remain high under professional city or county management. Elected officials still need to be kept informed, and they still have final authority over the budget and major policy decisions.

## THE PUBLIC LIBRARY BOARD

By far the most common form of governance for local public libraries is the lay board of trustees, although in Alaska, Maine, New Mexico, and Texas some other governance options are permitted.[5]

**Number and Powers of Trustees**

The number of trustees on public library boards varies from state to state, and even within a state, depending upon the type of political jurisdiction the library serves. Usually, however, the number ranges from 7 to 12 persons. Trustees are most commonly appointed by the chief elected official of the jurisdiction, but sometimes the county board or city council or the city or county executive may have this responsibility. In most cases, appointments require confirmation by the city council or county board.

Trustees are almost always required to be residents of the jurisdiction they serve. Terms of office are prescribed by state statute, as are the powers of the board, but both may also be contained or amplified in local ordinances.

The customary role of the trustee is to approve the library's policies of service, supervise the expenditure of funds and develop a plan for the effective operation of the library. Responsibilities for daily operation are vested in a chief library administrator, and it is customarily the responsibility of the board to select that individual.

The considerable powers granted library boards include the following:

• Constructing, leasing, purchasing and selling facilities for library service;

• Establishing regulations governing the use of the library's collections and services, including the levying of fines or other penalties for the abuse of borrowers' privileges;

• Levying taxes (to varying degrees);

• Entering into contracts;

• Accepting donations and establishing trust funds and other special financial accounts; and

• Establishing personnel policies and pay schedules.

**Composition of the Board**

In theory, the library board is representative of the community. However, there are seldom young people on a board, since tradition or statute usually requires that the trustees be of voting age. There is likely to be a high percentage of professionals on a board and a minority of blue collar workers. Those active in civic affairs are also overrepresented on a typical board, for this position is generally highly respected in the community.

Trustees are seldom compensated, except for occasional expenses. Thus, the typical trustee is a volunteer, willing to devote considerable time to the improvement of local library service, with the chief reward being the attainment of that goal.

## THE ROLES OF TRUSTEE AND ADMINISTRATOR

While statutes may prescribe the functions or roles of the administrator and the trustee, these job descriptions will probably require clarification. It is generally assumed that the trustee is concerned with policy, and the administrator is expected to implement that policy. But who has the responsibility for suggesting or initially drafting the policy? Furthermore, who interprets that policy?

### Typical Roles

In practice, it is customary for the administrator, based upon problems or needs reported by the library staff, to identify the need for a policy. The administrator usually drafts a recommended policy, based upon research on the problem, examination of policies employed by other libraries and professional experience. The policy is reviewed by the board, which may accept, modify or reject the recommendation. Whatever the outcome, the administrator then has the responsibility for implementing the decision and interpreting the policy for the staff and public.

The same roles apply in planning and in the development or modification of services. Again, the board's role is to review, approve, modify or reject. On occasion, the board can certainly initiate policies and programs, but usually the administrator is expected to gather the facts—such as costs, need, personnel and facilities requirements—and to organize the program into a form that allows its importance to be judged in relation to other priorities the library board has previously set.

### Role Reversal

There are times and situations where roles become confused. A board that is frustrated by a librarian reluctant or unable to take the initiative on policies and planning may begin proposing its own policies and plans. The librarian may then be in the position of reviewing those actions and implementing them, with modifications based upon his or her knowledge of the impact they will have on public service. This reversal of roles may continue for years, until either the board or the administrator changes and the new party challenges the old order.

A library board that has assumed administrative responsibilities is often—but incorrectly—called a strong board, and an administrator whose prerogatives and role have been assumed by the board is defined as weak. In fact, a board that has confused its role with that of its administrator will be both weak and ineffective. Lacking time to weigh thoroughly the implications of its policies and plans, it will have to satisfy itself with only limited achievements. The board's refusal to either change or motivate its administrator to assume his or her responsibilities in presenting policies, programs and plans for review and approval will also weaken the library.

### "Strong" Boards and Administrators

A truly strong board is one in which the members can interpret the needs of the community and continually review and modify policies, plans and programs to keep them relevant. To achieve this, the board must demand that its administrator prepare the reports and gather the information essential to this task. Such a board should question the administrator and his or her staff to ensure they have explored the alternatives and have arrived at the best recommendation.

A strong administrator is one who is able to take the initiative in proposing solutions to problems facing the institution and who can be creative in proposing new programs or modifying existing services to meet the changing needs of the community. The administrator should also welcome the questions from the board as an opportunity to review the study that led to a recommendation.

Both a strong board and a strong administrator are needed if a library is to be successful in achieving its goals. Without the resultant creative friction, the institution may stagnate.

## COMMITTEE STRUCTURE

The most effective boards have working committees to examine in greater detail the policies, programs and plans that will eventually be brought to the full board. Regardless of the size of the library, there is rarely enough time during a brief monthly meeting to satisfy everyone's concerns about the institution. Furthermore, committee assignments also more effectively employ the abilities of individual board members.

While the number and responsibilities of committees will vary from one library to another, it is well to keep the number limited and the responsibilities broad. Rather than separate committees for finance, personnel, facilities, equipment, public relations, program and the myriad other concerns likely to confront a library, two or three committees, each given a distinct set of responsibilities, will be best. On occasion, a special ad hoc committee will be needed, perhaps to screen new candidates for the administrator's job or to serve as a nominating committee for the next year's officers, but these are best given a brief portfolio and a short run.

A board committee can focus upon details that might bog down the progress of a full board meeting. It may find deficiencies in a report or recommendations, which can then be remedied before final presentation. It can initiate ideas for new programs or goals without the formality encountered in a regular board session. A committee may make time for greater staff input to introduce varied ideas and facts, thus giving both the board and the staff greater insight into an issue and into one another's concerns.

Some libraries also function with an executive committee, usually consisting of the officers of the board. This may be very useful, since it permits rapid action to be taken—assuming, of course, that full authority has been granted by the board for such action. Problems occur when executive committees continually bypass or fail to report their actions to the full board. Therefore, the authority of such a committee should be determined by the board. Further, such authority should not be exercised too regularly, or attendance at full board meetings will soon wane.

## BYLAWS

For both the board and the administrator, the most important document in maintaining efficient relations is a set of bylaws. This document should contain the following elements:

• Authority granted to the board;

• Number of members and terms;

- Procedures for removing or replacing members;

- Officers and their responsibilities;

- Procedures for electing officers and their terms;

- Duties of any special or standing committees of the board;

- Frequency of board meetings and procedures for changing meetings;

- Responsibilities or authority granted the administrator; and

- Protection granted the board, officers and staff against liability.

These are only the most essential parts of a set of bylaws. Certainly the library's attorney could identify others that could improve the document.

### Terms of Office

It is often recommended that the terms of board members and officers be limited to permit healthy turnover and infusion of fresh ideas. It should, indeed, be helpful to allow others in the community to gain an insight to the library and participate in decisions on its policies and services.

There is, however, an equal advantage in being able to retain trustees and officers who are familiar with the library and who have taken a strong interest in its needs and activities. A lifetime appointment is hardly desirable for anyone, but neither is an automatic termination after one or two terms. A board's policy should be flexible enough to permit keeping those members who continue to contribute to the work of the library and who are able to make the commitment. The library administrator should have enough rapport with the officials responsible for appointment to ensure they replace board members who are no longer effective.

### Administrator's Responsibility

Another important aspect of the bylaws is a description of the administrator's responsibility. This should not be a complete job description, but should cover some essential elements, such as responsibilities pertaining to personnel, budget and finance, and reporting. The bylaws represent an official document and policy adopted by the board, and the clarification of the administrator's duties in it avoids misunderstanding in the future.

## Legal Protections

Finally, the bylaws should contain some statement regarding the protection that would be extended to members of the board, administration and staff in the event of a lawsuit. We live in litigious times, and all sorts of lawsuits are being brought against boards, administrators and staff.

At one time, public bodies were granted immunity against these actions, unless real negligence was evident, but the courts have gradually removed this protection. Thus it is desirable to have a clear statement that the library will provide legal assistance in defending any action of the board, administration or staff, provided that action was undertaken in the best interest of the library and in the belief it was proper and legal. Errors and ommissions coverage and liability insurance, discussed in Chapter 9, provide important protection, but each library should provide for indemnification in the bylaws of the institution as an added precaution.

## DEVELOPMENT OF THE BOARD'S MEETING AGENDA

No meeting should ever be held without a written agenda. First of all, the process of developing that agenda aids in determining whether the meeting is justified. Second, the agenda allows the participants to be prepared. Developing the agenda for the board and its committees is a responsibility shared between the chairperson and the administrator. Generally, the administrator drafts an agenda for review by the chairperson, who may delete, modify or add items for discussion. It then falls upon the administrator to prepare the documentation for that meeting.

The agendas for regular and annual meetings are often specified in the library's bylaws. This practice is of dubious value. While some standardization may be desirable, most institutions change their procedures often enough to require flexibility in their agendas. Parliamentary procedure also influences the agenda of most boards, and it is a rare institution that begins meetings without roll call and approval of the minutes of the previous meeting, which provide an opening ritual.

## Organizing the Agenda

It's best to organize the agenda so that routine items and reports that might be prescribed by law, such as the approval of payment for monthly bills or submission of committee or librarian's reports, are dispensed with as early as possible. The main body of the board agenda—and of a committee agenda—should be action on old and new business. While some administrators provide information reports as part of their board agenda, this generally clutters up the meeting and might be best handled as written reports transmitted separately to the board or as part of the library administrator's monthly written report. If old and new business are restricted to action items for the board's consideration, with attachments containing summaries of the facts and the staff recommendation, the work of the board can proceed more efficiently.

## Agenda Attachments

The agenda should identify each matter to be discussed and, in a line or two, summarize the issue. The associated attachment should be thorough enough to state the problem or define the proposed program or policy, contain the alternatives the staff or administrator considered and end with a definite recommendation. A formal resolution should also be contained in the attachment, to allow the board to see exactly what it is voting upon and to simplify the development of the minutes.

Without this preparation, valuable time will be lost in the meeting, and the results may be misinterpreted by the board members or the staff. If proper documentation cannot be developed for the board, then it may be premature to bring the matter before them. Figure 2.1 is a fictional example of an effective board agenda.

## MAINTAINING EFFECTIVE RELATIONS WITH THE BOARD

Many factors, including personality clashes and financial problems, can undermine relations between the administrator and the board. The key to maintaining good relations is communication—the ability of both parties to keep one another informed about the library and its problems and to create a clear understanding of responsibilities and expectations.

## Figure 2.1: Example of an Effective Agenda

**Meeting of June 5, 1984**

1. Approval of minutes, meeting of May 4, 1984      ATTACHMENT A

2. Reports
   a. Monthly Financial Statement and Bills      ATTACHMENT B
   b. Librarian's Monthly Report and Statistics      ATTACHMENT C
   c. Finance and Personnel Committee Report
   d. Building Committee Report

3. Old Business

   a. Selection of New Branch Site: The Building Committee has reviewed 5 sites selected by the City Planning Commission and recommends 1200 Rosemont.      ATTACHMENT D

   b. Selection of the Architect: The Building Committee has reconsidered the criteria submitted last month based upon the suggestions of the board and has developed a new proposal for approval by the board.
   ATTACHMENT E

   c. Fund Transfers: The Finance Committee has reviewed expenditures and revenues for the first half of the fiscal year and recommends 5 transfers.      ATTACHMENT F

4. New Business

   a. Video Tape Selection Policy: The Public Relations Committee has reviewed and recommends a revision of the materials selection policy concerning this medium.      ATTACHMENT G

   b. Personnel Evaluation Policies: The administration has proposed several changes in these policies, which have been reviewed and approved by the Finance Committee.      ATTACHMENT H

   c. Arnold Bequest: The administration has reviewed the conditions of this recent bequest to the library and acceptance is recommended. A plan for the use of this bequest is also recommended for approval.
   ATTACHMENT I
   d. Other New Business

Adjournment

## Mutual Respect and Responsibilities

In some libraries, the board and the administrator are continually in disagreement; such institutions are unlikely to be very effective. Friction is certain to be communicated to the staff and the community and to be reflected in poor morale and reduced service and programming. This doesn't mean that boards and librarians must always agree on policy; there has to be room for differences of opinion. It does mean that, when consensus is reached, the board and the administration should stand together on the issue.

The primary responsibility of the administrator is to carry out the policies and goals of the board; if the administrator cannot do so, he or she should resign. In the same fashion, the board should respect the opinion of the professional library administrator and reconsider its action if that action runs counter to professional recommendations. Through this process of give and take, an effective balance can be maintained.

The administrator must also be aware of a responsibility to inform board members of problems or complaints and to treat those problems seriously. No one likes to convey bad news, but it must be done if a bond of trust is to be maintained with the board. Certainly the administrator and trustees cannot be on the telephone every day, but a clear understanding should be reached as to the type of problem that would merit immediate attention. Furthermore, the administrator should meet with the board president on a regularly scheduled basis, to discuss the general programs and services of the library as well as problems and new activities being considered.

## Employment Contracts

Employment contracts are quite common in the education profession but infrequent in public libraries. Administrators traditionally serve "at the pleasure" of their boards, which should remind administrators where their loyalty ought to be placed. While some major libraries successfully use an employment contract for their chief administrator, there remains some bias against it. There is concern that, if problems arise between the administrator and the board, the contract will be an impossible bond keeping the parties together. Most employment contracts, however, possess escape clauses in the event of conflict.

Employment contracts do offer the advantage of clarifying the respective roles of the board and the administrator. They generally set clear times for evaluation of the administrator, since as the contract nears expiration the board is forced to consider the performance of the administrator.

From the administrator's standpoint, the security offered by a contract lasts only until the contract expires. While a contract may define the roles, that is no guarantee that a new board will agree. Administrators under contract are generally compensated at a somewhat higher rate than the average for public libraries, perhaps in recognition that their tenure may be shorter. Without that financial incentive, it is doubtful many administrators would support this concept.

**Evaluation of Administrators**

The evaluation of administrators is not a common practice, which is unfortunate for both the board and the administrator. When evaluation is undertaken, the same tools employed for general staff are often used. They are not applicable. It is of limited value to rate an administrator on appearance, loyalty, attitude and the other general attributes common to the typical evaluation form.

There are several elements to an effective evaluation for library administrators. First, evaluations should be undertaken privately. Most boards feel they cannot conduct such a session because of local or state legislation on open meetings. Executive sessions are usually permitted, however, for personnel matters, including evaluation of administrators. Second, the best basis for evaluation of an administrator is the progress that has been made toward meeting the library's goals and objectives. Third, there should be opportunity for an appraisal of the board's relationship with the administrator. Evaluation is a two-way street, and this opportunity for objective appraisal may clear the air and set the foundation for more effective action in the future.

## THE PUBLIC LIBRARY IN THE POLITICAL PROCESS

Politics has become a dirty word. Often a library administrator is maligned as a "politician" because he or she has arrived at a compromise with local officials. Boards are criticized for becoming political if they are responsive to suggestions from elected officials. While politics can certainly have its darker side, in fact it is nothing more than the art of getting things done. Legislation permitting the creation and support of public libraries would never have been implemented without politics. Most federal legislation promoting the advancement of libraries would not exist without politics. In almost every jurisdiction today, it would be impossible for libraries to exist without politics.

## Understanding the Elected Official

The first step in the effective use of politics is understanding elected officials. Most men and women who accept the risks associated with public office do not do so for the money. They are underpaid for their talents and have to expend large sums to win office. They are on call 24 hours a day, 7 days a week, and they are certain to get only complaints and criticism for their contribution. The real motivations are many and varied; a careful administrator can usually identify those of a particular candidate from campaign positions and statements.

One motivation is certain to arise after the individual has been elected: to stay in office. Once that is understood, a good administrator should have no difficulty in gaining and maintaining the support of any elected official.

## Four Rules for Success in Politics

The first rule for success in politics is to know the official's position on any issue affecting the library. An official who has run on a platform opposing any new taxes should not be approached to endorse the library's new $35 million bond issue.

The second rule is to identify the official's major interests and to develop programs which relate to them. For example, if better youth programs in the community are a favorite cause, certainly the library can develop some related service.

The third rule is to make the official look good whenever possible. If a branch must be closed in a councilman's jurisdiction, it is of little value to claim that his position on the library budget is responsible for the closing. It is certainly important to communicate with that official to advise him of the consequences of a position. However, if a compromise cannot be reached, it is the library that should take the blame, not the official. After all, the library administrator is paid for making those decisions and does not have to be reelected.

The final rule is always to give credit to any official responsible for or associated with a successful program. That seems common courtesy, but there are too many instances where officials fail to receive the recognition they deserve. For example, if an official's support helps gain an improved book budget at a branch in his jurisdiction, this could be noted in the neighborhood newspaper. That may seem like a little thing, but little things add up to improved rapport.

While the methods discussed in this section may seem designed to do nothing more than curry favor at the expense of the library, the end is to be responsive to the community and its elected officials. Building good lines of communication with these officials can bring the library into the mainstream of community awareness and make it more useful.

**Political Cautions**

There are certainly many pitfalls in finding an appropriate place for the library in the political process. Certainly no library should promote an individual candidate or take sides in a political campaign. No library staff member should ever use his or her position to the advantage of a candidate for public office. The library must always remain clear of patronage and favoritism. Alliances with an elected official to advance a program or service he supports should always be made, in effect, with the office that person holds, not with the individual.

It is a careful line to walk, but there is ample evidence among the more successful public libraries in this nation that it can be done, to the benefit of both the library and the community.

## SUMMARY

While a majority of public libraries are municipal entities, a significant number are county agencies or special district libraries. Other less numerous forms include regional libraries in rural areas and township, school district and association libraries. The options a library administrator has in maintaining operations and obtaining services are determined to a large extent by the library's position in the hierarchy of local government.

The most common type of public library governance in the U.S. is the board of trustees. In dealing with the board, the public library administrator's main concerns are to have the separate roles of board and administrator clearly defined and to develop good communication with board members.

Public libraries cannot escape involvement in the political process. Administrators can certainly act to gain the support of public officials but must ensure that the library does not stray from a nonpartisan position.

## FOOTNOTES

1. International City Management Association, *The Municipal Yearbook, 1979* (Washington, DC: International City Management Association, 1979), pp. 63-64.

2. *American Library Directory*, 34th edition (New York: R.R. Bowker Co., 1981), p. x.

3. U.S. Bureau of the Census, *Public Employment in the U.S.* (Washington, DC: Government Printing Office, 1979), pp. 9-11.

4. *Ibid.*, pp. 28, 31.

5. Roberta Bowler, ed., *Local Public Library Administration* (Chicago: American Library Association, 1964), p. 22.

## SUGGESTIONS FOR FURTHER READING

Altman, Ellen, ed. *Local Public Library Administration,* second edition. Chicago: American Library Association, 1980.

Josey, E.J., ed. *Libraries in the Political Process.* Phoenix, AZ: Oryx Press, 1980.

Ladenson, Alex. *Library Laws and Legislation in the United States.* Metuchen, NJ: Scareacrow Press, Inc., 1982.

Mason, Marilyn Gell. *The Federal Role in Library and Information Services.* White Plains, NY: Knowledge Industry Publications, Inc., 1983.

Rochell, Carlton, ed. *Wheeler and Goldhor's Practical Administration of Public Libraries,* revised edition. New York: Harper & Row, Publishers, Inc., 1981.

Young, Virginia G. *The Library Trustee: A Practical Guidebook,* third edition. New York: R.R. Bowker Co., 1978.

# 3

# Financial Management

The public library administrator will probably spend more time and energy on questions of finance than on any other subject except personnel. A public library can go only as far as its budget allows. Learning how to get the maximum return from available revenues and resources, where to find alternative sources of income and how to manage costs through budgeting and other controls are the subjects of this chapter.

## LOCAL TAXES

Nearly 75% of all public library revenue comes from local sources, chiefly the property tax.[1] Although economists have long argued the relative merits of the property tax, it remains the major source of revenue to fuel municipal and county services, public education and many special services required by the nation.

### The Property Tax

The property tax is based on an estimate of the value of real estate, both commercial and residential. Often there is a formula that results in a comparatively higher rate for commercial property, based on the assumption that businesses are making profits using the property and can therefore pay more. Moreover, businesses don't vote, people do; it is therefore considered desirable to favor individual voter and taxpayer. In any event, real estate is taxed based on a portion of its true value, perhaps 15% to 25%.

Tax assessors face many difficulties in attempting to appraise property at true current value. There are just too many pieces of property, and not all the improvements the owner may make will be readily visible. Moreover, in a time of rapid inflation, the value of property may move faster than the assessor can keep up with it.

To complicate matters, once the total assessed valuation of the taxing jurisdiction is established, there will always be some revenue loss because of those who fail to pay their taxes. Corporations go into bankruptcy. Individuals' property can be tied up in an estate after death or in foreclosure. People can refuse to pay the tax. Thus, at best, the actual total assessed valuation, on which property tax revenues must be based, remains something of an estimate.

In theory, the revenue from the property tax should increase annually even when the tax rate remains the same, because property appreciates. In practice, there may be no overall increase, and in some instances revenue could even decrease. For example, in a severe recession property values might remain stagnant or actually drop, businesses could fold, and the percentage of delinquencies due to unemployment could rise. Local government is then faced with proposing either increased taxes or decreased services. Neither is likely to prove very popular with the public.

### State Regulation of Local Taxes

State law usually determines assessment and taxing procedures. States that grant "home rule" powers to local government may permit some special taxes, such as the so-called nuisance taxes on lodging, entertainment, alcohol and tobacco, discussed later in this section, but usually strict procedures on property tax apply statewide. Increasingly, the courts are requiring local assessors to reappraise property regularly thoughout the jurisdiction to avoid the inequity of older properties have much lower assessments than property that has been recently developed or sold.

In some states, local governments or special units, such as libraries, are granted latitude to tax up to a specific amount, or millage, on the tax rate. Beyond that amount they are required to gain approval from the voters through a referendum. In other states, any change in the tax, except for a decrease, requires a referendum.

## The Public Library's Role

The local public library is usually tied to the policies of its jurisdiction, unless it is a special district with complete autonomy. Even then, the special district board is likely to be strongly influenced by neighboring jurisdictions. While the boards of many municipal and county libraries may have authority to control their budget and seek additional tax revenues, they are not likely to proceed without approval from the parent jurisdiction. In jurisdictions where the library tax is considered part of the total tax for the municipality or county, it may not even be itemized on the tax bill. Whatever the case, the library tax typically represents only 1 to 2% of the tax upon the total jurisdiction.

Depending on the relative autonomy of the library, it may become involved in a tax levy campaign whenever its needs would require an increase in the property tax. Such a campaign should be designed to inform the voters why the increase is justified—whether to remodel, to construct new facilities or simply to cope with inflation. Whatever the circumstances, it is critical that the facts are communicated and that as many supporters as possible be motivated to go to the polls.

There are restrictions on the use of public funds for such a campaign. Thus, local Friends groups or other organizations are often recruited to raise funds for any advertising or to staff telephones and distribute literature on the referendum. Some advice on how to run a successful campaign will be given later in this chapter.

Increasingly, those libraries that depend on the property tax as their only or principal source of revenue are finding it necessary to seek special referendums. This is because in many major metropolitan areas—where most public libraries are located—officials are reporting relatively low rates of increase in property tax revenues. Contributing to this situation are the condition of the economy, special exemptions granted to groups such as senior citizens and taxpayer initiatives to halt or roll back the local property tax.

### The Income Tax

While the income tax has been the major source of revenue for federal and state government for many years, it has not until recently been widely considered at the local level. This was due in part to the states' control over this tax and in part to the previous adequacy of local property and nuisance taxes.

In theory the income tax is fairer and more elastic than the property tax. It falls upon every wage and salary earner, and, in a good economy, revenues rise as income increases. In practice, however, the income tax presents as many problems as the property tax. A serious recession could substantially reduce revenues for local government, while the property tax would remain somewhat more stable. Income taxes are also more easily evaded, since not all earnings are automatically reported.

Moreover, many states are reluctant to share this revenue source with local government, since they are themselves experiencing financial shortfalls. Local governments, in turn, are concerned that the imposition of an income tax could prompt businesses to relocate into adjacent communities that do not have local income tax.

### The Sales Tax

Another, and more common, local tax is the sales tax. Although sales tax is often imposed by the state, many municipalities and counties piggyback a percentage onto the state tax to supplement their revenues from the property tax. It is not common for a library or special district to impose a general sales tax, but the revenues such a tax brings into a jurisdiction certainly permit the property tax to be lower.

Sales tax income is closely tied to the condition of the economy, and it is highly elastic. Local governments that rely upon the sales tax must watch any changes in the economic barometer; a significant decline can make severe retrenchment and reduction of services necessary.

### Special Taxes

There are a host of special, or nuisance, taxes imposed by local governments. These include "sin" taxes on alcohol, tobacco or entertainment (which are really a form of sales tax) and "dedicated" taxes levied on certain types of materials, inventories, services or transactions and granted solely to a particular unit of government.

An example of a dedicated tax is the "intangibles" tax that supported public libraries in Ohio. During the Great Depression, the Ohio General Assembly placed a cap on property taxes to protect homeowners. This also had the unfortunate result of removing the primary source of income for the state's public libraries. To compensate for this loss, a special tax was imposed on the productive return from stocks and bonds. That did not amount to much during the 1930s, but in time the revenue grew significantly, at least in metropolitan counties.

The problems experienced with the intangibles tax are typical of those experienced in the administration of dedicated taxes. Because it was collected and distributed at the local (county) level, the amount of support varied considerably among the state's libraries. Because the tax was dedicated and easy to evade, it was comparatively expensive to administer. Taxpayers objected to being taxed twice—once for the earnings on stocks and bonds, and then again under the state income tax. In 1983 the tax was repealed and replaced with a percentage of the state income tax.

Some states grant authority to local government to allocate or dedicate the proceeds from certain activities other than taxes for special purposes. An example of this is the state of Michigan, which allocates library revenues from penal fines imposed by the courts.

**The Outlook for Local Taxes**

A host of taxes and fees can be imposed by local government for the support of public libraries, and state legislators and local governmental officials appear to be more creative each year in their pursuit of the perfect tax. Taxpayers are also becoming more vocal in their efforts to keep taxes down and to make them more equitable. The 1970s revealed some slight decline in the percentage of public library revenues derived from local taxes. However, for the foreseeable future, the bulk of revenues will continue to come from local sources, primarily from the property tax.

**FEDERAL AID**

Federal and state governments provided 14.5% of the support for local public libraries in the 1977-78 fiscal year.[2] Despite the difficulties being faced by both these levels of government, more recent reports indicate that this percentage has actually increased, primarily because of increased state appropriations.

The 1977-78 LIBGIS survey revealed that the total of federal funds allocated to local public libraries in that fiscal year was more than $122 million.[3] The largest single source was general revenue sharing (GRS), which amounted to almost $58 million, or more than 47% of the federal funds that went to local libraries.[4] The next largest sum came from the Library Services and Construction Act (LSCA), which provided almost $30 million for local library services, 24% of total federal revenues.[5] The balance came from a hodgepodge of federal programs, including the National Endowment for the Humanities, the National Endowment for the Arts, and the Comprehensive Education and Training Act.

### General Revenue Sharing

General revenue sharing is not allocated directly to libraries, but to local political jurisdictions (e.g., municipalities, villages, townships and counties), as well as to the state. Initially, libraries were cited as a priority in the program chiefly because appropriations for public library construction under LSCA were eliminated during the Nixon administration. The library priority was subsequently dropped, but libraries have continued to receive a significant portion of revenue sharing dollars.

Under revenue sharing, local political jurisdictions are required to develop plans for expenditure of funds and to hold public hearings on the plans, but there are no other strings. Some libraries have taken the initiative and submitted requests; many have received funds, though this often depends on the library's lobbying and the urgency of competing requests.

Initially many local governments treated the GRS program as "soft" money and were reluctant to use the grants for anything but capital improvements. However it has become evident that the program will be a permanent feature of local government financing. Increasingly, GRS has been committed to the support of operating functions of local government, including library service.

### Library Services and Construction Act

As noted in Chapter 2, LSCA is administered by the state library agency, and funds are expended in accordance with the state plan developed by that agency, often with input from the state's library community. LSCA is divided into several "titles," or categories of emphasis. Each year, Congress considers appropriations for each of the titles, and the approved funds are then distributed to the states based upon a formula reflecting the comparative populations of those states but guaranteeing a base amount for the smaller states and possessions.

The state library agency may elect to use part of its LSCA grant to administer its program, and it may commit part of the money to maintain certain statewide services, such as reference or interlibrary loan. It may develop special programs such as scholarships to recruit minorities into librarianship or to encourage professional librarians to serve rural libraries. It may also develop a direct grant program, using a formula to distribute LSCA funds to eligible public libraries throughout the state. Usually, however, the state agency encourages local libraries to develop project proposals that will satisfy needs identified in the state plan. On occasion, the state library agency may commission or contract with another agency such as a university to perform certain research deemed beneficial to the state's libraries.

Major emphases for LSCA in the past have been upon reducing the number of people unserved or underserved in rural and urban areas, extending service to the aged, the handicapped and minorities, sharing of resources, and increasing interlibrary cooperation. Construction of modern library facilities and removal of barriers to access for the handicapped have also been a priority, but Title II, which funds construction, has received no appropriations since 1975.

Although GRS has become the largest source of federal funds for public libraries, LSCA has been the most important federal program because of the impetus it has given to so many significant trends in the field. These include regional library development, improved long-range planning, automation of library service, increased use of audiovisual materials, service to special groups and multitype library cooperation.

Project proposals for LSCA funds are reviewed according to policies that are developed by the state library agency and that are published and made available to local libraries. Often, the review process includes panels or advisory committees representing libraries throughout the state. Emphasis is often placed on whether the project will be applicable to other libraries in the state and how well it relates to the state plan. The state library agency is also concerned with evaluating the results of the project and disseminating this information throughout the state.

## Other Sources of Federal Aid

Two other federal programs that represent appropriate funding sources for public libraries are the National Endowment for the Humanities (NEH) and the National Endowment for the Arts (NEA). In addition to grants to individual artists or humanists and challenge grants that permit local donations to be matched with federal dollars in a specific ratio, NEH and NEA offer program grants, which are of particular relevance to libraries. These grants allow the library to design arts or humanities programs for the public, based upon the use of materials from the collection. Libraries of all sizes throughout the nation have been able to bring artists and humanists of national stature to local audiences, to draw upon local talent and to stimulate greater awareness of the importance of the arts and humanities in society.

There are many other federal programs that are pertinent to libraries. The best source of information on these programs is the *Catalog of Federal Domestic Assistance*.[6] The catalog, arranged by subject, describes the myriad programs and eligibility requirements and tells how to obtain additional information and where to send applications. This publication is available from the Government Printing Office and is an invaluable reference tool for all but the very smallest library.

### Problems of Dependence

Libraries often resist the use of federal funds at the local level, for fear that they may become dependent on that resource. Should it then disappear, continuing the program will increase the local tax burden. It is true that during the 1960s and 1970s a great many programs were initiated that raised expectations but then failed because local support could not be found to maintain them.

Many administrators, boards and local officials are cognizant of that problem and are careful in the use of federal funds. Most federal agencies are also cautious in awarding grants to local libraries, because they want to be assured that the grantee will be able to maintain a successful program after federal funding ends.

### STATE AID

State aid programs have increased slowly but steadily since 1970. Although they provided less than 7% of total local library support throughout the nation in 1977-78,[7] state programs are evidence of a growing realization that public library support should be a partnership of local, federal and state government. In some states aid is provided on a formula basis designed to "equalize" support, i.e., to ensure that those libraries with the lowest per capita support are brought up to a minimum level sufficient to provide adequate services. To ensure that communities do not reduce their support as a result of the state's contribution, there is usually a "maintenance of local effort" clause in state aid programs.

Where state aid programs extend to all public libraries in the state, there is usually a formula for distribution that includes population and area served as factors. States will frequently impose eligibility requirements, such as participation in the interlibrary loan process and reciprocal borrowing privileges. In some instances, libraries must meet minimum standards, which may be developed by the state library association or which may represent basic features of service that the state agency believes every library should have, such as a telephone, a basic book collection and a minimum of operating hours and staff.

The combination of the carrot and the stick has proven successful in those states where development was needed. In those states that already had higher levels of support and more sophisticated services, the state aid program has fostered interlibrary cooperation and resource sharing, which might otherwise have required years to implement.

Not everyone greets state aid programs enthusiastically. Many local jurisdictions fear the imposition of state regulations and requirements, although they might sorely need the aid. Some states have avoided programs in which the state extends services to the local level. Others believe that the delivery of services such as centralized technical processing, consultant help and backup reference services are more effective than direct aid for helping local public libraries.

## OTHER SOURCES OF INCOME

After local taxes and federal and state aid programs, "other" revenues constitute the balance of public library income. "Other" represents more than 10% of total revenue, a significant amount, and consists of a variety of sources.[8]

### Income from Inactive Funds and Endowments

One of the largest of these other sources is income from inactive funds and endowments. Inactive funds are monies that the library has in its bank account but that it does not need to spend that month for payroll, book expenditures or other miscellaneous expenses. Libraries are likely to have inactive funds because local property taxes are usually collected only once or twice a year, while the library's expenditures tend to fall more evenly throughout the year. Thus, the library can afford to invest that portion it does not need immediately and gain additional revenues from the interest.

Interest is also earned from endowments, which are funds given to the library. Either the donor or the board decides the funds should remain intact, and the library uses only the interest earned from investing the principal. While there are many types of endowments, they fall into two basic categories: restricted and unrestricted. Restricted endowments may only be used for purposes specified by the donor, such as purchases for the children's collection, construction of a new wing or payment of the librarian's salary. Unrestricted endowments are those which can be used in any fashion the board wishes.

State laws usually restrict how libraries may invest funds. Often they can go only into "government-secured instruments," such as Treasury bills or certificates of deposit. Under no condition should such an investment be made unless it is fully backed by the financial institution. For example, if the library's accounts or investments in any single bank or savings institution exceed $100,000—the maximum covered by federal deposit insurance—the library must require protection for that excess in the event of failure. Even when boards are not limited in their investment options, they are likely to be conservative because of concern about loss. Trustees, as well as administrators, may be personally liable for misuse of funds if an investment backfires and public funds are lost.

Such a suit was brought against the board of a public library on Long Island (NY) in the early 1970s. The board elected to place some of the library's inactive funds in arbitrage (i.e., the exchange market). For some time the returns were high, considerably better than those for securities such as Treasury bills. Unfortunately, the market suffered reverses due to unforeseen government policy changes, and the library lost a significant sum. A taxpayer in the district filed suit against the board for misuse of public library funds. The courts ruled against the board, and the members were personally liable for the loss.

Later in this chapter we will discuss the development and management of library endowments and donations.

## Contractual Services

Contractual services are another significant source of funds for some public libraries. These are services that the library may perform either for other libraries or for individuals, organizations or other governmental agencies. For several years, the Cuyahoga County (OH) Public Library, serving suburban Cleveland, operated a major book processing center for other libraries and public schools. While this service was not intended to produce profits for the system, the revenues it produced helped to defray some of the library's expenses for its own technical processing and allowed it to extend the service to other libraries at a comparative savings.

An unusual service was performed by the Elyria (OH) Public Library for the National Aeronautics and Space Administration for several years during the height of the space exploration program. The library had experience with the administration of several public library cooperative film circuits. When it learned that NASA was seeking an outside contractor to administer its Midwest film library, the Elyria Public Library submitted a proposal and was awarded a contract.

Other types of contracts have included specialized reference services for corporations, maintenance of libraries for hospitals or correctional institutions, delivery services, consulting and audiovisual services. Many major urban libraries have contracts with state library agencies for the provision of service to the blind and physically handicapped. Contractual service can be a significant source of revenue for many libraries if they are cautious in estimating and controlling their costs and if they are sound and businesslike in the establishment of rates for their services.

The question is sometimes raised whether such services may jeopardize the institution's tax-exempt status or represent unfair competition with the private sector. If all expenses and overhead are considered, however, a library is unlikely to make an overall profit. As for unfair competition with the private sector, it is equally unlikely the type of services in question would represent an attractive proposition for a business seeking a reasonable profit with a limited investment.

Administrators who observe underutilization of desirable services, whether they are computer facilities, technical processing operations, audiovisual centers, printing facilities or public relations departments, might consider packaging, pricing and marketing those services to other institutions. In a similar fashion, services that libraries may not be able to support on an individual basis could be financed through a contract among several libraries in which one of the cooperating libraries agreed to assume primary responsibility for management.

The principal concern in any contract is to spell out the mutual commitments and the services to be offered. In addition, careful estimation of the costs, including overhead, must be part of the process, to avoid financial disaster.

### Fee-based Services

Fee-based services are the center of much controversy in the public library field and are likely to remain so for some time. The major objection to fee-based service is rooted in the long struggle libraries had to gain tax support and break out of the subscription library pattern. There is also the fear that fees will become a barrier to users. While the fees generally proposed in libraries today apply to such services as online computer searches, rather than to more traditional activities such as book loan and reference service, there is some concern that, once the concept is introduced, even traditional services might be metered. Indeed, a few communities, among them Denver (CO), have established charges for resident borrowers' cards, and tax revenues have been reduced as a result.

Fees for use are fairly common in almost every public library, despite these fears. For example, few libraries offer free photocopying. Most charge enough to cover the cost of the service and, often, enough to cover the library's internal photocopying needs as well. In a 1981 survey, the majority of libraries were found to charge patrons for online reference services, and the longer a library had offered the service, the more likely it was to charge for it.[9] However, the fee usually covered only the cost of computer connect time and telecommunications. It rarely extended to the cost of the terminal and the professional time devoted to the search. Often the primary motivation for establishing a fee is to permit the library to ration expensive services such as online database searching and so keep costs under control.

Another common fee is for the use of audiovisual materials, such as films and video tapes. In this case, fees might be expected to pay for repair or replacement of a comparatively fragile resource. For smaller collections, fees can be a rationing device and also provide funds to purchase additional titles. Public library rental collections are frequently justified on this basis. Such collections usually consist of bestsellers, and institutions are often reluctant to commit a limited book budget to satisfy what is seen as an ephemeral need.

If charging a fee makes it possible to offer a service or resource that would otherwise be unavailable, the administrator should certainly consider that approach.

**Fines and Payments**

Fines do not represent a significant source of public library revenue, public opinion to the contary. Still, fines remain an income possibility, if they are compatible with the philosophy of the local library. Most studies of fines and circulation procedures reveal that it costs the public library more to administer its delinquency and fine program than the fines bring in. For most public libraries fines are intended only as a nuisance to the patron to encourage return of material.

Some libraries have experimented with the elimination of fines, both to save costs and to determine whether there is any impact on book return. The results of these experiments have been mixed, and the tradition is strong enough that the overwhelming majority of libraries still set fines.

Many patrons actually appreciate overdue notices as a reminder and complain when one is not received. Libraries might consider— particularly if they are automating their circulation procedures— making this a service for which the patron pays the actual cost of preparing and sending an overdue notice. That charge would still be far below the cost of the book. If the circulation system was sufficiently flexible, a more nominal traditional fine could be continued for those patrons who are not interested in the convenience of a reminder.

Payment for lost or damaged books is another revenue source, although it is unlikely to cover actual costs in the typical library. Some institutions actually depreciate the book cost for the patron or charge an arbitrary sum and usually exclude processing costs, which are likely to equal the cost of the book.

**Contributions**

Donations, special grants and memorials are additional revenue sources, and later in this chapter there will be some discussion on how these may be encouraged. Public libraries have the benefit of being tax-exempt, and contributions to them are tax deductible.

## BUDGETING

Equally important as raising adequate revenues is managing their expenditure. The administrator's main tool for financial control is the budget. A budget should be more than just an accounting mechanism, however. It can also play an important role in planning. Too often, library boards and administrators separate the budget from the planning process or look into development or revision of the library's long-range plan *after* they have completed their budget. This is a mistake. The budget should be prepared either concurrently with development or revision of the plan, or afterwards.

Most political jurisdictions follow an annual budget cycle that includes preliminary development, review, final revision, submission and approval, followed by implementation, review and audit. It would be wise for an administrator and board to link this to a planning cycle. Chapter 4 will focus on planning, but it is well to consider budgeting and planning as a joint process, or the library will always have difficulty making meaningful progress toward its goals.

There are a host of different types of budgets in the public sector. Some are faddish and eventually fall into disuse or are modified. An example is the zero-based budget, or ZBB, which became popular during the Carter administration. In zero-based budgeting, every expenditure has to be justified every year. Each service or activity starts with a budget of zero and is evaluated in terms of its value to the organization. ZBB lost favor because it was too time-consuming, and frequently administrators defeated its purpose by relying on last year's expenditures as a basis for the coming year's budget and adding an allowance for inflation.

### Line Item Budgets

The most common budget types in the public sector are line item, program and performance. In a line item budget, all the *types* of materials, contractual services, personnel and miscellaneous expenses are ennumerated: books, audiovisual materials, salaries for librarians and clerks, postage, stationery, equipment main-tenance and replacement, etc.—rather like the family budget. This is still the most common type of budget in use today. It lends itself to careful analysis, because comparison with previous years makes it possible to identify trends and project future expenditures. Budget analysts can also quickly identify unusual changes that may require justification or further scrutiny.

The problem with the line item budget is that it does not provide convenient information about the costs of specific services or about what those services are. It is a nuts-and-bolts budget, useful for administrators or technicians.

## Performance Budgets

To correct this, many governmental entities have adopted the performance budget, which is organized in terms of output services or products. For example, technical services operations would include the personnel involved in that work, supplies consumed in processing, utilities and equipment costs, and any other expenses associated with that activity. The number of books and other materials to be processed would then be estimated, allowing determination of the per unit cost for this service.

In performance budgeting, line item expenses such as personnel, supplies and fringe benefits, are distributed throughout the document, making it difficult for aggregate expenses for these items to be readily identified. Overhead expenses such as costs for administration can also be distributed throughout the budget.

Another problem with performance budgeting, particularly for libraries, is that not all services lend themselves to determination of an output. Reference service and circulation do lend themselves to the process, but what is the "output" of the periodicals section, particularly if the materials are not loaned? Also, tabulating the statistics for performance budgeting is an added expense, which makes it unpopular with many libraries. Nonetheless, it does permit institutions to get a better handle on their costs of operation.

## Program Budgets

Performance budgeting was strongly favored by the International City Management Association for many years and gained some ground, but lately it has been competing more frequently with program budgeting. In a program budget, the library's services are divided into clear program areas, such as services to children, to the blind and physically handicapped, etc.

Once again, the expenses associated with those activities are identified: personnel, materials, contractual services and maintenance of the facilities required. A supportive function, such as technical services or management, is spread across those programs, in proportion to the amount of time and resources devoted to each program. Thus, if the technical services department devoted 25% of its time and materials to the processing of materials for youth, then 25% of the total expenditure for technical services would be assigned to the youth services program.

Sometimes elements of the performance budget can be used in program budgeting. For example, juvenile books circulated, reference services provided, programs scheduled and classrooms visited might be output measures for the program. In addition, advocates claim that program budgets are easier for the public to interpret, but there is no consensus on this.

Program budgeting also lends itself to "decision packaging." A decision package is a new or existing project or program that can stand alone, that is, for which the total dollar cost to the library can be separately stated. Examples could include services for senior citizens, development of a video tape program, construction of a new branch or maintenance of an existing unit. The board or the budgetary officials of the jurisdiction are then in a position to weigh the relative merits and costs of different packages and approve or reject them with a clear understanding of the impact of their decision.

The disadvantages of the program budget are that it is complicated and time-consuming to develop and it is difficult to identify aggregate costs. A top-heavy administration can be more easily hidden in a program budget, just as in the performance budget, because the expense of those individuals and their fringe benefits can be spread throughout the programs. There are techniques to correct this, but they usually involve the creation of a line item budget.

## THE BUDGETING PROCESS

Often public libraries that are independent districts or are autonomous in their budgetary process—i.e., when the board is the only body that reviews the budget—may develop whatever form of budget they find most useful. However, some states do prescribe a particular form. Libraries linked to a local political jurisdiction, such as a city or county, are bound to the format employed by that jurisdiction. The process by which the budget is developed and the manner in which it is presented will also depend on whether the institution is autonomous in its budget procedure.

## Autonomous Libraries

If only the board must approve the budget, then it can set its own deadlines for the cycle. Usually, several months in advance of the new fiscal year, the administration gathers information from the operating units and assesses new programs, equipment, personnel increases, and unusual amounts of supplies or contractual services that might be required for the coming year. Larger institutions may use formal budget requests. These would be evaluated by the administrative staff and modified based on the library's long-range plan. If changes to that plan are anticipated, they should be discussed with the board committee responsible for monitoring or developing it.

A preliminary budget is then prepared by the administrative staff and brought before the finance committee of the board. New programs or additional expenses beyond normal inflationary trends would be noted and justified. The anticipated revenue requirements would also be part of this document, providing some indication of whether an increase in the property tax or other revenue sources might be required.

After review and modification by the finance committee, the administrative staff would then prepare a final budget proposal for approval by the board. Following approval, the document and the library's fiscal requirements would be transmitted to that public agency or official responsible for collection of the library's taxes and to any other agencies required by state laws. The state library agency usually also requires reports on revenues, expenditures and usage as part of its statistical responsibilities.

## Libraries Subject to Review

If the library is part of a political jurisdiction that requires review and/or approval by another body, such as a city council or county board of supervisors, another series of steps is involved in the process, and the budget cycle must begin earlier. Larger cities and counties customarily have a budget or finance department perform part of the review. An analyst is assigned to scrutinize the preliminary budget after the board's finance committee has approved it. While the analyst does not have the power of life or death over desired programs, his or her recommendations are certain to be conveyed to the jurisdiction's budget officers, chief elected official and legislative body.

In some jurisdictions where stronger control over the library budget exists, preliminary meetings may be held at the very beginning of the budget cycle. At these meetings, budget officers or officials convey policy guidelines, such as what percentages of increase will be allowed or whether all new programs will be rejected. The rejection of a desirable program by the budget department of a political jurisdiction is not necessarily a final decision. When the preliminary budget is returned for approval by the board, the institution may still restore the program and lobby for its approval in the legislative body.

It is customary for all political jurisdictions possessing legislative bodies, whether they are village or city councils or county boards, to delegate authority for reviewing budget requests to a finance committee. Often this is the most powerful committee in the jurisdiction. The library will be called upon to present its budget request and respond to any questions that might be raised. This presentation may be made by the administrator, by a library board member such as the president or the chair of the board finance committee, or by both the administrator and members of the board. A combined presentation is preferable, for it permits a representative of the community to speak on the library's needs and services, while the administrator is able to respond to technical questions. However, custom often determines who makes the presentation.

It is before the finance committee and later, during final approval by the city council, that the greatest opportunity exists for preserving programs that the city budget office recommended not be funded. However, such an effort raises serious questions about the library's loyalty to the political leadership of the jurisdiction. The budget office reflects the policies of its chief elected official. If the legislative body is of a different political persuasion, then the library can be caught in the middle. The chief elected official can always veto a budget or replace members of the board as terms expire or make it difficult for the administator to function effectively. Conversely, a budget that favors the library and has the support of the budget office could be gutted by the legislative body.

Some libraries are able to restore desirable programs through the lobbying efforts of Friends organizations or allied civic groups such as PTAs. If the budget review process allows public comment or hearings, then groups have an opportunity to speak on behalf of desirable new programs or service restorations. If public comment does not help, of if it is not part of the process, then groups and individuals may also lobby individual members of the legislative body as well as the chief elected official. Some officials resent this as a lobbying effort engineered by the library. On the other hand, they may be swayed by their constituents. Whether to encourage citizen lobbying is a decision that the board and the administrator must make together.

## THE OPERATING BUDGET

Whatever form the budget takes, once it has been approved, it becomes an important tool that allows the administrator and the board to monitor the implementation of plans and the delivery of services. When costs exceed original projections, it is a signal to management to intervene and consider modifications in the delivery of services. Because of the importance of the budget, it is worth examining its use, the necessary reporting procedures and methods that can be employed to ensure the institution stays within its limits.

The major components of the operating budget are personnel and materials (books, audiovisual resources, periodicals, microform, etc.). Fringe benefits may or may not be considered part of the personnel budget. The personnel and the materials budget together will represent between 65% and 85% of the total budget of the typical library.

Personnel costs are determined by the table of organization an institution maintains. This is a list of positions and the classification or title they hold, which can be converted into dollars and cents for budgetary purposes. Fringe benefits can be linked to this table. Customarily, part-time personnel receive few or no fringe benefits, while full-time salaried personnel receive full benefits. The cost for these fringe benefits may vary depending upon the salary or classification of the individual, but it is usual to define fringe benefits in terms of a percentage of the personnel budget, which may range from 15% to 25% of total personnel costs. Therefore, it is important that personnel hiring be strictly controlled to ensure that the allocation for salaries, wages and fringe benefits does not exceed the budget. Often a board will require approval of personnel appointments, although this is just an added check, taken after the fact.

The materials budget is usually controlled through department heads or individual selectors within departments. Typically, they are assigned a portion of the budget based on criteria such as usage or the collection development plan of the institution. Some libraries have automated acquisitions systems that keep managers informed as to the balance remaining in their budget. Others rely on manual systems. Whatever the mechanism, both management and the board must be able to monitor expenditures to ensure overspending does not occur.

## BIDDING AND VENDOR CONTRACTS

Control over expenditures can also be maintained by requiring competitive bidding procedures for supplies and equipment, as well as for services. Frequently, this is dictated by law, but even where it is not, it is an extremely desirable management practice. Specifications for desired services, equipment or materials should be prepared by the staff, based on research into needs and available services or products. Advertisements for bids can then be placed, or invitations or formal requests for proposals (RFPs) distributed to firms known to be reliable.

### Specifications

Specifications should contain instructions to bidders to ensure that their proposals are received in a form which makes comparison easy. It is preferable for the library to prepare its own bid forms to ensure standardization whenever possible. Standard requirements, including liability protection, carriage of workmen's compensation and satisfaction of other pertinent state and federal regulations such as equal opportunity or prevailing wage, should also form part of the specifications.

Two other important clauses should be included. The library should retain the right to accept any and all irregularities in case a firm proposes some exception to the specifications that might be acceptable to the library. The library should also have the right to reject all bids in case they all exceed the library's allocation for the materials, equipment or services.

### Awarding Contracts and Selecting Vendors

When the bids have been received and evaluated, the contract can then be awarded based on the lowest and most qualified bid received. Sometimes, the lowest bidder may not be the most qualified. To ensure there is no question about how this conflict is resolved, the specifications or instructions to bidders should spell out the criteria for selection and who will make the final judgment.

That person is customarily the administrator or the purchasing officer. Following this award, the work should be confirmed with a written contract that includes start and completion times, payment arrangements, acceptance procedures and other elements required by law.

This formal a procedure is not appropriate for every expenditure, but it should be a practice to collect three quotations on supplies or equipment to ensure that a fair price is being paid. The quotations should always be requested in writing and confirmed by a purchase order to the lowest bidder to bind the price.

For purchases that cannot be handled on a bid basis—for example, book purchases—an effort should be made to work through jobbers whenever possible. Based on estimated annual purchases, discounts should be negotiated with jobbers and other suppliers the library uses regularly. Larger libraries should consider developing specifications for book suppliers and obtaining competitive bids, to gain the maximum possible discount.

Some states have very strict procedures for purchasing and contracts, and it would be well to confer with the library's legal counsel to ensure that the library's practices conform to the law. In other instances, the board may have a policy requiring competitive bidding for expenditures above a specified amount. There may also be state or local jurisdictional purchasing programs which will permit the library to benefit from bulk contracts with suppliers for materials like paper and light bulbs. Eligibility can be determined by contacting the state and local jurisdictional purchasing agents.

## Bid and Performance Bonds

Bid and performance bonds may be required or desirable on some major work. A bid bond is a surety that a bidder is commited to enter into a contract with the library if it is awarded the work. The bond is customarily a percentage of the bid price, such as 5%. If the firm subsequently decides not to undertake the work, it forfeits the bond, which can be used by the library to help defray any expenses caused by the delay.

A performance bond is a surety that the company or individual will complete the work as specified. Again, if the firm fails to do this, the library can use the bond to pay another contractor to complete the work. Performance bonds are usually equal to the cost of the project.

Bid and performance bonds are included in construction or

major equipment contracts, such as computer purchases, but are infrequent on smaller work because they may discourage firms from submission of bids. Nonetheless, whenever a purchase is important to the library and it is desirable to weed out unqualified firms, these bonds may be appropriate.

## OTHER FINANCIAL CONTROLS

There are a number of other ways in which expenditures can be monitored and controlled.

### Purchase Orders

Purchase orders are another means of controlling expenditures and verifying receipt. Whenever a commitment is made to a vendor, a purchase order should be issued and recorded, and firms should be directed to cite the purchase order number on bills and shipments. Upon receipt of the materials, the purchase order can be pulled and the receipt noted, permitting verification when the bill is received. Purchasing of supplies and equipment should always be centralized, and even in the smallest library someone should be designated as a purchasing and receiving agent.

### Handling Cash

Libraries often handle a great deal of cash, accumulated from fines or fees for services such as photocopying. Cash should be accounted for daily by a responsible member of the staff, verified by a second individual and deposited as soon as possible. Expenditures for supplies or small services should never be made from receipts in the cash drawer. This encourages sloppy record keeping and pilferage. If libraries require cash for everyday transactions that cannot be handled through the library's finance or purchasing department, a separate petty cash fund can be established. This should be as small as practicable, and receipts for expenditures should always be required and verified by the finance officer.

Employees who regularly handle cash or checks or who work in the library's finance department should be bonded. A bond provides surety that, if some fraud occurs, the library will be protected for the loss, up to the limit of the bond. Often the library pays the cost of the bond; however, some states may forbid this.

## Reports

Reports on expenditures and receipts should be prepared monthly for review by the administrator and the board, and their review should be a normal part of every regular board meeting. There should also be regular reports on the library's investments, indicating amounts, return, the nature of the security and its maturity date.

## Audits

Every year the library's financial records should be audited by an independent certified public accountant selected by the board's finance committee. Professional services such as these are always negotiable, even when that profession may have standard fees. Estimates of the cost for the service should be requested in writing as one of the factors that will aid the board in making its selection. It is well to change auditors at periodic intervals.

Besides reviewing the accounting records of the institution, the auditor should be requested to identify any desirable or necessary improvements in the library's financial procedures. Upon completion of work, the auditor will customarily meet with the administrator and the financial staff and discuss any findings or errors. Clarification can be given prior to the submission of a final audit report to the board. In some states the audit process is a function of the state, and in some larger local political jurisdictions there may be an internal audit department.

## THE CAPITAL IMPROVEMENTS BUDGET

The foregoing discussions have applied to the library's operating budget. There is often another type of library budget, a capital improvements budget. Frequently, this budget has separate revenues and different accounting procedures. Capital expenditures may be for buildings and property or for major pieces of equipment, such as furnishings or computer systems. Segments of the general appropriation to the library may be assigned for capital purposes, or special bonds may have been issued to furnish the revenues.

Associated with the capital improvements budget is a plan defining specific projects. This may be an annual plan, or it could be long term, running 5 to 10 years.

Increasingly, local governments are working on long-range

development plans in order to avoid duplication of expensive projects and assess long-term cash requirements. While some capital improvements might be financed out of general appropriations, it is more customary either to borrow or to gain voter approval through referendums. Legal requirements may prevent a unit of local government from borrowing without voter approval, as well. Few libraries have the authority to issue bonds for capital improvements; most depend on their local political jurisdiction for this. Critical factors in the decision whether to issue bonds or seek a referendum are the current interest rate and the political jurisdiction's credit rating. A low rating will increase the interest rate and substantially increase the cost of the project. Governments can generally offer lower rates when they borrow because the interest earned by the lender is tax-exempt. Nonetheless, many jurisdictions may not want to bear the additional indebtedness for a project if they are near the limits of total indebtedness permitted by local ordinance or state statute.

A form of short-term indebtedness often employed by libraries is a tax anticipation note. A local lending institution may advance, at a comparatively low interest rate, a major portion of the revenues that the library anticipates from a referendum that has passed but that have not yet been collected. This may permit a project to be started at a more favorable time. The tax anticipation note is more frequently used with the operating budget, but it can also be applied to the capital budget in many states.

## MANAGING RETRENCHMENT

Budget control and capital improvements are obviously desirable and, with good management, usually achievable. There may come times, however, when despite the best of efforts, some retrenchments will be necessary to bring expenditures into balance with receipts. Some unanticipated disaster may require transfer of funds, or a shortfall in estimated receipts may demand cutbacks. There are some general guidelines that an administrator can follow to deal with this type of emergency.

Since the two largest categories in a public library budget are personnel and materials, it is logical to examine those first. In the personnel category, freezing employment is a customary first step in retrenchment. If cutbacks are necessary, labor contracts and civil service requirements may dictate the order of layoff. If they do not, the most common practice is to reduce or eliminate part-time employees, followed by full-time employees according to seniority. In the case of either a freeze or layoffs, transfers are almost always necessary to equalize the impact of unfilled positions. Among libraries that have branches, some institutions have elected to close temporarily those least used. Others have tried to keep a geographical balance, to permit library service to be maintained in each area of the city or county. Some libraries have assigned certain staff members to two or more branches, allowing all facilities to remain open but with limited hours.

Probably the most common retrenchment practice in libraries is to reduce the materials budget temporarily. Unfortunately, that may permanently harm the collection, since materials that are not purchased during that period may never be acquired, thus leaving a permanent gap in the collection. Balancing the reduction throughout the collection is preferable to an outright stoppage in any one area. The administrator should always remember that one of the primary functions of the institution is to acquire materials for public use. When that does not happen, it will have an adverse long-term impact on public opinion, no matter how much the public sympathizes with the library's plight. Every effort should be made to keep that percentage of the library's budget spent for materials at 15%-20%.

Cancelling purchases of equipment, supplies and services that are not essential to the operation of the library is a final retrenchment strategy. Standing orders and contracts should be evaluated to identify appropriate cancellations.

The above guidelines represent only a starting point and were not presented in any order of priority. Retrenchment should not be implemented unilaterally by the administrator. Possibilities for cutbacks should be reviewed with other members of the library's administration, the appropriate committee of the board and eventually the full board, as well as affected local officials before any steps are undertaken. A plan should be written and disseminated to the staff and public, so that everyone is aware of what will occur.

No one can look forward to retrenchment, but sometimes it reveals inefficiencies and services that do not justify continued support. More often, retrenchment justifies an increase in local support.

## GOING TO THE PUBLIC

Some libraries do not have the legal authority to approach the public directly for tax increases. For them, cutbacks can only set the stage for requests to their jurisdiction for an increased appropriation to permit restoration of essential services. For those institutions that can go to the public for a referendum or tax levy increase, the board and administration will find this their greatest challenge.

All states have fairly specific procedures on how such an election is to be held, the language of the ballot, the time of the election and the percentage of votes cast required to gain passage. These requirements should be thoroughly studied, and legal assistance should be obtained to assure that the effort on the referendum will not fail because of a technicality. Despite these technicalities and widespread anti-tax sentiment, a number of libraries, including the Pikes Peak (CO) Regional Library District and the Columbus and Franklin County (OH) Public Library, have mounted successful tax referendums in recent years.

### Developing the Plan

Estimates of the amount of revenue that will be needed from the levy must be made. This, of course, requires a plan that identifies services to be restored, activities to be maintained and new programs or facilities to be created, together with any other expenses that will have to be paid for from the proceeds of the levy. This plan represents the platform for the campaign. It should be clear and simple, since it will have to be stated again and again during the campaign.

The major elements of a successful campaign to "sell" the library's plan include financing, endorsements, communications, personal contact and organizing voter registration and turnout.

### Financing

As noted previously, there are strict regulations governing the use of public funds for elections. Almost certainly the library will have to gain independent financing for any expenses associated with the campaign. It is also important to find independent leadership. While the board, administrator and staff have to become involved in the effort to ensure passage, it is essential to have a nonpartisan citizens' organization officially working for voter approval. Sometimes a Friends group can provide the nucleus. Other times, it may be more efficient to persuade another civic organization to perform this service, or the administrator may take the initiative in establishing a new group with leadership willing to assume the task.

Whatever the group, it will usually be required to register with the state and submit reports on contributions and expenditures. There are special categories of tax-exempt status that can be granted by the IRS to this type of organization to permit contributions by individuals and firms to be tax-deductible, even for a political campaign.

The campaign committee can raise funds through individual solicitation or special events such as rallies. Dinners, cocktail parties and informal coffees are popular because they bring together individuals with a common interest and increase the sense of commitment to the campaign. However, they can be expensive to set up; generally donors are sought to absorb any costs so the proceeds are free and clear.

## Endorsements

Endorsements by local organizations that are prominent in the community and that reflect the range of library use are equally important and provide valuable public relations material. Groups such as the PTA council, the chamber of commerce, civic associations and labor unions are likely supporters. It is especially important to seek the endorsement of the news media, including local radio and television stations as well as the newspapers. Presentations before their editorial boards will provide them with the facts on which to base their support.

## Communications

Because of the expense of political advertisements, which generally cost more than normal ads, it is important to place them carefully. They should be spread evenly throughout the media to ensure that favoritism isn't shown to any particular newspaper or broadcasting station. Larger campaigns may find it important to retain an advertising agency to place their ads, since an agency can determine the best times and media for reaching the desired target audience.

The administrator or a suitable member of the board should appear on talk shows and at service club and civic meetings to communicate the need for the refendum. A basic brochure on the library and the purpose of the referendum, paid for by the campaign committee, is also an essential tool. In addition, Federal Communications Commission (FCC) regulations permit a campaign to request free air time on television and radio, and this may be another means of reaching the voters. However, under the fairness doctrine, anyone who opposes the campaign may gain equal time.

### Personal Contact

Successful politicians report there is nothing like personal contact to gain votes. The campaign should have its members, the board, the staff and the administrator as visible as possible. Another popular option is the telephone poll. The campaign committee can either develop a calling list based on a random selection in the telephone directory or work on a particular target group such as library users. Identifying themselves as members of the campaign organization, callers can determine levels of registration and support for the levy. They can also answer any questions, using information provided by the library. If a random sample is used, selected by a statistically sound method, it may be possible to assess how the campaign is going, although the primary purpose of the poll is to make more voters aware of the issue and gain their support.

### Voter Turnout and Registration

Registration is a critical element in the campaign, since statistics reveal that a fairly high percentage of the American public is not registered to vote. Some libraries can serve as voter registration locations, through special arrangements with the jurisdiction's voter registrar. This has the advantage of attracting people to the library and allows libraries to register new borrowers and voters at the same time.

Getting the voters to the polls is the final step in the process and can often be done in concert with other organizations such as senior citizens groups. It is important that the "right" voters get to the polls, however, and therefore emphasis should be placed upon working with those organizations that have endorsed the library levy.

After the campaign has ended, and the issue has been decided, it is essential that everyone who was associated with the effort is thanked and recognized. This includes the campaign committee, the media and all the organizations that endorsed the campaign. The next step, if the campaign was successful, is to implement the plan that served as the platform. Promises must be kept, for the library is certain to suffer the consequences the next time it approaches the voters if it reneges on its commitment.

## ENDOWMENTS

Endowments were mentioned earlier in this chapter, but deserve further attention, in terms of both how they should be managed and how donations can be encouraged. Estimates are that public libraries in the U.S. have between $500 million and $1 billion in endowments and other inactive funds. This money is usually placed in local financial institutions, and it is not always effectively managed to provide the best yield for the library.

### Management

Some administrators and boards pride themselves on their financial acumen and manage these endowments by themselves. However, the investment field is growing increasingly more complex, and the lay investor is aware of only the most common options. A better choice for the public library board is the creation of an investment advisory committee or the retention of an investment manager for the library's portfolio. The committee or manager should keep the portfolio sound and should be knowledgeable about legal restrictions against certain investments.

An advisory committee consists of representatives from the local financial institutions who volunteer their services in advising the board how to best invest its endowment funds. Many financial institutions will do this as a free public service for a library.

For libraries that retain the services of an individual investment manager, it is important to realize that these services will cost money. Nonetheless, if the endowment is large enough and the aboard has latitude in the manner in which the funds can be invested, professional services should be paid for easily out of the increased yield.

Whichever method the library employs, it will need to set some goals for the endowment. If the intention is to accrue the return to build a larger base or to earn a return of a specific amount each year, that will need to be communicated to the committee or manager, as a foundation for investment strategy.

## Development

The development of endowments and donations is a major function of the administrator. While some institutions have established special trusts to receive bequests and donations, most public libraries can accept them without jeopardizing their tax-exempt status. The IRS recognizes public libraries as governmental entities. The only problem may be for association libraries, which can certainly qualify under other provisions of the Internal Revenue Code.

A useful device for many libraries is a descriptive brochure which explains the tax benefits of bequests and donations, contains the official name for inclusion in a will or other legal documents, defines how restricted endowments may be established if that is the donor's intention and provides some examples of how other endowments or donations have been used. This can be distributed whenever the library provides a program for local service clubs or can be mailed to professionals such as attorneys, who may wish to refer them to clients.

Memorial contributions can also be encouraged, such as purchasing books in memory of someone who has died. A simple procedure can be arranged to provide a letter to the nearest living relative, an acknowledgement to the donor for income tax purposes and a book plate noting by whom the book was donated and in whose memory. Many libraries have found that memorial gifts can be significant supplements to their book budget, and that they can sometimes lead to substantial gifts or an endowment for an additional memorial. These memorials should be displayed and publicized whenever appropriate to encourage additional donations.

It is good pratice to encourage departments to have a list of needed projects ready to suggest to an individual or organization interested in donating to the library. Of course, the donor may have a specific project in mind, but often people are searching for worthwhile projects to sponsor and need several suggestions as a basis for their decision.

The administrator should never hesitate to bring an appropriate project to a civic group or service club. While these organizations may have adopted other permanent service projects, a library proposal might be developed in conjunction with that project. Sometimes a group may be seeking to broaden its scope. Groups that are reluctant to make a donation to a tax-supported entity can always be reminded that tax revenues are never sufficient to satisfy the library's needs.

## GRANTSMANSHIP

Besides seeking individual donations and improving the return on the library's inactive funds and endowments, the library administrator is generally the institution's principal grant seeker. Federal and state grants were discussed earlier in this chapter. As noted, the major source of information on federal grants is the *Catalog of Federal Domestic Assistance*, which will identify any programs appropriate for the library. While there is no comparable compendium for state aid, there are some parallels between many states and the federal government. For example, most states have their own version of the National Endowment for the Humanities and the National Endowment for the Arts.

State humanities councils and arts councils get their funding from NEH and NEA, and many are further subsidized by their state legislatures. A project that is inappropriate or too small for consideration for a federal grant might be welcomed by the state organizations. Guidelines and deadlines can be obtained by contacting the state councils.

There is an increasing trend toward funding projects that involve more than one type of agency or that have the endorsement of other agencies. Often local schools and academic institutions are seeking endorsements or cosponsors for such projects. Making it known that the library is interested in similar projects can improve rapport with those institutions, gain endorsements and perhaps stimulate an invitation to join in an interesting project.

### Corporate and Foundation Grants

Corporations and foundations are also potential sources for grants. Federal tax regulations permit private corporations to deduct up to 10% of their profits as donations to nonprofit institutions. Some large corporations have separate foundations for charitable giving; others act through committees or through their executive office. By watching the papers or through personal contacts, the administrator should be able to identify those corporations in the community that offer funds.

Significant donations have been received by many libraries. For example, Borg-Warner Corp. supplied the Chicago Public Library with teaching machines and volunteer trainers. Playboy Enterprises, Inc. donated $35,000 to that same institution to purchase the John Peter Zenger papers for its special collections division. Many libraries can cite similar examples of the generosity of local companies.

The advantage to the company, besides tax credits, is building good will in the community and improving local services that will benefit its employees. Besides the direct benefits that come to the library in terms of dollars, materials or services, there is also the possibility of a long-term commitment to the library. That corporation is likely to use the library more frequently as its executives become familiar with it and to increase its investment through additional donations in the future.

While libraries often receive donations from national foundations, such as the Carnegie Foundation, the Council on Library Resources and the Ford Foundation, it is the local foundation that deserves the most attention from the library. Most national foundations are seeking to support programs that have long-term national impact, such as research in the preservation of library materials or the development of management internship programs. Grants to aid in building programs are not common and are likely to go only to very large libraries.

Local foundations, in contrast, are searching for ways in which they can improve their own community. Many cities have community trusts, which are really collections of many smaller trusts and endowments that are given to foundation officials to administer. Individually, these trusts might not have significant impact, but, when they are pooled, substantial grants may be possible. For example, the Columbus (OH) Foundation donated $150,000 to the Columbus and Franklin County Public Library toward the purchase of an online circulation system.

Local foundations usually understand the library and its needs, making it easier for the library adminstrator to prepare a proposal and justify it. Preliminary meetings can be arranged with local foundation officials to discuss the proposal. An astute administrator can use these meetings to emphasize those components of the project that interest the official.

In working with foundations, great care should be taken to report the progress of the project and to provide a sound evaluation of the results. Foundations are under constant scrutiny by the IRS and other governmental agencies, as well as the donors and the foundation board. Documentation to support the effectiveness of the foundation's grants is greatly appreciated and underlines the efficient use of the foundation's money.

**Writing Grant Proposals**

Writing project proposals is both an art and a science. There are many good books on this subject, but three simple guidelines are given here.

• Always read the guidelines and requirements published by the agency. Agencies devote considerable time to preparing them, and they neither appreciate nor favor an application if there is evidence its authors failed to study the requirements.

• While every agency has a preferred format to be followed, always remember that a proposal must define a need, state goals, describe the methods proposed to attain those goals, set up a timetable and include a budget. There may be many more elements requested, but this information must be there.

• Use the language of the specialist, but keep it simple and free of jargon.

Even when a proposal is rejected, some valuable lessons can be learned that improve the library's chances with its next proposal. Many federal and state agencies, for example, will provide comments regarding the proposal made by the reviewing panel or individuals. These should be requested whenever possible.

While grantsmanship can be time-consuming and highly competitive, it can bring both immediate and long-term rewards. In the short term, of course, the project is funded. As noted, private corporations may assume a long-term commitment to the library once they are more familiar with it. A local foundation may also draw upon the library's resources and find the library a valuable means to implement other projects.

## SUMMARY

Local revenues provide the major source of funding for public libraries. Property taxes remain the primary source of these revenues, but other local taxes that may also generate funds include the income tax, the sales tax, and various special and dedicated taxes. Federal support for library services has come principally through general revenue sharing funds and the Library Services and Construction Act. State governments are also providing increasing levels of support. Other sources of revenue include interest income, contracts to provide services, fees, fines, and grants from federal and state agencies and from corporations and foundations.

Whatever the sources of income, the library administrator is responsible for converting money into library services. The library budget should be a major tool in both planning for and providing those services, as well as for controlling expenditures. Other financial management concerns include contracts with vendors, the capital improvement budget and techniques for dealing with times of retrenchment.

In addition to managing revenues, the library administrator can play an active role in increasing the library's funding. In most cases, the administrator will have to lobby for passage of the library budget. Whenever there is a referendum to increase tax support for library services, the administrator should be directly, if discreetly, involved in the campaign. Finally, the administrator is also responsible for maximizing the return on invested funds and for actively seeking donations, endowments and grants.

## FOOTNOTES

1. U.S. National Center for Educational Statistics, *Preliminary Report. Library General Information Survey, LIBGIS III: Public Libraries, 1977-78* (Washington, DC: U.S. National Center for Educational Statistics, 1982), Table 12.

2. *Ibid.*

3. *Ibid.*

4. Frank W. Gaudy, "General Revenue Sharing and Public Libraries, An Estimate of Fiscal Impact," *Library Quarterly*, January 1982, p. 17.

5. *Ibid.*

6. U.S. Office of Management and Budget, *Catalog of Federal Domestic Assistance,* 17th edition. (Washington, DC: Government Printing Office, 1983).

7. *LIBGIS III*, Table 12.

8. *Ibid.*

9. Mary Jo Lynch, *Financing Online Search Services in Publicly Supported Libraries: The Report of an ALA Survey* (Chicago: American Library Association, 1981), p. 10.

## SUGGESTIONS FOR FURTHER READING

Alley, Brian and Jennifer Cargill. *Keeping Track of What You Spend: The Librarian's Guide to Simple Bookkeeping.* Phoenix, AZ: Oryx Press, 1982.

Boss, Richard W. *Grant Money and How to Get It: A Handbook for Librarians.* New York: R.R. Bowker Co., 1980.

Breivik, Patricia and E. Burr Gibson. *Funding Alternatives for Libraries.* Chicago: American Library Association, 1979. .

Chen, Ching-Chih. *Zero-Base Budgeting in Library Management: A Manual for Librarians.* Phoenix, AZ: Oryx Press, 1980.

Corry, Emmett. *Grants for Libraries: A Guide to Public and Private Funding Programs and Proposal Writing Techniques.* Littleton, CO: Libraries Unlimited, Inc., 1982.

Getz, Malcolm. *Public Libraries: An Economic View.* Baltimore, MD: The Johns Hopkins University Press, 1980.

Leerberger, Benedict A. *Marketing the Library.* White Plains, NY: Knowledge Industry Publications, Inc., 1982.

Mason, Marilyn Gell. *The Federal Role in Library and Information Services.* White Plains, NY: Knowledge Industry Publications, Inc., 1983.

# 4

# Planning

The administrator is the library's chief planner. Indeed, planning is one of the primary responsibilities, burdens and joys of the job. Although the board must review, modify and approve the goals and objectives of the institution, the administrator is responsible both for initiating and for implementing those goals and objectives.

The development of a long-range plan involves the participation of many people. Staff participation is especially important. It is a fundamental rule that the individuals who have to implement a plan must help to develop it, or it will fail. Board members and community representatives must also be included. Nonetheless, authority and responsibility for planning remain with the administrator.

Planning is also a complex process, with many steps, including appointing a planning committee, evaluating the library's mission, gathering information, setting goals and objectives, developing strategies, establishing priorities and, finally, implementing the plan. The review of these steps in this chapter provides a basis for their application in many specific areas discussed in other chapters, such as budgeting, personnel administration and automation. The long-range plan—and the statement of the library's mission—provide the framework in which specific goals and objectives can be developed.

## PLANNING: PRO AND CON

There are many who object to formal planning processes, for a variety of reasons. Some believe that a plan raises false expectations, particularly if it comes during a time of economic problems. They feel that the goals and objectives set will require additional resources, and that this can happen only through the termination of existing services. Others are disturbed by the time that must be committed to develop a meaningful plan that is based on sound information. Others reject the concept of trying to anticipate future needs and resources.

### Raising Expectations

It is well to admit that there is a bit of truth in all of these concerns. Many plans do raise expectations that cannot be fulfilled. However, many others succeed because the community believes it is worth the commitment to develop them into permanent programs. Furthermore, without planning, an institution stagnates.

In times of economic crisis, planning is more important than ever. When resources are short, care must be taken to ensure they are effectively used. For example, if it appears future revenues will not support the staffing of a new branch library, then funds allocated in the capital budget for that new branch should be shifted to some other purpose—perhaps automation of circulation to permit more effective use of existing personnel.

### Termination of Services

Planning does sometimes result in a decision to terminate existing services, when it is determined that another program will better satisfy public needs. No law requires the library to maintain forever services that are past their usefulness. Planning helps prepare both personnel and the public for these changes.

### Time Commitment

The time required for planning can be reduced as experience in the process is gained and as planning becomes an integral part of management and budgeting procedures. Planning is not a task that requires any set time to complete; rather, it is a continuous cycle. Later in this chapter this cycle will be discussed at greater length.

## Predicting the Future

Finally, forecasting change *is* risky and can result in expensive errors. On the other hand, waiting for future needs to knock on the library's door is almost certain to lead to management by crisis or to valid public criticism that the institution has failed to exercise any vision.

The library cannot just respond to current public needs. It must also anticipate those needs. Collections and services are built on assessment of trends and reasonable judgment of what the community will require, not just today, but in the foreseeable future. Good planning involves use of projections and statistics; however, it need not be bound by them. For example, a community may wish to maintain a strong commitment to programs and services for children even if they are not a growing segment of the population.

The library needs to plan as a basis for training and developing its staff, for redesigning its operating and capital improvements budgets to meet anticipated needs, for reorganizing and refining its collections and services to keep them pertinent, and for influencing the development of the community. Ten years ago, not many people realized the impact that online database searching would have on public library users. A few libraries did take the risk to invest in and develop this service, and its use has spread widely.

## THE CHARGE AND THE COMMITTEE

The first steps in planning are the creation of a charge and the appointment of a committee. The charge—or instruction to the committee—must be carefully drafted to define what the committee is to produce, when it is to be completed, and how and to whom it is to be presented. Customarily, the charge is determined by the board, based upon the recommendation of the administrator.

Usually, the charge specifies a time span—for example, a 3-year plan or a 10-year plan. It may also focus on a particular area of increased service, such as reaching special user groups. More often, however, the charge is quite general—for example, to produce a 5-year plan to improve library services, with an emphasis on developing ways to obtain the revenues necessary for those services.

The board should also specify the support it will provide for the committee, including such items as financial assistance for conducting surveys and clerical support for preparing reports and minutes of meetings.

The planning committee should include representatives from the board, the staff and the community. There is no perfect number, but 12 is convenient and workable. Too large a group discourages full participation. Too small a group prevents a broader view from being developed. The ratio should be 50% community representatives, 25% board members and 25% staff. The library administrator should serve as the chair or coordinator.

Once the committee members have been selected and have accepted the position, the staff and the public should be encouraged to send suggestions and recommendations to the members.

At its first organizational meeting, the committee should discuss the charge and consider the steps required and the time they will take. Ideally, the process should be completed within six months, since a longer period will result in loss of impetus. The committee should also discuss the type of information needed to complete the task and how it can be collected.

Regular meeting dates should be established, so they can be fixed in everyone's calendars. Minutes of all meetings should be taken and distributed for the benefit of those unable to attend each session and as a basis for subsequent interpretation of the plan.

## THE LIBRARY'S MISSION

All planning should take place in the context of a statement of the library's mission. Many libraries have role statements or funtional descriptions in their bylaws or in the enabling ordinance that created them. If there is no such role statement, one should be developed. It will form an important benchmark for the plan, and goals can be tested against it. Sometimes, however, planning discussions may reveal different perceptions regarding the institution. Thus, it may be necessary to revise the role statement by the time the plan is complete.

Developing a role statement is usually among the most difficult components of planning, because the role of the institution is generally stated in abstract terms (see the examples in Figure 4.1). It is also the first time the group has focused attention on the institution. Although it may be useful to study the role statements of other institutions, care should be taken not to accept another's statement unless it reflects the same concerns as those of the planning committee. The principles statement of the Public Library Association (PLA) is also a valuable reference for this process; an excerpt was given in Chapter 1.[1]

## Figure 4.1: Sample Role Statements for Public Libraries

•

The Willson Public Library shall serve the adult population of Horicon County and the youth of the county in concert with the County Board of Education and the Higher Education Council, providing this audience with wholesome books and audiovisual resources to satisfy their recreational, educational and informational needs. In addition, the Willson Library shall provide information services and cultural programming in cooperation with the Upper Valley Library Federation and other pertinent social service and cultural organizations of Horicon County.

•

The Baltis Public Library shall serve all the people who reside or work in the city limits of Baltis, without regard to age, race, creed or color, drawing upon a balanced collection of print and nonprint resources, maintained by an adequate staff of professional librarians and supportive personnel. The collection shall reflect the needs of the community, as determined by regular survey. Cooperation with other libraries, educational, cultural and social service agencies will be ongoing to ensure unnecessary duplication of resources and services is avoided.

•

The Temps Memorial Library will provide free books, audiovisual and other appropriate resources to any resident of Freemount County through its central library and extension services departments. As needs are identified for the provision of specialized reference and cultural services by the library's professional staff, with the approval of its Board of Trustees, these shall be either extended by the Temps Memorial Library or offered in concert with the other libraries and/or institutions located in the county that have a pertinent interest in the service.

•

Another resource is the statement of the American Library Trustees Association, which was adopted by the organization during the meeting of its board of directors in January 1984, and which reads:

> The mission of the public library is to serve the public and to ensure to all of the people the freedom to read and to freely choose from all sources of information and knowledge.
> Libraries have existed since the beginning of recorded history and public libraries, as we know them today, have

grown and developed over the past 150 years. While public libraries perform many functions, they primarily enrich our personal lives, encourage self-education and promote enlightened citizenship.

The public library affords access to resources far beyond the normal reach of any individual. It provides to everyone with motivation or curiosity the accumulated wisdom and experience of all mankind. It widens the horizons and whets the thirst for knowledge.

The United States, the leader of nations that cherish political freedom, has accepted the concept that the education of all its people is necessary for the highest possible levels of individual development; it is necessary for the growth of our democratic society. The public library is, and always has been, one of the major institutions which enhances educational opportunity for everyone.

If the committee has difficulty in developing the statement, it may be helpful to focus on identifying specific elements that members wish to include. These can then be combined into more general topics to produce a comprehensive statement. As a rule, committees do not write well. One or two members should be appointed for the actual drafting of the statement, which can then be modified by the committee if necessary before adoption.

## DATA COLLECTION

The next step in the planning process is to gather reliable information on which to base the selection of goals and objectives to be included in the long-range plan. It is important, however, not to overload the committee with so much data that it is overwhelmed.

Among the types of information needed are financial history, statistics on usage, comparison to state or regional standards, ranking with other libraries, summaries of demographic trends and current census data. The planning department and the finance office of the local governmental jurisdiction should be able to provide useful assistance. Specialists on the library staff may report on trends and the current status of the library in their area of specialization.

As data are collected, they should be compiled in written reports. These reports should be distributed to committee members as background to be studied in advance of discussion. Valuable meeting time should *not* be devoted to review of these data. As the plan begins to take form, it can be tested against the facts that are known. For example, do the statistics support the need for increased services to senior citizens?

## SURVEYS

One of the most valuable information gathering tools is the survey. *A Planning Process for Public Libraries*, developed for the Public Library Association, recommends a number of surveys that should be considered by the planning committee, including surveys of library users, citizens (i.e., both users and nonusers in the general population) and staff.[2] With the exception of the staff survey, *A Planning Process for Public Libraries* proposes use of a random sample. Sampling procedures are discussed later in this chapter.

Questionnaires included in that publication may offer an alternative to the development of a questionnaire by the committee or staff. However, the questions should be modified to be appropriate to the library and the community. Very long questionnaires may discourage participation. The committee should carefully weigh the value of the information a question will generate. Unless it will make a clear contribution to the plan, the question should not be included.

### Citizen Surveys

Hundreds of libraries have used citizen surveys because including nonusers as well as users gives a truer picture of how the community views the library. The results, which have been frequently reported in the professional literature, have been fairly uniform throughout the nation. Although a large percentage of the population expresses satisfaction with the library and its services, many surveys reveal public ignorance of all but the most traditional library resources and services. Nonusers report other sources for information or only limited need for the resources and services offered by the library, and they assert that there are few actions the library can take to attract them.

#### *Value of Citizen Surveys*

Nonetheless, such a survey may be useful in reassuring the planning committee (as well as the board and other public officials) that library service is generally satisfactory. Emphasis can then be placed on responding to any suggestions for needed improvements that do appear in the survey results. A citizen survey is also good public relations, since it shows the library is making an effort to keep its services responsive to community need.

*Conducting Citizen Surveys*

Citizen surveys are usually handled door-to-door or by telephone and require considerable organization to ensure that the results are valid. While some libraries have attempted surveys using the mail or by publishing questionnaires in local newspapers or newsletters, they do not provide valid responses. In addition to questions about library use, citizen surveys should emphasize what could be done to attract the nonuser.

Some libraries have employed marketing research firms to undertake citizen surveys. These firms base their charges on the number of interviews completed. Additional charges are assessed for editing, tabulation and reporting of the results. While marketing research surveys can be expensive, depending upon the size of the sampling and the complexity of the survey instrument, they have the advantage of being objective. Also, because the survey personnel are experienced, there is less chance of adverse public relations than if a volunteer or a member of the library staff conducted the survey.

If a marketing firm is retained, the administrator, in consultation with the board, should prepare the survey specifications carefully. These should include the following:

• A copy of the questionnaire to be used;

• A description of exactly how the sample should be taken;

• When the interview should be held in terms of hours of the day, day of the week;

• The specific age group to be surveyed;

• How the results are to be presented;

• When the survey is to be completed;

• Prior testing requirements to determine if changes in the instrument are needed.

The marketing firm should be directed to record the name of the individual interviewed and the address and/or telephone number, so that the library may verify, on a sampling basis, that the interview took place and assess the quality of the interview.

## User Surveys

The results of user surveys closely parallel those from citizen surveys. The user survey can provide, however, a valuable insight into who in the community uses the library, as well as the amount of nonresident use. It can provide information on when usage is heaviest, which services and resources are most in demand, and a host of other facts pertinent to the function of the library—provided that those questions are asked in the survey.

Much of this information may already exist in the library's management reports. For example, a good registration system should be able to reveal the nature of the users and the level of nonresident usage. The circulation system, particularly if it is automated, should be able to supply statistics on which resources are most in demand. Nonetheless, a great many libraries have very simple statistics and do not possess much information about the nature of their usage. If that is the case, then a user survey may be a very important facet of the planning process.

A good user survey should provide the following information:

- Ease of access to the library;

- Need for additional agencies or facilities;

- Reason why the user patronizes the library;

- Adequacy of hours;

- Frequency of user visits to the library;

- Services and resources used;

- Level of satisfaction with services and resources;

- Deficiencies in terms of services or resources;

- Services and resources that are most and least valued;

• Degree of awareness of library services and resources;

• Other libraries the patron uses and reasons for that use;

• User information such as community, education, age range, sex and length of residency.

User surveys are easier to undertake than citizen surveys. Representative times of day and days of the week are selected for the survey. Volunteers or staff can distribute surveys to people as they enter the library at those times. The surveys are then collected as patrons leave, or they can be placed in a return box on the circulation desk.

While these surveys can be time-consuming, they can also provide essential information for the planning process and serve as a reference point to measure the impact of the plan. For example, if the premise of the long-range plan is to improve public use and satisfaction within five years, the level of satisfaction reported at the beginning of the planning period can be compared with the results of a similar survey taken five years later. While library statistics usually provide evidence of increased or decreased usage, they cannot provide qualitative results. That is where the surveys become more valuable.

## Staff Surveys

A survey of the staff is often the most efficient means of identifying problems and deficiencies in public service. The staff hears the complaints of users and is well aware of gaps in the collection as a result of interlibrary loan and reserve requests. While the public may have a generally low level of expectation and may be grateful to be able to locate any information in the library, the staff should be more knowledgeable of what should ideally be available. Thus, a staff survey should be considered even if citizen and user surveys will not be conducted.

Administrators occasionally fear that a staff survey will produce complaints about mismanagement, low morale, lack of communication and similar grievances  These might cause the planning committee to shift its concern to an assessment of the library's management. The survey could also result in a list of petty gripes or become self-serving in its focus upon the need for improved salaries and fringe benefits.

The best way to avoid these problems is to prepare the survey carefully so that it elicits information that contributes directly to the development of the long-range plan. Keeping the questions objective and avoiding open-ended questions that require a narrative response will contribute to that end and also make tabulation of the results easier.

Information that should be sought in a staff survey includes:

• Services or resources that will increase public use or satisfaction;

• Services or resources that should be eliminated because of limited use;

• Adequacy of the collection and the degree of duplication;

• Quality of reference services and programming;

• Assessment of major strengths and weaknesses in the library's operations;

• Degree of job satisfaction;

• Adequacy of communication;

• Assessment of work load;

• Satisfaction with training and supervision;

• Deficiencies in working conditions.

The staff survey form contained in *A Planning Process for Public Libraries* can be used by the planning committee. Analysis of the results collected by libraries using this questionnaire reveals that most staff welcome the opportunity to contribute to the planning process. They use the survey to identify community needs and problems in service that would normally be missed by administrators, boards and citizens.

Two final notes about staff surveys: Staff should be encouraged to submit the questionnaires anonymously, and the results should be reported to them. If the questionnaires are signed, the results are certain to be skewed. If the results are not reported, staff will believe that the administration is trying to hide unfavorable information.

## SAMPLING PROCEDURES

Surveys are of value only if they are done correctly. Because a staff survey involves the entire organization, there can be little doubt of its validity—unless only a minority participated, or the questions were slanted. For a user or citizen survey, however, no library can afford the time and expense associated with a poll of all its users or the entire community. Even if it could, a substantial percentage of the users or citizens would probably fail to participate. For those reasons, most user and citizen surveys are conducted by polling only a sampling of the users and citizens.

To understand sampling procedures, it is important to know the types of errors that are possible in a sampling study. These, in turn, will determine the size of the sampling that should be taken.

### Tolerance

"Tolerence" is the measure of the accuracy of the result of a survey. For example, we may say that 25% of our users are students, but we know that it is rarely possible to pinpoint that figure precisely unless we go through the process of surveying everyone who uses the library. Therefore, we may simply say that between 23% and 27% of our users are students, based on our observations. This tolerance is generally written as 25%±2.

### Confidence

"Confidence" is a measure of how certain one is that the true answer lies within the limits stated in the tolerance. For example, a confidence of 90% means that there is one chance in 10 that the true value of the number being predicted by a survey lies outside the tolerance set. In other words, if the survey is repeated 10 times, using the same sample size and tolerance, but different sample audiences, the results would fall within the specified tolerance for nine of the replications.

Most libraries find that a tolerance of five and a confidence level of 90% will produce satisfactory results.

### Size of Sampling

Once the administrator or planning committee determines the degree of tolerance and confidence they will accept for a sampling survey, the information given in Table 4.1 can be used to determine the size of the sampling. Thus, if the planning committee should decide on a survey with a tolerance of five and a confidence level of 90% the necessary sample size is 271.

## Random Sampling

Sampling must also ensure that the individuals who are

### Table 4.1: Determining Size of Sampling

| Confidence | Tolerance | Size |
|---|---|---|
| 99% | ± 0.5% | 66,358 |
| | 1.0 | 16,590 |
| | 2.0 | 4,147 |
| | 3.0 | 1,843 |
| | 5.0 | 664 |
| | 7.0 | 339 |
| | 10.0 | 166 |
| 95% | 0.5 | 38,416 |
| | 1.0 | 9,604 |
| | 2.0 | 2,401 |
| | 3.0 | 1,067 |
| | 5.0 | 384 |
| | 7.0 | 196 |
| | 10.0 | 96 |
| 90% | 0.5 | 27,060 |
| | 1.0 | 6,765 |
| | 2.0 | 1,691 |
| | 3.0 | 752 |
| | 5.0 | 271 |
| | 7.0 | 138 |
| | 10.0 | 68 |
| 80% | 0.5 | 16,435 |
| | 1.0 | 4,109 |
| | 2.0 | 1,027 |
| | 3.0 | 457 |
| | 5.0 | 164 |
| | 7.0 | 84 |
| | 10.0 | 41 |

Source: M. Carl Drott, "Random Sampling: A Tool for Research," *College & Research Libraries,* March 1969, pp. 119-125.

surveyed are truly a random and unbiased selection. For example, conducting a user survey only on weekday afternoons would yield a disproportionately high number of students and a low number of business and professional people, given typical school and working hours. Thus, hours and days selected for the user survey should be balanced to ensure true usage is reflected.

If a citizen survey is conducted based on the formula that every fifth house will be visited in each block of the community, then some similar random formula will have to be applied to apartments. In addition, the surveyor must repeatedly seek to contact the inhabitants of houses or apartments specified. If the surveyor simply goes from door to door until he or she finds someone at home, the survey results will not be valid.

## GOALS AND OBJECTIVES

Based on the information gathered, the committee can begin to develop a clear set of goals and objectives for the plan. Figure 4.2 illustrates sample goals and objectives, and the relationship between them.

A goal is a measurable achievement that can be attained

**Figure 4.2: Sample Goals and Objectives**

---

**GOAL:** To improve library service through the construction of a new branch library.

**OBJECTIVE A:** Locate a site central to the community through survey and assistance from the county planning agency.

**OBJECTIVE B:** Develop a building program using the assistance of a consultant, extension personnel and the county architectural department.

**GOAL:** To improve reserve response for the system through the implementation of an automated system.

**OBJECTIVE A:** Prepare a set of specifications based on research into the present reserve procedures, review of the available systems and discussions with circulation personnel.

**OBJECTIVE B:** Solicit bids from qualified contractors and award a contract to the lowest bidding and best qualified firm.

---

through the completion of one or two objectives. Goals are intentionally broad, but not so broad as to prevent evaluation of progress toward them. To be useful, a goal should not be unattainable or ongoing. Unattainable goals might serve as incentives for some individuals or organizations, but usually they become ignored in the long term. Ongoing goals really become job descriptions or duty rosters and have limited value in long-range planning. Thus, the tests of a good goal are whether the steps to attain it can be logically determined and whether it meets a need identified by the planning committee as a result of the data it gathered.

Objectives are the specific steps a library takes toward achieving its goals. An objective should represent only one task. If several tasks must be completed to achieve a goal, each should be written as a separate objective.

The process of setting goals can be difficult, as the committee must turn from hard facts to decisions about what "should" be. In this stage and the two that follow—determining strategies and setting priorities for implementing the plan—the services of a facilitator may be especially valuable. The use of facilitators is discussed after the section on setting priorities.

## STRATEGIES

After goals and objectives are set, the committee must examine them to identify the various alternatives the library might take to attain them. Defining alternative strategies is among the most important aspects of the planning process, for it reveals whether the goals and objectives are practical. For example, the strategies needed for the examples in Figure 4.2 would include assignment of funds and personnel to implement the tasks. If neither is available, then both goals and objectives will require revision.

### Deadlines and Responsibilities

The committee should set a deadline for completion of each goal and should determine which department or individual will be assigned the responsibility for implementation. Without a deadline, it is impossible to measure and evaluate progress. Even if the deadline is just a guesstimate that is revised as more information is obtained, it must be there.

Obviously, goals and objectives cannot be met unless it is clear who is responsible for taking the necessary action. The responsible department or individual should, of course, be involved in this decision. Otherwise, commitment may be lacking, and the plan is not likely to succeed.

## Special Considerations in Larger Libraries

As the size of the library and the complexity of its services increase, it is important to increase participation in planning. The most typical approach is a "goals down, plans up" planning process. In this process, the planning committee concentrates on defining the mission of the library and setting general goals, as well as some limited objectives.

Supervisory staff then carry the partially developed goals and objectives to their units, where they can explain to their staff the considerations of the planning committee. Additional objectives can then be defined by the staff, and strategies for attaining the library's goals and objectives can be established. Each unit should focus on those objectives and goals that are particularly relevant to it. For example, a goal of making the collection more accessible would be extremely pertinent to the staff of the technical services department. Based on their knowledge of technical operations, they could establish measurable objectives and define the strategies to achieve them.

## SETTING PRIORITIES

Often the process of developing a plan will reveal a natural set of priorities. Finding additional revenue sources or personnel may have to precede other goals. Completion of a marketing analysis should come before implementation of a new service. Evaluation of collection losses is required before a decision is made to purchase and install a theft detection system. The deadlines that are established for the different goals will reflect the natural priority or sequence of activity.

The planning process may also reveal conflicting priorities. Some members of the board or planning committee may favor emphasis on automation while others believe the library must first improve its personnel resources. If the library cannot simultaneously pursue goals with equally high priorities, the plan may falter unless a compromise can be reached. Often the compromise is made on a subjective basis by a committee or board who are swayed by the strongest personalities. However, there are other, more objective, methods an administrator can employ in establishing priorities for the institution.

The political jurisdiction of which the library is a part may have a long-range plan or other programs that include elements related to the library's long-range plan. If the plan or programs were issues in a recent election, some insight may be gained into concerns held by a majority of citizens.

Another alternative is to undertake another survey, using a sampling of the community to assess their preference. Examining the state library plan may also suggest which goals and objectives should have priority, particularly if additional revenue sources are needed to implement them. A project proposal to the state library agency might be an appropriate strategy. Review of the library's role statement may also reveal emphases that can be used to weigh goals. Finally, if the board or committee appear deadlocked on priorities, the best solution may be to propose concurrent progress on the goals but to extend the deadlines because of the limited capacity to undertake two major goals simultaneously.

## FACILITATORS

Getting the participants in a planning process to work effectively requires special skills. The focus must keep to measurable goals, and it is important to provide an opportunity for even the least assertive participant to make a contribution. If the group becomes divided on key issues, such as construction of new facilities versus expansion of services, it is particularly difficult to maintain the momentum and balance necessary for the group to satisfy its charge. The administrator, in attempting to maintain the balance, may feel his or her own goals and objectives are being submerged. For these reasons, some libraries choose to retain an outside facilitator.

Experienced library administrators sometimes act as consultants. In addition to supplying technical expertise on the alternatives being considered, such an individual can also function as a facilitator during the discussions of the planning committee. Libraries may also benefit from the services of an individual with expertise in group dynamics, who can remain neutral and objective as the committee proceeds with its work.

The administrator must assess his or her own skills and appraise the composition and strengths of the members of the committee in order to determine whether the group will need a facilitator. When a facilitator is required, there are several sources of assistance. Most state library agencies can supply the names of individuals who are familiar with the planning process and/or possess skills as facilitators. The Public Library Association also maintains lists of people qualified to provide this assistance. Another resource might be the administrator or a staff member from a nearby library that has developed a sound long-range plan through participatory techniques. Some cooperative library systems provide this kind of consultant service or can identify specialists with these skills.

## EVALUATION OF THE PLANNING PROCESS

Upon completion of the planning process, the administrator should seek an evaluation of the effort from the participants. A sample evaluation form is given in Figure 4.3. An evaluation will identify problems that should be corrected for future planning sessions.

## IMPLEMENTATION

After the completed plan has been reviewed and accepted by the library board, the administrator must begin its implementation. Too many plans fail because the administrator assumes that various departments will automatically identify objectives and strategies that apply to them and will proceed with their implementation. It rarely happens that way.

### Staff Coordination

At a postplanning process session for the administrative staff, assignments and responsibilities should be clarified, and action delegated. The staff should also be oriented to the plan and its relation to their work. If the administrator has regularly reported on the progress and direction of the plan and conferred with appropriate department heads in determining reasonable deadlines, there should be no serious problems with this phase of implementation.

There will, however, be problems of coordination. Often, different departments must complete separate objectives for the same goal. One department may have to wait until another component of the plan is complete before it can carry out its

## Figure 4.3: Planning Evaluation Form

1. Did you receive sufficient information to help you in the development of this plan?

    _____ Yes       _____ No

    If not, what specific information was lacking?

2. Do you feel that the information provided to you during the course of this planning process was presented in a manner which made it clear and useful?

    _____ Yes       _____ No

    If not, what changes would you suggest which would improve clarity and usefulness?

3. Do you feel the committee had enough time to study and discuss the mission, goals, objectives and strategies?

    _____ Yes       _____ No

    If not, how would you have changed the discussions to permit more time?

4. Do you feel the coordinator (or facilitator) carried out his/her responsibilities adequately?

    _____ Yes       _____ No

    If not, what changes would you make regarding the coordinator's (facilitator's) role in the future?

5. Do you feel the committee membership was well balanced and appropriate for the task?

    _____ Yes       _____No

    If not, what changes would you make in the appointment of future committees?

6. Do you feel that the goals, objectives and strategies developed by the committee are essentially sound and appropriate for the community?

    _____ Yes       _____ No

    If not, what are the most serious deficiencies?

7. Additional comments: Use back of sheet if necessary.

responsibilities. The administrator must coordinate carefully to avoid duplication and wasted time. Progress reports can help ensure that time is not lost and allow the administrator to determine where additional resources are required.

## Evaluations

Personnel evaluations can be a major means of facilitating the implementation of a new plan. Typically, personnel evaluations are based on the individual's performance in ongoing responsibilities, such as management of the technical processing department or handling the timely flow of interlibrary loan requests. While these are certainly valid and important, there is no reason why the evaluation cannot also include the individual's contribution to the attainment of long-range goals. This is particularly appropriate at the supervisory and administrative level, where critical responsibility does rest for implementaton.

In fact, the best measure available to a library board for evaluating the performance of the library administrator is the library's progress toward its long-range goals. The administrator possesses the ultimate responsibility for the coordination of the institution's resources toward the attainment of those goals.

## Progress Reports

Requiring regular progress reports form the library's departments will also ensure both awareness of and implementation of the plan. It is often valuable to incorporate these reports in summary fashion in the administrator's monthly reports to the board. An annual review of the long-range plan should also be scheduled for the board as part of the normal order of business.

## THE PLANNING CYCLE

This chapter has emphasized the creation of a long-range plan for the library. However, once that plan has been produced, planning should become a continuous process, integrated with the budget and personnel cycles. The administrator should establish a regular schedule for monitoring progress, and major administrative decisions should be assessed for their relationship and contribution to the plan.

Prior to, or concurrent with, the development of the next

budget request, the plan should be evaluated to determine whether additional funds are needed to complete an objective or whether a deadline should be extended. As goals are satisfied, amendments may be required in the plan and the budget. When personnel are evaluated, supervisors should reflect on whether additional training may be required to facilitate an individual's progress on the plan. Appraisal should assess whether an individual is inhibiting the unit's progress on an assigned task or has contributed significantly and deserves recognition and reward for the extra effort.

Every administrator has a calendar that guides his or her work flow. Preparation for board meetings, implementation and reporting on board action, department head and staff meetings, and review of progress with local governmental officials are among the components of this calendar. By plugging into this calendar the key elements required to monitor the plan, the administrator will have established a planning cycle to assure that the plan is maintained. These elements include monitoring, reporting, collection and evaluation of information (such as new census reports or population projections), prebudget meetings and annual review. Without such a cycle, the long-range plan becomes merely another document that is filed away and dusted off once a year.

## SUMMARY

While planning can sometimes lead to false expectations, result in termination of existing programs, be subject to misleading projections and consume valuable time, lack of planning can result in wasted resources, duplication, stagnation and management by crisis. Once it has committed itself to long-range planning, the board should appoint a planning committee that includes members from the board, the staff and the community.

The committee should review the library's mission as a benchmark for testing the goals, objectives and strategies that evolve from the planning process. Next, the committee must seek data about the library and the community. Much information may be available from historical records, published census data and departments of the local political jurisdiction. However, the committee may want to conduct staff, user and citizen surveys as well.

The committee must then evaluate the data to determine what they reveal about needs for new or improved library services and resources. Strategies for achieving goals and objectives should be defined, using input from the staff members who will be responsible for implementation. Priorities may also need to be set if the library does not have the resources to pursue all goals simultaneously. Many libraries find the services of a facilitator to be helpful in this process.

While the administrator plays an important role in initiating the planning process and directing (or at least participating in) the committee, he or she bears full responsibility for the implementation of the plan once it is adopted. The administrator must coordinate staff actions in support of the plan's goals and should require regular progress reports. Evaluation of supervisory personnel can also be an important means of monitoring progress.

Ultimately planning should become a continuous process, with regular review and modification of the plan as goals are achieved or conditions change.

## FOOTNOTES

1. Public Library Association, Principles Task Force, *The Public Library: Democracy's Resource. A Statement of Principles* (Chicago: Public Library Association, 1982).

2. Vernon E. Palmour, et al., *A Planning Process for Public Libraries.* (Chicago: American Library Association, 1980).

## SUGGESTIONS FOR FURTHER READING

Bommer, Michael R. and Ronald W. Chorba. *Decision Making for Library Management.* White Plains, NY: Knowledge Industry Publications, Inc., 1982.

Martin, Allie Beth, coord. *A Strategy for Public Library Change.* Chicago: American Library Association, 1972.

McClure, Charles R. and A.R. Samuels, eds. *Strategies for Library Administration: Concepts and Approaches.* Littleton, CO: Libraries Unlimited, Inc., 1982.

Palmour, Vernon E. *A Planning Process for Public Libraries.* Chicago: American Library Association, 1980.

U.S. White House Conference on Library and Information Services. *Summary* (of Proceedings). Washington, DC; U.S. Government Printing Office, 1980.

# 5

# Personnel Management

A library administrator's major resource is the institution's personnel. Whether this resource is wasted or effectively employed depends on the administrator's organizational skills, leadership ability, sensitivity to employees' needs, knowledge of their skills and capacity to motivate them. This chapter will focus on the organization required for effective management of personnel, some important basic policies and procedures, and motivational techniques.

Given the small size of the majority of the nation's public libraries, most are unlikely to have a personnel department as a formal entity. Nonetheless, there is always some individual who is responsible for personnel administration. Whether handled by the administrator, a full-time personnel officer, another staff member on a part-time basis or several score employees in a very large urban library, certain basic functions must be performed. These include recruitment, selection, enrollment, orientation, evaluation and counseling, administration of fringe benefits and personnel policies, termination, and the maintenance of personnel records.

## MERIT AND CIVIL SERVICE SYSTEMS

For libraries that fall under a merit or civil service system, recruitment and testing of applicants will be the responsibility of another department of local government. Merit or civil service programs were designed to combat the evils of patronage and to base selection and promotion upon individual skills, training and knowledge. While civil service systems do create some problems, which will be discussed below, the systems have by and large raised the level of professionalism in local government and thus work to the advantage of both the public and public administration.

## Problems of Patronage

Some people argue in favor of a patronage system in the belief that it makes local government more responsive to community needs. Under a patronage system, elected officials are able to award jobs to those who supported them in their election. If public service is poor, then the official and his or her followers can be voted out of office at the next election. Presumably that fear of job loss will keep local governmental services efficient, and as long as the elected officials' policies have the support of the majority of the electorate, all will be well.

In practice, patronage systems are notoriously inefficient, and payrolls tend to become bloated because of the need to find jobs for those who have contributed time and money to the officeholder. Morale suffers because jobs and promotions depend on the favor of a key official, rather than on effective performance.

## Selection Under Merit and Civil Service Systems

Both merit and civil service systems rely on test procedures and weighted interviews to arrive at objective employee selection. The relevance of test questions and the weights assigned to key factors are critical. However, with frequent professional input and review, they are likely to be valid. Thus, administrators must develop both good communication and good rapport with merit and civil service personnel.

Candidates for a position must be selected from a list of those eligible and qualified. Usually the choice is restricted to the three to five candidates with the highest scores. For upper level management positions, interviews before panels representing local and regional professionals may be employed to weed out unqualified candidates. The final choice among the top-ranked candidates is left to the administrator.

## Problems of Civil Service

Problems sometimes arise when tests are scheduled infrequently and lists are outdated. Many candidates may then have already taken other jobs. When no one on the list is interested or available or when all candidates are rejected as being unsatisfactory, merit and civil service systems may allow for interim appointments in order to fill key positions. While this ensures that library operations can continue, serious problems may result if tests are subsequently held, and the individual who has temporarily held the position does not rate high enough to assume the job on a permanent basis.

Despite these difficulties, many public libraries with civil service or merit systems are able to recruit and develop outstanding staffs. The key is good understanding of the procedures and good communications with civil service or merit system personnel.

## RECRUITMENT AND SELECTION

Merit or civil service systems are most common in larger units of government, and the majority of public libraries are not likely to deal with them. Instead, it will fall upon the library's personnel officer to recruit, test and select applicants for positions in the library. There are several tools and procedures to aid in that process.

### Job Descriptions

The basic tool of every library personnel officer is the job description, the specification for the position that must be filled, whether administrator or page. The job description should contain the job title, characteristics of the work, typical examples of the duties the individual will perform, requirements of the job, such as formal training and experience, and any attributes necessary or desirable for satisfactory performance. If a job description does not already exist, one should be prepared. Staff members currently performing those duties, other libraries with similar positions, and the literature can all help provide the necessary information. There are many compilations of job descriptions that can be used as a base, but care should be taken to adjust the description to meet any unique needs in the local library.

The temptation to prepare a job description for every position on the staff should be resisted. Everyone believes his job is unique, and there will be distinctions at almost every level of employment. Nonetheless, job descriptions should be written broadly, and titles should be uniform. Rather than having an order clerk, a receiving clerk, a processing clerk and similar unique titles, the library would be wiser to designate them all as clerks. Where there are actual distinctions in terms of responsibility, clerks can be classed as senior and junior or ranked numerically. This will permit comparison with other libraries and units of government and aid in establishing a comparable salary schedule. Pay plans and job descriptions of other units of local government will help considerably in this process.

## Attracting Applicants

Drawing on the job description, the personnel officer should be able to draft advertisements and notices and define a standard for selection of candidates. The personnel officer can also contact the employment services offered by all state governments. Typically, a state employment service is strong on clerical and skilled trades, but professional personnel may also be listed. Many employment services are computerized so that they can match an opening to qualified candidates both locally and across the state. Some have reciprocal agreements with other states, if more specialized skills are required and they cannot be located withing the state. Professional journals, graduate schools and employment services of professional associations are good places to advertise for professional or administrative vacancies.

Including the salary and the job requirements in the notice, whether the position is clerical or professional, will help enormously in the process of recruitment. If the salary is flexible, then a range should be stated, noting that placement is dependent upon qualifications. Later in this chapter there will be discussion on the pay plan.

## Application Forms

Another fundamental tool for the personnel officer is a standard application form. Sample forms can be found in some of the additional readings cited at the end of this chapter, and a representative form is given in Figure 5.1. Typically, an employment form will provide space for name, address, telephone number(s), education, experience and any general remarks the applicant may wish to make regarding his or her qualifications for the position. A simple and well designed employment form will be a considerable aid to the employment officer, since it will speed screening of

## Figure 5.1: Sample Application Form

| EMPLOYMENT APPLICATION ANYWHERE PUBLIC LIBRARY | 1. Title of job you are seeking: | 2. Date |
|---|---|---|

3. Name:          Last:          First:          Middle:
   PRINT

4. Present Address:          City:          State:     ZIP:

| 5. Home Telephone: | 6.  Business Telephone: | 7.  Social Security No.: |
|---|---|---|

8. Education:          Name and City     Dates Attended     Major Subject     Diploma/Degree

   High School

   College(s) _____

   Graduate        _____
   Schools

   Other           _____
   Training

9. Honors received:

10. Previous employment. Begin with your present job and work back.
    Name and Address of Firm     Job Title     Dates     Reason for Leaving

    If more space is needed, continue on other side of this sheet.

11. List your best qualifications for the position desired:

12. Have you ever been discharged or asked to resign? Yes___No___ If yes, explain.

13. May we contact your present employer? Yes___     No___

14. How soon after receiving an appointment can you begin work?

15. List any persons we may contact who are familiar with your work performance.
    Name          Firm and Address          Title          Telephone

16. I verify that the information I have supplied on this application is correct, and
    I understand that any falsification may result in the loss of employment.

    SIGNED:

qualified candidates and ask all the essential preliminary questions. Whether you elect to use a standard application form or develop your own, the form should be reviewed by the library's attorney and by the local or state equal opportunity employment agency. There are a great many things that state and federal laws prohibit an employer from asking a job applicant, either on the employment form or in an interview. Among them are questions about age, religion, ethnic or racial background, certain types of criminal record, sex and dependents—and the list continues to grow each year. Some exceptions are allowed, but again it would be well to check with the library's legal counsel beforehand.

**Other Application Procedures**

It is common in the professional field, and in many para-professional areas, to require the submission of a resume. While a resume can be a critical aspect of the recruiting and selection process, individuals should also be required to fill out the library's application form. The form may reveal deficiencies or problems, such as gaps in employment that might be hidden in the form of resume used by the applicant.

For certain types of positions, it may also be advisable to require the applicant to complete the form in the library and in the presence of a staff member. The author recalls a custodian who was badly burned handling chemicals because he couldn't read the label. His wife had completed the application form for him at home, and no one in the library was aware that he was illiterate. While that is an extreme and unusual case, the principle holds for less bizarre situations. For example, an individual who requires an hour to complete the form may not be the individual to staff a busy circulation desk.

An applicant should always be asked to sign the application, and as a protection for the library, there should be a statement to the effect that any false statements on the form could lead to dismissal. Some libraries automatically require references, or the names of previous supervisors and their telephone numbers or addresses, but practice varies on this. If only a general reference is requested, the applicant might list a friend, relative, minister or teacher, who might not provide an objective appraisal. On the other hand, a former supervisor might be equally, but negatively, subjective, out of resentment that the individual was no longer employed there.

It is desirable to accept applications and retain them on file, even when the library does not have any vacancies or after an advertised position has been filled. If there is an unexpected departure or the new employee does not prove satisfactory, that file could avoid the necessity of reopening the search. Applications should not be kept indefinitely, however. They should be filed in chronological order, and periodically the oldest files should be discarded.

**The Selection Process**

The selection process will certainly vary depending upon the size of the library. In larger institutions the personnel officer typically eliminates unqualified candidates and arranges the interviews with the supervisors for those who are qualified. In a smaller library the administrator, as personnel officer, may perform all functions.

The fundamental rule, however, is that the person who will be responsible for supervising the position should be the person who makes the selection. If there is some question about the capability of the supervisor to make that decision, then the responsibility may be shared with the administrator or personnel officer. On occasion, candidates might be interviewed by a team of supervisors, particularly if the position being filled is complex and affects the operations of several departments. Candidates for administrator are typically interviewed and selected by a committee of the board of trustees or by the entire board, unless the library is under a city manager or county executive.

*Interviewing*

The interviewing process can be greatly simplified and improved if the candidates are given copies of the job description and summaries of the fringe benefits offered by the institution. The purpose of an interview is to learn as much about the individual as possible. If the interviewer must devote a major portion of the time to conveying data about the library and the job, valuable time will be lost. The candidate should be put at ease, and the interview should always be conducted privately and never over a busy desk with the telephone breaking in.

There are three things every interviewer should determine:

1) Why did the individual apply for the position?

2) What can this person offer the library?

3) How much will the library have to pay?

However the interviewer wishes to phrase these questions, they are the basis of the interview. Any questions placed to the candidate should be open-ended, to encourage the individual to reveal as much as possible that is relevant to the scope of the job and the applicant's experience and training. On occasion it may be necessary to be more specific to steer a wordy or disorganized candidate back on the track. It is also well to establish a time limit for the interview, at least in the interviewer's mind.

Certainly the candidate should be granted an opportunity to ask essential questions about the job. One, of course, will be the salary or wage offered. If the library has a salary and wage plan, that should solve the question. If there is a range for a particular position, the policies regarding placement of the individual in that range should be reviewed. Candidates are also likely to have questions about working conditions, benefits, and the responsibilities and authority involved.

### Selecting among Candidates

There are many formulas for selection, but the most common process is to establish weights for those attributes and elements contained in the job description. If good communications skills are more important in a specific job than experience, they are ranked accordingly, and emphasis can be placed on assessing the desired attributes during the interview.

Testing is not a common practice in libraries, but it may be desirable in some situations. Typing skills and ability to use office or data processing equipment may be tested if the candidate's qualifications cannot be verified. Personality and intelligence testing are not customary and may be discriminatory. Some state employment services will conduct specialized tests, if they are required for the job.

Generally, however, the library will state the requirements for a job in the job description and discuss them during the interview. Continued employment is based upon the individual's ability to demonstrate the required skill in the performance of his or her duties. If the person hired as a typist cannot in fact type upon reporting for work, he or she can be discharged for falsely claiming to possess that skill.

Common courtesy requires that each applicant be informed once the library has made a decision. A telephone call or standard note is sufficient, and it should be handled as soon as the decision is made. The candidate who is selected should be contacted personally, and any open details such as salary and starting date should be resolved. All details should be confirmed in a formal letter to the finalist. Depending upon the nature of the position, the library may request an acceptance from the individual to ensure that there is a commitment and that there is no confusion regarding the terms.

## ENROLLMENT AND ORIENTATION

The personnel officer must formally enroll the new employee as a member of the library staff. That will involve having the individual fill out payroll and tax information forms. The employee must also enroll in the fringe benefit programs offered by the library.

### Employment Packets

To ensure these procedures are handled efficiently and consistently, the personnel officer should prepare standard packets containing the forms and any necessary explanatory literature for employees. If there are differences in procedures or benefits for different categories of employees, separate packets for each category should be prepared. These packets should be reviewed with each employee, for there frequently are options available to staff enrolling in these programs.

Employees should be instructed to retain the explanatory literature on fringe benefit programs such as health and life insurance, since these represent official documents defining their rights. Unfortunately, in the confusion of starting a new job, many employees fail to understand their benefits and responsibilities, and a large part of the personnel officer's time is devoted to clarifying questions that can usually be answered by referral to this literature.

### Student Employees

Many library employees are likely to be students, and the personnel officer must be sure that the institution's policies and job requirements conform to the state's child labor laws. Work permits are usually required for students still in high school, and there are limitations on the hours they may work. Once again, the library's legal counsel can advise on these regulations. Because this may be a youngster's first job, special attention will have to be paid to orientation, explanation of responsibilities and the many routine practices that are commonly known by the adult staff.

## Staff Handbooks

Another extremely useful tool for every personnel officer is a staff handbook. Every library, regardless of size, should possess a handbook that can be easily duplicated and given to new employees. The purpose of this handbook is to orient the individual to the role of the library and describe briefly the essential facts of the library's policies and practices.

A typical handbook should describe the library's governance and its primary sources of support, fringe benefits, vacation and sick leave procedures, evaluation procedures, working conditions, the library's statement of purpose, emergency information and termination procedures. For a very small library, the handbook may consist of only a few photocopied pages. A larger urban library may have an illustrated manual with as many as 50 pages. Whatever its form, the handbook should be reviewed by the library's legal counsel, since it becomes a document on the individual employee's rights and responsibilities.

## Orientation

Some larger library personnel departments have formal orientation programs for new employees, but typically the administrator or personnel officer is more likely to introduce new personnel, provide a tour of the facilities and let the employee's supervisor take over from there. A policies and procedures manual is an extremely valuable tool in training and orienting new staff, since it explains in detail the operations of the departments and the major policies of the institution. (The policies and procedures manual will be discussed further later in this chapter and in Chapter 6.)

## EVALUATION AND COUNSELING

It is customary for every new employee to be on probation, i.e., subject to discharge without review during the early period of employment. The period of that probation should be explained to new personnel, as should the criteria by which their work will be evaluated.

## The Evaluation Process

Once past the probation period, a formal evaluation procedure is customary. Usually at an annual anniversary date, or some other standard date, the supervisor will meet with staff members individually, to assess their work and to allow employees to identify any needs or problems in the performance of that work.

At least, in theory that is what occurs. In actual practice, personnel evaluation is one of the most difficult aspects of management. Supervisors are often reluctant to discuss deficiencies, and, for employees who have held the same job for many years, the evaluation session can be a meaningless rubber stamp process. Because of this and because of widespread misunderstanding about the process, the personnel officer may also be brought in to provide guidance or to supervise the evaluation process.

The readings at the end of this chapter include many examples of forms and procedures that can be employed. A great many libraries spend considerable time refining the form that is used, but in fact the form is the least critical part of the procedure. A blank sheet of paper may be the best evaluation form of all, since it forces the evaluator to focus on the individual performance and how it can be improved.

Fundamentally, the procedure should compare the individual to the job description and assess whether the work required of the position is being performed and whether it is satisfactory. Second, the procedure should allow the supervisor to comment upon exceptionally good or poor performance and provide examples to illustrate them. If the library has a long-range plan and the individual has a role in its implementation, the evaluation should note the degree of progress made and permit comment on exceptional performance or the need for improvements.

## After the Evaluation

The form records that an evaluation has taken place. Often the form requires the signatures of both the supervisor and the employee to verify this. There may also be a provision for the employee to respond, if he or she does not agree with the results or feels that the evaluation was unfair or inaccurate. The forms normally go into the personnel file for future reference. The evaluation may be linked to the library's pay system, so that if an unsatisfactory performance appraisal is received, the individual may not be eligible for a pay increase.

The personnel officer or the administrator can monitor the evaluations and identify any problems, either with the supervisor or the employee. A good evaluation system should grant the employee the right to appeal, preferably to some impartial individual. Often either the personnel officer or the administrator is the court of last resort.

### Employee Counseling

The personnel officer also finds that he or she functions as a counselor. Questions on personnel policies and fringe benefits are frequent, but so are personal matters. An employee who is continually ill may be an alchoholic, or a female employee may be annoyed by the advances of a male supervisor. Employees may be faced with financial or marital problems. Whatever the circumstances, the personnel officer must be familiar with the social services and counseling available to the library's employees so that referral can be made. Of course, it is essential to maintain confidentiality concerning both the employee and the problem. Often, the only thing an employee may require is someone to listen to a problem and provide reassurance.

For many people, their jobs are the most important thing in their lives. Whether that is good or bad depends on your outlook, but it is a fact. Consequently, the personnel officer and the administrator must be cautious and sensitive to the impact policies or changes in policies can have upon the morale of the staff. An objective approach, a warm, open and understanding attitude, strict confidentiality, accurate information and a positive commitment to the employee are the requisites of a personnel officer in the role of counselor.

## FRINGE BENEFITS AND PERSONNEL POLICIES

The personnel officer is the authority on fringe benefits for the institution and must have a solid understanding of them. Typically, fringe benefits consist of retirement benefits, health and life insurance, vacation and sick leave, and holidays. More elaborate plans may include training and tuition reimbursement, dental insurance, health maintenance programs, personal business days, leaves of absence, exchange programs and employee discounts. Sometimes vendors—such as book jobbers, magazine agents and equipment suppliers—are willing to provide special benefits by advancing discounts to employees at no cost to the library.

## Choosing Fringe Benefits

Determining which fringe benefits to offer the staff is a decision for the board of trustees. However, their decision will have to be based on what comparable units of government offer their employees, general practice in the area and the overall compensation program of the library. For example, if the library is a department of municipal government and all the departments provide one day per month sick leave, cumulative up to 90 days, than this would be sound justification for a similar policy. Holidays vary considerably from one region of the nation to another. Mardi Gras would be appropriate in New Orleans and Mobile, but out of place in Seattle. On the other hand, common practice among local governments might be to allow two weeks of vacation each year, but in the library profession it is common to offer four weeks for professionals, to compensate for the evening and weekend hours they must work.

If it is the policy of the board to offer competitive or comparable benefits for library personnel, then this will require continual evaluation of fringe benefit packages offered by other libraries and local government. Many state libraries and professional associations survey their members to indentify trends and practices on fringe benefits as well as salaries. These surveys will provide valuable information for maintaining the library benefit program.

Selection of fringe benefits is similar to choosing any other product or service. Once the library determines what types of fringe benefits it wants to extend to its employees, specifications should be prepared and bids should be obtained. It is also a fundamental rule that the larger the group is, the better the price will be. For that reason many libraries cooperate with other local governmental units to provide certain benefits—for example, the establishment of a credit union. Only a very large library can justify the creation of such a service, but in concert with other city or county departments, a strong institution could be established.

## Policies and Procedures Manual

The types of policies reviewed in this chapter require continual interpretation and change by the administrator and the library's personnel officer. Almost every library maintains a policies and procedures manual, which includes personnel policies. These policies explain benefits and the practices the library will adhere to in its operations. For example, funeral leave may be defined in terms of the time employees may take, for whom they may take it and how it is to be charged.

The staff handbook mentioned earlier may contain summaries of primary policies, but the policy manual contains all policies in their entirety. These manuals are generally in looseleaf form to permit easy updating and revision. The date a policy is instituted should also be indicated.

The personnel officer must keep personnel policies current and in conformity with common practice and the law. Maternity leave offers a good example: Recent court cases and rulings by the Equal Employment Opportunity Commission (EEOC) have required many changes in organizational policies. An advisory committee made up of staff members can provide insight on various concerns among the staff and offer valuable assistance to the personnel officer in developing policies for consideration by the board's personnel committee.

## TERMINATION

It has been said that while our Constitution has a Bill of Rights, those rights do not extend to the workplace. The courts have been changing that, and increasingly an employee is considered to hold certain rights regarding his or her job.

Employees cannot be arbitrarily terminated. "Due process"— the phrase that has crept into use regarding this right—requires that an employee must be informed of deficiences in performance, granted reasonable time to correct them and advised that he or she will be discharged if there is no improvement. In addition, evidence to support the cause for discharge must be gathered. The personnel officer is the guardian of due process and also serves to evaluate the evidence against the employee. Increasingly, the courts have forced both local government and private employers to rehire employees, often with back pay, if the employer failed to document deficiencies and apply due process.

Personnel evaluations are increasingly important in the termination process. Evaluation can serve as documentation and proof of due process. As noted previously, many supervisors do not know how to evaluate and so lose the benefit of this tool. Often a supervisor will approach the administrator or the personnel officer to request that an employee be discharged. When the employee's file is examined, it may show that six months earlier the same supervisor had written a highly complimentary evaluation report and that no disciplinary actions have occurred since then. The supervisor should be instructed to return to his or her department and build a case, starting with a special evaluation identifying the deficiencies.

Of course, not all terminations are due to worker deficiencies. People get other jobs, relocate, retire, return to school and take a host of other actions that result in resignation or leave. Some libraries arrange exit interviews, usually administered by the personnel officer, or use a questionnaire to determine why the employee is leaving and whether there are problems or any policies that require revision. Almost all libraries require the employee to give written advance notice of the intention to resign. The extent of notice may vary but is designed to allow time for the library to hire another person and to allow time for training as well. The resignation letter can also provide information on the cause of termination, which may be useful to the institution.

## PERSONNEL RECORDS

A personnel file should be started by the personnel officer as soon as an individual is hired. The file should include the original application, letters of reference, resumes, information regarding changes in status such as pay or job title, data on whom to contact in the event of an emergency and personnel evaluations. This information is confidential, and access to the file should be limited to as few persons as possible. If library policy allows the employees to have access to their own files, care should be taken to ensure no employee removes materials from the file without the knowledge of the personnel officer.

While all of these records do not need to be retained forever, some summary must be maintained for future reference. Verification of past employment may be requested decades after the employee resigned. Questions regarding fringe benefits, injuries or pay are likely to arise at any time. The best recourse is to maintain both "live" and "dead" personnel files, in alphabetical order. This effort is sometimes frustrated by name changes, but it is more reliable than other filing systems such as those that employ the Social Security number, since numbers can be easily transposed.

Other types of records that the personnel officer may be responsible for maintaining include vacation and sick leave, leaves of absence, holidays, time cards and personal business leave. These may be part of the individual personnel file, but are more likely to be a function of the payroll process or finance department. Strict provisions govern the retention of these records, and each administrator should examine state statutes and obtain the advice of the library's legal counsel before disposing of time and salary records.

## COMPENSATION PLAN

The library's compensation plan consists of both its fringe benefits and its pay plan. A logical pay plan is vital to proper budget preparation and ensures consistency and fairness to all employees. Fringe benefits were discussed in an earlier section; however, both fringe benefits and wages must be reviewed whenever the library considers revision of its compensation plan. Typically, a fringe benefits program ranges between 15% and 25% of salaries, making it a significant element in the library's budget.

Pay can be an hourly wage, which would be typical for part-time employees and temporary or seasonal workers, or it can be an annual salary, which would be based on a set number of hours per week of work for full-time employees. The level of both wages and salaries may be determined in a number of ways: by a survey of the geographic area, by a survey of the field, by negotiation or by task analysis.

In a survey of the geographic area, information is gathered on salaries and wages paid locally for positions similar to those in the library; the information is then used as the basis for determining compensation. A survey of the field consists of gathering salary and wage information from other libraries of comparable size. In negotiation, personnel are queried regarding their needs, and wages are established based upon the capability of the library's budget to satisfy those needs.

### Task Analysis

Task analysis is a more involved procedure. Each job is thoroughly reviewed, and a new job description is prepared. The various responsibilities of the job and factors such as working conditions, necessary education and experience, desirable attributes and special skills are all assigned weights reflecting their scarcity and relative importance to the institution. For example, a job that requires the individual to work evenings and weekends will receive more points than a job that does not. These points are tabulated, and jobs with similar totals are grouped together. The pay plan is broken into ranges. Jobs with low totals are assigned to the lower ranges; those with high totals, to the upper ranges. Because this is an objective process based upon careful analysis of the work performed rather than the individuals performing it, it is widely favored in government and private industry. Variations of this method are also often used by management consulting firms.

Establishment of a pay plan based on task analysis is a sound management practice. If salaries are based on individual negotiation, favoritism is possible, and those employees who are less vocal may be at a disadvantage, as may those who have been with the library for long periods without an opportunity to renegotiate. Survey methods are very common among libraries, but they have the disadvantage of locking wages into an abnormally low level. This is particularly true of field survey methods, since library salaries are notoriously low, and this method simply perpetuates that situation.

**Adjustments**

There are three different types of adjustments possible in a typical pay plan: cost-of-living, longevity and merit. A pay range for a typical job will have a number of steps representing percentage increases. These increases could be granted based upon growth in the job, represented by the number of years of service, which would be a longevity increase, or the increase could be granted based on increased productivity or greater responsibilities, in which case it is a merit increase. If the entire pay scale is changed by some percentage reflecting the increase in consumer prices, it is a cost-of-living increase.

All three of these may be operational in one pay plan. The administrator may learn that most local governments are planning to grant a 5% cost-of-living increase to their employees in the coming year. Assuming sufficient revenues exist to permit this, the board may approve a 5% revision to the salary and wage plan. The plan may also provide for a 5% one-step increase for current employees after one year of service. This ensures their salaries are above the level of someone newly hired by the library, and also reflects their increased productivity. In addition, supervisors may identify individual employees who have assumed additional responsibilities during the year. While their jobs have not changed sufficiently to merit promotion, they would be eligible under the library plan to receive a 5% merit increase.

**Other Considerations**

Wages for part-time positions should be the equivalent of the hourly rate for salaried personnel with similar titles and responsibilities. Otherwise, there could be grounds for a lawsuit based upon discrimination. It is also a wise practice to plan an annual geographic survey, just to observe any trends. The pay plan and job descriptions should be revised on a regular basis, at least every five years. Jobs and responsibilities change very rapidly, and the volatility of the economy requires this review to ensure library staff do not become victims of inflation.

## UNIONS AND STAFF ASSOCIATIONS

At one time most states had legislation forbidding public employees to form unions. That situation is rapidly changing, and public employee unions are being established even in those states where the legislature has not acted. Public sector membership is now growing faster than any other category for unions.

Almost any type of union—from the Teamsters to the Laborers' International—may attempt to organize a library, although there are also unions that represent only governmental employees, such as the American Federation of State, County and Municipal Employees (AFSCME). Depending on the size and nature of the bargaining unit, library employees may be included in a larger unit with all the employees of the local political jurisdiction; they may form a separate unit composed only of library employees; or the unit may include only certain departments or classes of employees within the library.

**Organizing**

Procedures for organizing a bargaining unit are strictly regulated by both federal and state governments. Even when state law does not officially recognize public employee unions, the regulations generally are interpreted as extending to that sector. Administrators may not prevent organizing efforts from taking place. However, there are limits to the steps union organizers may take. For example, they cannot interfere with the work of the institution or actively campaign on the library property.

If the board and the governmental jurisdiction do not favor

union representation, there are some steps administration may take. It can identify the benefits and concessions the staff has gained without union representation. Disadvantages of union membership can be pointed out, including dues, strike requirements and other obligations. The administration can also identify the causes for organizational effort (which might be cited in the union's organizing literature), such as low salaries and fringe benefits, and lack of participation in decision making on personnel policy. If possible, steps can be undertaken to correct these problems.

If a significant percentage of the staff does sign cards or petitions requesting an election, one must be held. The library's attorney should be consulted during the election procedure. A certification election is a strictly defined process held under the supervision of either a state agency or the National Labor Relations Board. The election will have to prescribe carefully the bargaining unit to be created, i.e., whether it will include all library employees, exclusive of management, or only certain categories. Generally, a union will seek the largest number it believes will support its side in the election. Should a local unit be approved, official representatives will then be elected and are responsible, in concert with union officials, for negotiating future agreements between the board and the unit.

## Bargaining Relations

Depending upon the rapport established between management and the union, collective bargaining can be beneficial for the library and resolve many long-standing problems. The contract can clearly specify the role of management and the rights of the members. Pay and fringe benefits may be defined, and this can provide a sound basis for financial and long-range planning. Without good rapport, divisiveness and poor service can be the outcome. The key to good rapport is communication and participation. Labor and management must realize that they both work for the public, and their obligation is the best possible library service the community can afford. Under those circumstances, with the union as a partner, there should be no disadvantage for the library.

## Staff Associations

Staff associations are probably much more common than unions throughout the nation. Many are very loosely organized without officers or bylaws, and their primary role is social. Others have been considered "house unions" because of their link to management. In fact, the staff association is a potentially strong organization than can play an important role in the operation of the library.

An administrator who is seeking greater participation from staff in the decision-making processes of the library can draw upon the association for advice, representation and support on matters involving personnel policies, planning and library development. The staff association, like the union, is also a good training ground for leadership. The organizational skills gained from the association can be transferred to the departments of the library.

Staff associations are also able to speak on subjects that might be difficult for administration. For example, administration may be prevented from taking an official role in a referendum campaign, but staff associations or unions may not have the same restrictions.

## MOTIVATION

So far in this chapter we have discussed the mechanisms necessary for effective personnel work. While these are important to the library, they do not ensure that the staff will be motivated to carry out the plans and programs developed for the institution. The pay plan and fringe benefits are certainly vital, but research has shown that they do not provide as strong a motivation as one may suspect. Frederick Herzberg, a psychologist and writer on management, has called pay and fringe benefits "hygiene factors." Like working conditions, they will have a positive impact if the employees know they are equal to those of individuals with similar responsibilities, and a negative impact if employees believe they are being exploited.

The work of psychologist Abraham Maslow has also had a tremendous impact on management theories. Maslow argues that there is a hierarchy of needs common to everyone. At the bottom of the pyramid, he places those elements that represent survival, such as adequate food and housing. Beyond that come pay and benefits, then recognition and status. At the very top of the pyramid is self-actualization, where the individual is motivated because of pride and satisfaction in the work itself. Thus, if one accepts Maslow's theory, an organization's compensation plan is important, but it cannot serve as the only tool of management to motivate personnel.

## Training

One primary motivational tool is training. Investment made by the library in developing its personnel will have a dual impact. It should increase the productivity of the individual at an ultimate savings to the taxpayer, and it will enhance the individual's sense of his or her own worth to the institution. There is always a certain amount of satisfaction in being able to improve one's skills, and a greater sense of security in the job should result. For this reason, staff development programs should be an integral part of the library budget. If the library is too small to afford to establish its own programs, then it should develop joint programs with other libraries in the region.

Training programs can be internal, allowing specialists to share their skills, or they can be arranged through contract with local or state academic institutions or other local agencies with expertise in the desired field. In addition to the traditional skills required by a library, the explosion of automated services, the expanded use of audiovisual and microform materials, and new planning and management techniques are all suitable topics for training programs.

## Job Enrichment

Job enrichment is another technique that can be applied in some settings. Research into the causes of employee turnover reveals that many employees leave because their existing job provides no challenges for them and has become dull routine. Job enrichment seeks to avoid this problem through rotation or expansion of responsibilities.

Some positions lend themselves better to rotation than others. For example, a branch head may benefit from a short-term transfer to another extension unit, which would allow him or her to meet new people, observe different techniques and work in a different environment. New ideas can be brought back to the branch as a result of this. Similarly, a branch reference specialist could be assigned to a central library subject department and gain greater insight to the collection of that unit, become familiar with new tools and improve referral techniques upon return to the branch.

Expansion of responsibilities may seem like overloading. However, an individual who has mastered all the components of a present job may no longer be fully occupied and may start to feel bored.

## Exchange Programs

Exchange programs are another motivational tool, and some libraries that have experimented with domestic and foreign exchange of personnel have found that it can provide many long-term benefits by introducing new techniques to the institution. Exchange programs are complicated to set up, since job descriptions, benefits and pay scales may vary, and there are not many persons willing and able to disrupt their personal lives for the period of the exchange. However, such problems can be dealt with if the will is there.

## Participatory Management

Participation in decision making is another method that can have good results for some personnel. Not everyone is anxious to assume the responsibilities that come with decision making, but for those who are eager for growth and desire a voice in the decisions that affect their work, this can be a stimulating opportunity. Smaller libraries may not find a formal participatory process critical to their needs, since individual responsibilities are diversified and the hierarchy is fairly simple. In medium-sized and large public libraries, however, such a process is often the only way newer staff members can have the opportunity to exercise their talents. For this reason, many large libraries have elaborate committee structures with representation from various units.

A fundamental factor for administrators who use the participatory management technique is to define the scope they can grant the committees and the time they have. Participatory techniques require more time than unilateral decision making, but the results are usually better. However, not every issue can be resolved through committee consensus, and sometimes a hard decision may have to be made by the administrator alone.

There is one fundamental rule that every administrator who uses participatory decision making should apply: If the authority has been fully delegated to a group, then the administrator must make a commitment to accept and implement the group's decision. Otherwise, staff will realize that the decision was never meant to be shared.

## Innovation

Innovation is another significant motivator and should not be ignored. A classic study of the application of innovation was done at the Hawthorne General Electric plant in Chicago. Different groups of employees were told they were being tested on the impact that different working conditions would have on their productivity. As the tests continued, it became evident that the productivity of most groups increased, even those serving as controls. Industrial psychologists originally concluded that the Hawthorne experiments primarily showed the untrustworthiness of traditional testing methods, and coined the phrase "the Hawthorne effect" to describe the effect of innovation on productivity. Subsequent research has confirmed that innovation, in and of itself, can be an important motivator if staff are involved in the application of new services or programs in the community, particularly if they were involved in the decisions leading up to the application. If the results will make a contribution to the community or the profession, there will be even greater commitment to the project.

**Employee Activism**

Encouraging staff to participate in civic and professional activities is also important and satisfies the motivation that all of us have to increase our skills and worth. Policies that unduly restrict employees from participation of this type should be reviewed and liberalized. While not everyone is able or willing to make such a contribution, it is poor practice to erect barriers for those who do wish to do so.

## SUMMARY

Personnel represents the most important resource a library possesses. Whether the major responsibility lies with the administrator, a personnel officer or a personnel department, basic tools and techniques of personnel management will help in making best use of this human resource. Helpful tools include job descriptions, application forms, staff handbooks, and policies and procedures manuals.

Supervisors, personnel officers and administrators should all seek to develop skills in interviewing, counseling and performing evaluations. In addition, administrators must often be able to work effectively with unions or staff associations and should make good use of such motivational techniques as training, job enrichment, participatory management and innovation.

A library must have clearly defined personnel policies and procedures regarding hiring, compensation, fringe benefits, evaluation and termination. However, these procedures are often influenced or even determined by institutions outside the library, including civil service systems, local government, state and federal regulations and union negotiations.

## SUGGESTIONS FOR FURTHER READING

American Library Association. *The Personnel Manual.* Chicago: American Library Association, 1977.

American Library Association. *Personnel Organization and Procedure: A Manual Suggested for Use in Public Libraries,* second edition. Chicago: American Library Association, 1968.

Creth, Sheila and Frederick Duda. *Personnel Administration in Libraries.* New York: Neal-Schuman Publishers, Inc., 1981.

Martin, Murray S. *Issues in Personnel Management.* Greenwich, CT: JAI Press, Inc., 1981.

O'Reilly, Robert C. and Marjorie I. *Librarians and Labor Relations: Employment Under Union Contracts.* Westport, CT: Greenwood Press, 1981.

Rizzo, John. *Management for Librarians.* Westport, CT: Greenwood Press, 1980.

Sager, Donald J. *Participatory Management in Libraries.* Metuchen, NJ: Scarecrow Press, Inc., 1982.

Van Zant, Nancy, ed. *Personnel Policies and Procedures in Libraries.* New York: Neal-Schuman Publishers, Inc., 1980.

# 6

# Management and Organization

Regardless of size and staffing, certain functions are common in almost every public library. The most fundamental are circulation, adult and reference services, juvenile or youth services, and technical services, as well as general administration. Larger systems often have an extension unit, an audiovisual section, specialized subject departments and other clearly defined units. The role and staffing of these departments will vary depending upon the goals and objectives of the local library and the needs of the community.

## ORGANIZATIONAL ALTERNATIVES

There are a number of ways in which these units are typically organized. The most common type of organizational pattern in public libraries is the hierarchy. Other forms include matrix and delegational organization.

### The Hierarchy

The board is at the top of a hierarchical structure. Directly below the board is the administrator plus any of his or her immediate staff. Reporting to the administrator are the major department heads, and below those individuals are any smaller units, grouped logically under an appropriate department head.

In this type of structure there are two types of relationship— line and staff. In a line position, the individual has clear authority over one or more operating units. Supervision of these units includes the power to hire and fire and to evaluate. A staff position is advisory or coordinative. While there may be some supportive personnel assigned to a staff position, they are usually not numerous.

The head of branches in a larger library is a line position, because that individual has authority over those agencies. A coordinator of youth services or a public relations coordinator would be a staff position, because these positions coordinate a category of service throughout the system. They may also include some limited line responsibilities, such as supervision of the central library children's department or a printing department.

Figure 6.1 illustrates a typical hierarchical organization. This diagram, known as an organization chart, is among the most fundamental tools in management, since it identifies the lines of authority that exist in the library.

**The Matrix**

An alternative to the hierarchy is the matrix, which is often applied to task-oriented or service organizations. In the matrix, the functions of the organization are grouped along one coordinate and the supportive operations are aligned along the other. The assumption is that all are equal in importance and that decision making is shared among the units, depending upon the function.

Figure 6.2 illustrates the matrix structure. Defined along the Y-axis of the grid are the public service departments: reference, circulation, programming, readers' advisory work and outreach. On the X-axis are the units that facilitate these services: technical services, data processing, custodial service, personnel, public relations, finance, materials selection and administration (the administrator is considered to be in this unit although he or she, of course, retains overall authority). Because these units are task-oriented, the matrix is particularly well suited for program budgeting. Relationships between the supportive and public service departments are more clearly stated and allow the units to interact without going through a bureaucratic structure.

Matrix organizations tend to be more informal and are less likely to result in layers of supervision to coordinate operations. The distinction between line and staff also tends to vanish. Projects often employ a matrix organization because it fosters communication and because there is no need to create formal lines of authority.

**Figure 6.1 Hierarchical Organization Chart**

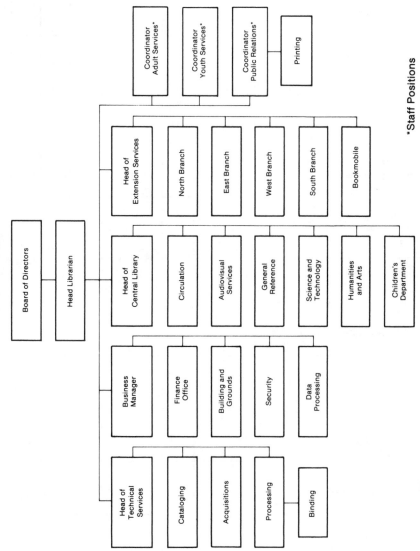

*Staff Positions

Board of Directors

Head Librarian

Coordinator Adult Services*

Coordinator Youth Services*

Coordinator Public Relations*

Printing

Head of Extension Services

North Branch

East Branch

West Branch

South Branch

Bookmobile

Head of Central Library

Circulation

Audiovisual Services

General Reference

Science and Technology

Humanities and Arts

Children's Department

Business Manager

Finance Office

Building and Grounds

Security

Data Processing

Head of Technical Services

Cataloging

Acquisitions

Processing

Binding

## Figure 6.2: Matrix Organization

**Public Service Tasks or Functions (Y-Axis)**

- Centralized General Reference Services
- Centralized Circulation
- Public Programming
- Centralized Art and Humanities Services
- Centralized Science and Technology Services
- Extension Service to North Community
- Extension Service to East Community
- Extension Service to West Community
- Extension Service to South Community
- Centralized Youth Services
- Service to the Handicapped

Security · Materials Selection · Personnel · Data Processing · Building and Grounds · Public Relations · Finance · Technical Services · General Administration

**Supportive Services (X-Axis)**

In general, governments have not made use of this form of organization, because it is common to define lines of authority to conform to legislation. By statute, the library board has authority over the library and is also authorized to retain a chief administrator responsible for the daily operation of the institution. Most administrators simply extend that hierarchical pattern downward into the organization. A clear line of authority must exist between the administration and the governance of a library. However, there is no compelling reason to establish a hierarchical order for the whole library, unless the administrator finds that this traditional structure is the most convenient format.

**The Delegational Structure**

Probably the most common form of organization in American libraries, other than the hierarchy, is delegational. In this pattern everyone reports to a chief administrator, who delegates responsibilities as conditions dictate. This informal structure is suitable for the majority of public libraries, which are small and have an average staff size of three full-time-equivalent persons. Staff members may shelve books, register borrowers, handle reference questions, or select and process books, depending upon the need of the moment and the direction of the chief administrator.

Delegation can be an efficient method of organization and can maximize the human resources of the institution. Under such a system, staff members may specialize in routines such as shelving or circulation, but these would not be inflexible assignments.

In time, however, the administrator may discover that so many persons are reporting to him or her that adequate supervision cannot be given. There is no magic maximum number that applies in every case; much depends on the leadership style of the administrator and the complexity of the organization. For some administrators the maximum may be three persons, while others can manage 15 or 16 without any problem. The test is how well the administrator can measure the quality and quantity of each individual's work and budget time to assist them, while still performing the administrative duties assigned by the board.

## POLICIES AND PROCEDURES MANUAL

Chapter 5 discussed the value of a manual containing the personnel policies and procedures of the library. In fact, a manual is important for all the functions and operations of the library. Every institution needs formal stated policies and procedures for the services it performs. Otherwise, services will be inconsistent, and training for incoming personnel will become sketchy and based on oral tradition. The manual should be the "bible" for the institution—a common reference tool when questions arise about board and administrative policy and the model by which units implement those policies and their general functions.

A *policy* is a written statement, approved by the library's governance and/or administration, designed to deal with a perceived problem or need. It is prepared to guide the conduct of personnel in the performance of their duties. A *procedure* is the detailed explanation or specification as to how a policy is to be implemented and interpreted, or the description of how a service is to be performed. Sometimes it is difficult to separate a policy from a procedure, and for that reason many libraries combine the two into the same manual.

### Organization of the Manual

Customarily, policies and procedures manuals are organized by subject to permit easier reference. Some libraries have separate manuals for the various functions or departments. A book selection manual may contain the board's selection policy together with ordering procedures. A circulation manual may contain the registration and circulation policies approved by the board, and the instructions prepared by the department on how clerical employees should process registrations, overdue notices and the like.

If separate departmental manuals do exist, they should be centrally indexed to prevent conflicts in policies and procedures and to provide a guide to departments when they need to know the practices of other units. Individual policies should also be dated, and the manuals should be loose-leaf to permit easy revision. If a list is maintained of all those who have manuals, a standard distribution system can be designed to ensure that any revised or new policies reach all manual holders. The administrator should control who may develop policies and procedures and should prescribe some consistency of format.

### Importance of the Manual

Written policies and procedures are important for more than

just training and consistency. In the case of formal complaint, such as in book selection or nonresident registration, the patron can receive a prompt explanation for the procedure. By breaking down the steps of a procedure, the manual can also aid in determining costs for some functions such as technical services. Interrelationships between various units of the organizations can be clarified. Finally, the administrator can explain readily to the board how policies are being interpreted and implemented.

**Contents**

A good policies and procedures manual may contain any number of subjects, but the following list appears basic for almost all libraries.

• Materials selection policy: standards and guidelines used by the institution.

• Personnel policies: benefits and staff responsibilities.

• Gift policy: types of materials accepted by the library.

• Patron privileges and obligations: loan periods, registration requirements, fines and fees.

• Complaints: steps the public or staff may take in bringing complaints on policies or services to the administration and board.

• Board bylaws: the formal organization and procedures of the board.

To be of value, a manual requires constant review and referral. Consulting it before the development of any new policy or procedure will help avoid duplication and inconsistency. A library with word processing equipment should consider using it to keep the manual current.

## CIRCULATION FUNCTIONS

Libraries have experimented with elimination of many different types of functions, but circulation seems to be the most durable of public library functions. This reflects the need to keep track of public property, to know who has which material and when it will be returned. Whether the library is a small room or a facility with hundreds of thousands of square feet, there is always a circulation desk near the door to remind the patron of the need to charge or discharge the library's materials.

Circulation is generally divided into a number of subfunctions: registration, charge and discharge of materials, overdue processing and, on occasion, interlibrary loan. (The last function is sometimes associated with an adult services or reference department, which has more sophisticated resources and search techniques to verify bibliographic information.)

## Registration

Registration procedure involves the recording of basic information about an individual applicant for a borrower's card (name, address, telephone number). Some libraries require references and various forms of identification. Traditionally, younger patrons must have their parents' signatures, to verify parental consent and assumption of responsibility.

Many lawyers consider library application forms to be legal contracts. Forms frequently contain rules and regulations to which the applicant must consent in order to gain borrowing privileges. The abuse of those rules is then grounds for action against the individual. Libraries should gain formal approval of those requirements and obligations by their local governmental jurisidiction to underline the importance of the policies. As quasi-legal documents, the registration and loan policies of a library merit review by the library's legal counsel.

## Charge and Discharge Procedures

Charge and discharge procedures are dictated by the type of circulation system a library has installed. Four basic types of circulation systems are in use today: manual or hand-charging, mechanical or machine-assisted, photocharging and computerized.

### Manual and Mechanical Systems

With a manual or hand-charge system, the staff member or the patron removes from a pocket in the book a card identifying the material and fills in the borrower's name or identification number.

The card is filed by due date, and the book is stamped with that due date. When it is returned, or discharged, the circulation personnel can locate the card in the file and restore it to the book. Those cards remaining after a specified period represent overdue items.

Mechanical or machine-assisted systems work basically the same way. However, the borrower's card will have a name or number on it which the machine will imprint on the book card.

## Photocharge Systems

Photocharge systems are transaction-based. In other words, charges are numbered sequentially through the day, and only the exceptions are actually traced, by number, to determine the borrower and the material. Circulation personnel normally record a simple bibliographic description of the material being loaned and the identification of the borrower, using a small microfilm camera. A numbered transaction slip is inserted in the book pocket. When the material is returned, the slips are sorted by date and number. The missing numbers represent exceptions, and the developed microfilm is then searched to locate the material and borrower.

## Automated Systems

Although a survey undertaken in 1981 indicated that automated circulation systems were used by only a few hundred public library systems,[1] that number has been increasing dramatically. Many libraries are cooperating in the purchase and operation of mini-computer-based units, and some libraries are acquiring micro-computer-based systems.

The typical automated system records the name of the borrower and the materials loaned and can also discharge the material. Devices such as light pens or lasers are often used to read the numeric or alphabetic codes assigned to the patron and the material. The computer also automatically generates overdue notices at prescribed times.

Automated systems have the advantage of greater accuracy and the capacity to generate statistics. They can also reveal more readily than other types of systems who has a specific book and when it will be returned. Computerized systems are more expensive to install than other systems, and data must be converted to machine-readable form, which is also costly. However, libraries are often able to integrate automated circulation control with other processes, such as acquisitions and cataloging, which makes automated sytems more cost-effective by reducing labor. (See Chapter 7 for a discussion of automation and its impact on public libraries.)

*Hybrid Systems*

There are various hybrid systems and combinations of these techniques. For example, some libraries use machine-readable transaction cards with their photocharge circulation systems, which permits a computer to sort and print a list of exceptions for subsequent searching. All systems have their advocates, and the "best" method depends on the goals and needs of the institution. Generally, the larger the library and the more branches it has, the greater the need to seek automated systems that are reliable and not too complex.

## Overdue Procedures

Overdue procedures require the preparation of a notice to the borrower by circulation personnel. Libraries have experimented with different loan periods, granting renewals and varying time periods before overdue notices are sent. No uniform practice can be said to exist. Factors that influence the decisions include the library's policy on patrons' convenience, available personnel and the type of circulation system used. Because they allow greater flexibility in these areas, automated systems are increasingly popular.

Most libraries have one or more notices that are sent at standard time periods, sometimes followed by a telephone call, and then a final notice or bill. The greater the time between the due date and the first notice, the more materials will have been returned, and fewer first notices will have to be mailed. Postal regulations permit a bulk mailing rate to be used if the notice is not individualized with the overdue titles. However, this savings may be offset by the time needed to satisfy the inquiries of patrons who do not recall what they borrowed.

Some libraries have a policy of using collection agencies or credit bureaus for long-overdue materials. These organizations charge a fee or percentage of the fine for their services. Other libraries suspend borrowers' privileges after repeated failure to return materials. Some few even employ local ordinances to have police retrieve the material. Many libraries simply ignore the loss, accepting it as part of the cost of service. While there are no national statistics on the extent of loss through circulation, the author's experience is that it ranges between 1% and 2% of total circulation. Accurate record keeping and periodic inventories of sample sections of the collection can allow an administrator to determine the extent of loss. The administrator can then propose a suitable policy on delinquencies to the board.

### Other Responsibilities

Circulation departments also handle a variety of other responsibilities, such as shelving materials, processing reserve requests, voter registration and simple directional activities. Because these tend to be routine responsibilities that can be assumed with limited training, personnel in the typical circulation department are primarily clerical, with many part-time employees, including students and retirees. Careful attention should be given to maintaining the quality and performance of this staff, since the efficiency of their service creates an important impression on the public. Too high a turnover rate or too high a percentage of part-time personnel can adversely affect service—and, therefore, public relations.

### Interlibrary Loan

Interlibrary loan (ILL), another function of many library circulation departments, has become a highly standardized procedure in most states. Networks are usually established by the state library agencies. These agencies can inform the administrator about the required procedures and where to forward requests for materials not in the local library collections. Customarily, out-of-print materials, best sellers and ephemeral materials such as light romances are not available through ILL, but this may vary depending on local or state interlibrary codes.

Automated circulation and cataloging systems greatly facilitate the flow of interlibrary loan requests, as can electronic mail systems. If library holdings can be accessed online, it is easy and quick to determine whether a specific library owns the desired material, thus saving much time and paperwork. Almost all systems require full bibliographic information on the material and verification regarding the source of that information.

In addition to formal ILL networks, many adjacent library systems have long-established informal procedures. The effectiveness of such procedures depends largely on how familiar the administrators and staff of those libraries are with each others' collections, specifically their strengths and weaknesses. While interlibrary loan constitutes only 1% of total circulation in U.S. public libraries,[2] it is a growing and important service, providing access to resources that would otherwise be unavailable to a library's patrons.

## ADULT SERVICES

The major components of adult services are collection development, reference assistance, readers' advisory work, and programs and exhibits. These services may be centralized or departmentalized by subject. For the majority of public libraries, they are centralized; subject divisions are more common in the central libraries of major urban institutions.

### Collection Development

The principal tool in collection development is the materials selection policy of the library. It should be based on analysis of the community, including business and industry, demographic composition and social trends. The book selection policy is usually not a document specifying how many titles in particular categories the staff should select each year. Rather, it highlights the areas of emphasis and the retention practice the library will follow. On occasion, a bequest or special source of income will influence selection. For example, the library may receive a large sum for acquisition of financial reference material or art books.

*Selection*

Selection is generally delegated to staff members who have special training or familiarity with a subject category. Those who do the selection should work with the public on a regular basis, so that they will be familiar with the type of information currently being sought. Those individuals should also regularly review that portion of the collection for which they are responsible, to weed it of materials no longer up-to-date or in demand.

*Evaluation*

There are various methods of evaluating the collection. The American Library Association publication *Output Measures*[3] is one source for information on detailed evaluation procedures. The circulation system—particularly if it is an automated system—may reveal which parts of the collection do not appear to be in demand. Certain categories of materials, however, including the reference collection, poetry, religion or philosophy, may require other techniques, such as comparison with collection development guides, like the *Public Library Catalog* [4] or *Books for Public Libraries*,[5] and lists of notable or award-winning books.

Evaluation standards depend on the philosophy of the library. For some institutions it is important to develop a collection representative of the best quality that can be acquired. Other libraries emphasize purchase of those materials in greatest demand by the public. For the majority of public libraries, there is a balance between those extremes. Larger systems sometimes have a specialist who can study trends, evaluate recommended bibliographies, and develop purchase or selection lists. This can permit greater control over the system's collection. For most libraries, collection evaluation is an individual process that is influenced by professional reviews, patron requests and the selector's own knowledge of the field.

## Reference Service

Reference service in public libraries is growing steadily, reflecting the changing patterns of the public's need for information and its perception of the institution. Previous generations were accustomed to visiting their local library, asking for assistance on a subject, and being directed to a section of the collection or receiving an armload of materials that might contain brief articles of interest.

Today the public has a somewhat higher expectation and is less tolerant of partial assistance. Reference questions are likely to be much more specific, and resources are likely to be keyed to detailed aspects of a subject. Rather than devoting the time to locate the answer to a question themselves, patrons are more likely to request the answer from professional staff.

### Types of Reference Service

Reference service is arbitrarily divided today into three areas: ready or quick reference, subject specialization and online database searching. All of these may be provided by one individual in a smaller library, but they are compartmentalized in larger libraries.

In quick or ready reference, questions can typically be answered in a few minutes by checking a relatively small collection of encyclopedias, dictionaries or handbooks beside the desk. Longer questions are usually shunted to staff members who specialize in that field or to a subject department, if one exists in the system.

While only a limited number of public libraries are using online databases at the moment, the numbers are certain to increase as more bibliographic and nonbibliographic databases are created, and as more libraries acquire the hardware, trained personnel and financial ability to tap them. Ideally, the use of online resources should be integrated with quick and subject searches, but there is a tendency for libraries to treat online database searching as a separate service, usually because it is fee-based. Search techniques also differ greatly from one database to another, and extensive training is required before staff can make full use of the resources.

### Evaluation

Reference service is measured in a variety of ways. *Output Measures* is once again useful as a detailed guide. The actual number of telephone and walk-in questions processed is one measurement. However, it is important to determine whether these questions are quick or specialized, whether they are directional or truly reference questions and, of course, whether the staff is able to satisfy them. Whenever possible, this determination should be made based on state and national definitions of the different types of reference.

### Reference Staff

Because of the intensive nature of reference service, it is well to rotate staff assigned to this duty during the day. Time on the desk assisting the public can be balanced with time for collection or program development. Reference staff are traditionally professional, but some libraries have found that with limited training paraprofessional staff can be assigned responsibilities for ready reference and directional assistance.

### Directional Assistance

Administrators should closely monitor the volume of directional assistance given to the public. Frequent phone requests for hours, for example, might be reduced by inclusion of the library's hours in the telephone book. A high level of directional requests within the library may indicate the need for more and better signs.

## Readers' Advisory Service

Readers' advisory work is designed to help patrons who are seeking materials to continue their self-education in a specific field. At one time libraries established formal offices for the public, where an assessment of reading level or special interests could be undertaken. Today that assistance is more likely to be informal and less individualized, but it still offers the professional librarian's knowledge of the collection.

This service differs from general reference work because of the emphasis on expanding the patron's knowledge on a broader basis than the satisfaction of a specific question. For example, a patron seeking an introduction to computers would look to the librarian for suggestions on the best resources for getting started. To be successful in this area, a librarian must have the opportunity to work more intensively with the individual and must possess an interest in bringing the right books to the right person at the right time.

## Programs and Exhibits

In some larger or better supported institutions, programs and exhibits may be the function of a separate department or specialist. For the majority of libraries throughout the nation, the design of programs and exhibits to promote greater awareness of the library's adult services resources remains another responsibility of the adult services staff.

Exhibits may range from simple displays of new resources or booklists of recommended titles on specific subjects to galleried exhibitions, drawing upon the library's or other institutions' collections and designed to educate and inform in their own right. Programs may include book talks by library staff or lectures by nationally renowned authorities.

A local resource file can be a valuable tool for the adult services department in fulfilling this responsibility. It may also occasionally be useful in reference activities. The local resource file lists people in the community to whom the library may turn for the development of exhibits and programs: the person with the collection of rare plates, the local historian, the head of the zoo's snake department.

Many libraries justify programs and exhibits because they may stimulate circulation. Others view the programs and exhibits effort as a means of attracting the nonuser to the institution. Still others consider programming and exhibits as an educational responsibility, in the belief that books and audiovisual resources alone cannot fulfill the library's commitment to education, information and enrichment for the community. Whatever the motivation, the fact that public libraries attract more than 8.5 million persons each week to their programs and exhibits is evidence of the importance of this function.[6] Further discussion of programs and exhibits can be found in Chapter 8.

## Subject Departments

Subject departments follow no fixed pattern. Most typically they are divided between the arts and humanities and the sciences and technology, but social sciences departments are also common. Many libraries have a government document division, although this may be largely because of the unique indexing and classification of government documents.

In theory, subject divisions allow the patron with a special interest to gain immediate access to the resources he or she needs and also allow library personnel to specialize in more selective subjects. These goals may be defeated by libraries that divide the collection into media formats, such as audiovisual, periodicals and books, for more convenient handling.

### The Need for Subject Departments

There is no formula for the creation of subject departments. They are not established once a library reaches a certain budget or collection size, nor are they determined by the size of population served. Only the use and requirements of the community can determine whether subject departments are needed. An overwhelming number of questions on finance and business may reveal that, even in a small suburb, a business and finance department is desirable if it is also affordable. Collection strength and endowments may also influence the decision.

Just as librarians have debated whether to divide the fiction collection into genres or to follow a strict alphabetic sequence by the last name of the author, they have debated the segregation of the collection. On the one hand is the advantage of specialization, allowing the staff to focus on narrower areas of the collection and the more experienced user to gain quicker access to information. On the other hand, subject departments may confuse new users, who must be referred to different locations to find needed materials.

### The Local History Department

Among all the subject departments, one unit deserves special mention—local history. There may be a simple collection of pamphlets and index cards, or a full-fledged department, packed with the original papers of prominent pioneers, indexed local newspapers, collections of local authors' works or realia on permanent exhibit in the institution.

The local library is under particular obligation to concentrate on its community's history if there is no local museum or historical society—a situation that applies to the majority of the communities throughout the U.S. Guidance in preserving local resources and other special archival techniques can often be obtained from the state library agency or the state historical society and archives, if the library lacks trained personnel.

Whether or not a local historical society exists, the local library has a special responsibiltity to preserve its own records. Too many libraries lack records of their creation or the full minutes of their board meetings. Valuable files, financial and legal records are all too often dumped in an attic where environmental conditions destroy them. Every institution should have a written policy and preservation program regarding these materials.

## JUVENILE SERVICES

At one time public libraries were only for the use of adults, on the assumption that it required an education to understand the materials and the tools to access them. To this day there remains controversy as to the role public libraries should play in the provision of youth services. Some feel that the schools should assume this role, since they can best perform the educational steps essential to understand libraries. At the other extreme, some public libraries administer local school libraries, in the belief that this better prepares the individual in the library procedures used in adult life. Some libraries separate out only their picture books for preschoolers from the adult collection, on the premise that age level is an arbitrary distinction in the world of books. The adult may find something of value in simply written materials for youth, just as the advanced young person may better satisfy his or her information needs with adult titles.

## Juvenile Services Policy

Each library should have its own juvenile services policy, based on analysis of the community. Service to children with learning disabilities, as well as the gifted, to parents, teachers, youth organizations, preschoolers and the handicapped merit thorough consideration, and there is no standard formula that should be applied.

These will be highly controversial issues. While adult services are generally based on open access and the design of a balanced collection representing all viewpoints, opinions change rapidly when minors are considered. However, even minors have rights. The administrator should ensure that the policies of service are not overly protective and limiting to the emotional and intellectual growth of the young person.

The public library often provides the child's first educational experience outside the home; it may also be a significant early step in the socialization process. The story hour introduces the child to the world of fact and fantasy and stimulates the child's curiosity and imagination. Youth services should be exciting, colorful and creative and should provide experiences that will encourage the child to return again and again.

The wise administrator will do everything possible to provide the encouragement, support and resources this department requires to do its job. Without the foundations laid by youth services, there will be poor public awareness and appreciation of library service in the future.

## Collection Development

Collection development has always played an important part in youth services. Because of the importance of illustrations, legibility and other physical elements of a book, materials are usually physically examined before selection. At one time the vocabulary was carefully weighed to categorize the book into the right age and grade grouping. (In fact, publishers supplied authors with lists of appropriate words to fit the market they intended to reach.) While vocabulary is still an important factor in the development and selection of youth materials, there is equal awareness of the vast range of reading abilities within any given group. Greater emphasis is now placed on the issues the material presents and the overall quality of the book or audiovisual material, rather than on whether the author has departed from an established formula.

There are many selection aids for juvenile works. Awards also play an important role. While a Nobel prize or other notable award will certainly influence the selection of adult materials, nothing is more certain to magnify the sales of a children's book than the Caldecott or Newberry award. This impact is intensified by the greater tendency to purchase multiple copies of highly recommended children's titles.

### Reference Service

Youth reference service places a greater emphasis on guidance in the selection of materials, both for the child and parent or teacher. Children are just as likely to have specific questions as adults, but often a reference interview will be necessary to identify their needs. Some libraries have well-developed referral techniques so that younger children who need adult reference materials or assistance can readily obtain that service. Usually, however, the process is initiated in the youth department.

Librarians in this department also perform an invaluable service in familiarizing children with basic reference tools such as dictionaries and encyclopedias. These tools should be current, and duplicate copies should be available. Many children's librarians also provide valuable service in guiding parents in the selection of these materials for home purchase.

### Programs and Exhibits

Programs and exhibits are a major activity in service to youth. Preschool and school-age story hours, summer reading programs, puppet shows, craft demonstrations, educational exhibits and similar events can introduce the child to the rich array of reading and audiovisual resources that can be borrowed from the library.

Libraries may offer these programs individually or with other libraries in cooperative systems. In either case, there should be a sound plan based on the achievement of specific learning goals. All too often, however, the children's program and exhibit series is a random array, dependent upon the resources available to the staff and not linked in any way with the local school systems or youth organizations. As discussed in the following section, whenever possible, the library should coordinate its programs with the needs of these other groups.

Exhibits should be simple and clear in their purpose and should focus on topics of interest to youth. Every children's department should have bulletin boards and display cases that can feature nature displays, children's artwork, hobby collections, traveling exhibits from other libraries or museums, simple science displays prepared by local industries or businesses, and the like. Often the preparation of exhibits in the children's department is relegated to a staff member who has an interest in art or to the newest staff member. Instead, it should be developed by the entire staff, with a logical plan based upon the seasons and the programming of the department. Youth services administrators should also see that, whenever feasible, the library's books and audiovisual resources are incorporated into the exhibits and that the labeling is clear.

### Cooperation with Other Youth Agencies

Another requisite for effective youth services is close communication with other youth service organizations. Professionals involved with servicing youth in a specific neighborhood or community should meet and share insights. While it is desirable to keep the library's program and exhibit series for youth informal and avoid converting it into an extension of any organization's curriculum, the library may often be able to draw on its collections and services to reinforce a mutually desirable goal.

Many public libraries are fortunate to have sufficient staff and time to permit them to visit local schools, conduct class visits to the library and plan joint programs with educators. Collections should be developed to complement or supplement school media center holdings. Teachers should be encouraged to inform the library of assignments involving library research by many students. School media specialists and children's librarians in the public library should have good rapport, sharing resources when necessary.

The library staff and the leaders of the Girl and Boy Scouts, church groups, 4-H clubs and similar organizations should develop projects that can contribute to the goals of both the library and the group. Of course, this requires a shared understanding of the goals of each organization. Tours and visits should be planned to fit the age group and time of these groups, and children's librarians should be encouraged to make visits to these organizations in the community whenever possible. Registration and story hours should be provided offsite, and an array of literature such as colorful and well-designed booklists and program announcements should be provided for distribution in and outside the library.

## YOUNG ADULT SERVICES

There is no doubt that young adults constitute an important clientele for all public libraries. Some feel that this group is among the heaviest users of library services. Unfortunately, there is no agreement regarding the best method of serving young adults, and libraries differ in even their definitions of the group.

### Defining the Group

For some, this group consists of junior and senior high school students. Others consider the young adult as anyone under the age of 18 or 21. Some libraries have separate collections and departmental personnel to cater to the specialized needs of young adults. Some lump them with children and require parental permission for them to use the services and resources of the adult section of the institution. For some libraries, young adult services represent a legal problem as to who is responsible for library materials used— the young patron or the parent.

### Importance of Young Adult Services

Because librarians are usually heavily burdened in responding to classroom assignments, there is often an assumption that they are already serving young people very well. Yet young adults have many needs beyond fulfilling class assignments, and the public library can perform exceptional service by developing collections and services that respond to those needs. Young adults face tremendous pressures from parents, peers and teachers to achieve. Plans have to be set for careers, family and a host of other responsibilities, and there is heavy competition for the young adult's time. The public library must be effective in designing programs and services for that age group, or they will be lost. There is little question that a sizable portion of young adults never darken the library's door after graduation and from high school and liberation from restrictive policies and procedures.

Careful market analysis of the information needs of the young adult, cooperation with schools and other youth organizations, and a commitment to treat the young adult as an individual with unique needs are required of every public library. While not every public library may find it desirable to establish a separate young adult department, even in the smallest library someone should be assigned responsibility for developing programs, services and materials for this clientele.

## TECHNICAL SERVICES

Traditionally, technical services are divided into three functions: acquisitions, cataloging and processing.

### Acquisitions

Acquisitions rarely includes the selection of materials, since this is usually performed by the staff in the public service departments such as adult and youth services. The acquisitions process includes the following steps: obtaining any missing bibliographic information on requested items, to ensure the correct item is acquired; determining whether the material is already on order: preparing the order forms; selecting the appropriate jobber or supplier; verifying the correctness of the order upon its receipt; and undertaking the necessary financial accounting to ensure the selector knows the impact of the request on the order budget as well as the status of the order.

Firms that supply materials from many publishers and audiovisual manufacturers (i.e., jobbers) offer a variety of services for the library. Besides offering discounts for the library's business and eliminating the need to submit direct orders to individual publishers, these firms can often provide books fully processed and cataloged for the library at a modest fee and also offer online ordering and financial accounting services. Some publishers do not permit orders through jobbers because of the larger discount they must offer those firms; in such cases libraries must order directly from the publisher.

#### Automated Acquisitions

Because of the complexity of this process, it is often partially or fully automated in those libraries that can afford it. Some of the bibliographic networks, such as the Online Computer Library Center (OCLC), integrate acquisitions with their other services. The local member library can verify bibliographic information on the cataloging database maintained by OCLC and then generate an order for the number of copies it desires. OCLC's profile of the library indicates which jobber the institution uses and either forwards the order electronically or mails standard forms. Verification and accounting records are also provided to the local library.

*Manual Acquisitions*

The majority of smaller libraries, however, perform the acquisitions steps manually. After searching the standard bibliographic tools for the detail necessary for the order, the acquisitions staff will invariably check its on-order file to determine whether previous orders were submitted and, if so, verify whether the selector wants to duplicate. Selection of a jobber then follows. Most libraries can determine from the jobber which publishers they represent. Selection is often based on the number of publishers represented, as well as the discount and services the jobber offers. Upon receipt of the shipment, the acquisitions staff will verify the order, often removing the record and transferring it to an in-process file.

**Cataloging**

The cataloging function may be initiated concurrently with the acquisitions process, but often it is delayed until the book is in hand to guarantee the cataloging is correct. Libraries that catalog in advance of receipt are usually concerned with getting the material in circulation as soon as possible and gamble that the vast majority of their orders will not be cancelled. Some libraries may circulate new materials without cataloging and retrieve the items for processing when the bibliographic data are obtained.

*Impact of Automation*

As will be discussed further in Chapter 7, cataloging has undergone more change as a result of automation than has any other technical service. An increasing percentage of public libraries purchases cataloging from various sources rather than perform the time-consuming task of doing original cataloging. In addition to saving time, purchased cataloging also saves money and offers greater accuracy and standardization.

A major reason for the success of purchased cataloging has been the development of cataloging information in machine-readable format (MARC tapes) from the Library of Congress. These tapes can be purchased by local library systems, bibliographic utilities such as OCLC and commercial processing centers, greatly expediting the availability of bibliographic data.

*Sources of Cataloging*

Libraries can purchase cataloging in several different fashions. Some may use a commercial processing center. In some states these are operated by a regional library system or the state library agency, and the costs may even be subsidized from state or federal grants to encourage local libraries to participate. Jobbers may offer cataloging as an incentive to the local library to order books from them. The online bibliographic utilities such as OCLC offer online (computer-based) cataloging. Cards can be custom-designed to satisfy local library requirements.

Data can also be supplied in the form of computer tapes for the institution's computer output microform (COM) catalog or online public access catalog. (See Chapter 7 for a discussion of these catalogs.) Some firms specialize in converting this online cataloging information into microform, which is sold to smaller libraries that use economical microform readers to extract the needed bibliographic information. Whatever method the library employs, it is highly recommended that the library purchase its cataloging whenever possible, in order to standardize its bibliographic records and reduce costs.

**Processing**

Processing services can also be purchased by local libraries. Processing practices can vary significantly from one institution to another. At one extreme is a full assembly line for total processing by the institution itself. At the other is contractual delegation of the entire responsibility to a commercial or cooperative processing center. Usually there is a little of both. Most of the library book jobbers offer processing for a nominal cost, as an incentive to attract the business. The library can develop a "profile" or description of where the book pocket is to be placed, whether plastic covers are needed, spine label placement and similar details.

*In-house or Contract Processing*

A larger public library system may establish an assembly line processing operation based on industrial applications, with a conveyor track to move the materials from one work station to another and with specific tasks assigned to technical processing personnel. Few libraries are able to acquire everything they require fully processed. In any event, local materials, specialized audiovisual resources and those titles ordered direct from the publisher will require individual processing, as will any gifts the library elects to keep.

While wages and the degree of processing a library uses will be factors, it is generally more economical to contract as much processing as possible. Where it is necessary to assume processing, every effort should be made to standardize and simplify. Is it necessary, for example, to use accession numbers, multiple ownership stamps, special bindings and protective covers to extend the life of certain ephemeral materials? Supplies should be ordered in sufficient quantity to permit the best possible discount. Joint purchases with other libraries in the area should be explored to benefit from the economy of scale.

*Mending, Binding and Preservation*

Mending, binding and preservation are other assignments that frequently fall to the processing section of the technical services department. Many state and regional libraries regularly schedule mending and preservation workshops, and even the smallest library should send some staff to these sessions. Expert processing and mending can greatly extend the life of library materials and avoid or reduce the cost of rebinding. Titles on mending and preservation listed at the end of this chapter can provide useful assistance in this process.

As the cost of binding has increased and various alternatives such as microform become more economical, there has been a decided decrease in binding in public libraries. The result has been a tremendous decrease in the number of qualified library binderies and an inevitable increase in the cost of binding. However, despite the improvements in microform readers, the public still prefers hard copy to microform, and libraries will continue to need binderies. (Administrators should also realize that staff time is required to explain microform equipment to the patron and to maintain it; hard copy does not require that level of support.)

*The Binding Program*

The library's binding program should be developed as part of the budget planning process and should complement its materials development policy. Areas of the collection that are to be strengthened will require greater binding allocations. Certain heavily used materials, such as reference materials, children's titles and paperback originals of lasting value, may require prebinding. Periodicals that are to be permanently maintained for reference also need binding. It is generally preferable to have the individuals responsible for selection also determine which materials should be bound, and they should be assigned a budgetary allocation for binding.

Selection of a binder should be through competitive bidding. The specifications should call for a certified library binder and simple procedures for accounting, shipment and delivery. Again, the citations at the end of this chapter should be useful in the development of these specifications. References should also be sought from the bidders, to determine the quality of service provided to other institutions.

## AUDIOVISUAL SERVICES

There is a tendency in public libraries to segregate materials by format and to employ different circulation and classification techniques for audiovisual materials. A few libraries have integrated their collections, placing recordings, films, video tapes and multimedia kits in the shelves alongside books. Alternatively, integration may occur just in cataloging. More likely, the public library patron will find a separate department or section of the library for films, recordings and similar formats. Recordings may be in a separate catalog or in separate drawers in the catalog. Films, filmstrips and video tape may be in a printed catalog.

There is a logic to the separation. Knowing that the library has a filmstrip on the life of Shakespeare does not help a patron who does not own or have access to a filmstrip projector. With a separate audiovisual section, those patrons who have the appropriate audiovisual equipment can go directly to that section and select the items they need. In addition, some audiovisual formats are relatively expensive or require inspection after use. For example, it is always recommended that 16mm films be inspected after use to ensure damage can be repaired prior to the next use. This requires special equipment and training for the personnel performing this function.

The usual catalog entry for many of these formats is also different. While the descriptions for a book, a film and a recording may have some common features, a film or video tape may require an annotation and a recommended age level. In addition, a separate catalog may be very useful to those patrons making regular use of the library's audiovisual collection.

## Cooperation

Smaller and medium-sized public libraries should work cooperatively with other libraries to share the costs and maintenance of audiovisual collections, particularly for costly formats such as 16mm film and video tape. Some libraries are able to house and maintain these collections centrally, delivering films to participating libraries when they are booked by patrons or by library staff for programming. Other libraries have formed "circuits," which periodically rotate films or video tapes to provide a variety of titles for on-the-spot use by patrons. Even larger libraries, or those institutions with the financial support and usage to justify individual collections, may find it advantageous to contract with smaller libraries in the area to spread their costs.

## Factors in Choosing Formats

Before investing in collection development for a particular format, administrators should take care to consider that format's maintenance requirements and the general availability of equipment in the community. For example, a sample marketing survey conducted over the telephone or in the library lobby can estimate the number of homes with video tape equipment and the percentage with Beta or VHS format. Contacts with local merchants and a survey of the literature can also provide information on public preference and the availability of titles suitable for library circulation.

**Managing the Collection**

The library should purchase equipment for staff and public use for each format the library acquires. Staff can then inspect reported problems such as torn tapes or scratched phonodiscs. In some instances, equipment to make the necessary repairs can be purchased from library supply houses. In other instances, commercial repair services may be needed.

Circulation procedures will vary with the format. Phonodiscs and audio cassettes can usually be handled just like books, but 16mm films may require advance booking to permit programs to be planned well in advance. Some libraries originally handled video tape like film, but the heavy demand for this format, particularly for the popular titles, has led many libraries to change their policies to "first come, first served."

The library should concentrate on a few audiovisual formats. Collections that are large and varied in a relatively few formats will be used more than small and restrictive collections in a dozen different formats. The consumer electronics industry is always developing new hardware to tempt the public. It often takes years before a standard format finally dominates the market and a respectable library of software is available. Time also has a tendency to make even the most common formats obsolete. There is almost no interest in 78 rpm phonodiscs anymore, and that same fate may befall the 45 and 33 rpm phonodisc as the compact disc and laser technology become more commonplace.

**The Library's Role**

Public libraries have generally been very conservative in their adoption of audiovisual resources and equipment. Less than 2% of the library budget goes for these resources.[7] It is well for administrators to be cautious. It is equally important that they realize the important role that libraries have in helping the public get experience with the formats and gain "literacy" in their selection and use.

Many libraries have introduced public access microcomputers, for example, to help patrons learn the capabilities and limitations of this equipment. The availability of good quality video tapes and audio recordings can also improve the selectivity of many young people (as well as their parents). While developing these collections and services almost always requires a major financial and personnel commitment for the library, it is essential in order to keep the institution current and to provide the public with information, education and cultural enrichment in a variety of formats.

## EXTENSION

Branch libraries, bookmobiles, mail order and book deposit stations are among the more traditional extension methods employed by public libraries. There are also new options available through cable television and videotex.

### Bookmobiles

Of all the methods, the most common extension service is the bookmobile stop. However, there is clear evidence that bookmobiles are decreasing in number, chiefly because of their cost. Bookmobiles are large and complex vehicles, prone to breakdown. Furthermore, bookmobile drivers generally command large salaries, expecially in unionized areas. These factors, coupled with the need for supportive collections and staffs, fuel expenses, and publicity to make the public aware of service points make bookmobiles among the most expensive forms of public library service.

Tests and studies conducted in various locations to assess the degree of usage that might compensate for the higher operating costs indicate that usually only when bookmobiles serve the public schools will the volume increase to the level that equals or exceeds branch service. However, most public libraries are reluctant to serve schools for fear that this inhibits the development of adequate school library service.

### *Uses for Bookmobiles*

Bookmobiles are used in both metropolitan and rural areas, but are less common in suburban communities. In the city, bookmobiles may be justified when rapid changes make it difficult to find the best location for a permanent branch. Bookmobiles are also more effective in serving areas with different ethnic or racial communities, since placement of a branch in one neighborhood often raises barriers to access by other groups. In a rural community, bookmobiles offer library service to a population that is scattered or divided by physical barriers, such as bad roads, rivers and extremes in terrain. Some libraries use bookmobiles to move collections and services to locations where they could not afford floor space, such as regional shopping centers. Others use them for special events such as neighborhood festivals and county fairs.

## Vehicles and Collections

Bookmobiles come in various sizes, and there is no magic formula an administrator can apply to determine which is best. Industry statistics indicate a preference for larger models with capacity for several thousand volumes, which can offer greater variety of materials to the user. Few bookmobiles have reference collections, and most emphasize popular titles, children's picture books, recordings and current magazines. These still require considerable shelf space. Just as consumers are attracted to larger stores, they are attracted to larger library collections. In some instances libraries have experimented with specialized collections, such as all paperbacks or collections solely for senior citizens. None of these has made much lasting impact on general bookmobile services.

## Administrative Concerns

As with any major expenditure, the administrator must consider a number of factors in the selection of a bookmobile. The manufacturer should have an established reputation for construction of special application vehicles and use a standard chassis and engine that can be easily repaired in the community. A few libraries have experimented with modification of more common vehicles such as RVs and house trailers. The majority of bookmobiles in use today, however, are built by manufacturers specializing in this type of design. *Bookmobiles and Bookmobile Service,* which is included in the bibliography at the close of this chapter, contains a good checklist of features that should be considered in a bookmobile and the basis for a set of specifications.

The administrator will also be involved in selection of book-mobile routes and stops. Among the concerns are bridge and underpass clearances, adequate turnaround area and parking space, and provision of electrical taps at stops. Signs noting the days of the week and time of the bookmobile should be posted at stops whenever possible.

## Branch Libraries

While bookmobiles can extend library service to the greatest number of locations in the service area, branch libraries are the preferred extension technique in many communities. Branches may range in size from one-room prefabricated "kiosks" to regional "super branches" able to serve several hundred thousand people.

### The Need for Branches

There is a variety of formulas to determine when establishment of a branch library is appropriate. One, based on population, recommends a branch for every 25,000 persons served above a 50,000 base population. In support of that formula, statistics reveal that communities serving between 50,000 and 99,999 persons have a median of one branch and a mean of two branches.[8] Similar ratios exist for larger service areas (see Table 1.2, Chapter 1). Another formula, based on circulation, provides for establishment of a branch when the circulation exceeds 60,000 items annually. Other formulas concentrate on the amount of travel time required to reach a library outlet and the extent of the geographic area to be served.

Politics and economics probably determine more than any other factors whether a library has branches and where they are located. For example, it would be logical to believe that a community of 10,000 is too small to justify having more than a central library, yet the LIBGIS III statistics reveal that 538 such libraries operate branches.[9] Sometimes physical barriers such as expressways or rivers divide a community, and another outlet is required. The demands of a neighborhood willing to tax itself for the additional convenience of a branch may also lead to this action.

### Trends in Branch Libraries

In recent years two contradictory trends have been occurring in branch development. On the one hand there is growing pressure to consolidate smaller service units into larger facilities that offer richer collections, longer hours and better staffing. When construction funds were more readily available during the 1960s and early 1970s, many library systems took the opportunity to close small rented storefront agencies and construct "regional" libraries, consisting of upwards of 10,000 square feet and serving populations of 50,000 persons. Larger units were also constructed in the Sun Belt states, where greater reliance was placed on automobiles rather than public transportation. In many respects this paralleled the development of the regional shopping center, which offered ample parking and multiple services. Many libraries actually located their regional libraries in or near these shopping centers when they could afford the land or the rent.

At the same time that this trend was cresting, libraries also began experimenting with the creation of mini-libraries. Often these were funded with federal grants and aimed at attracting groups that have traditionally not used library services, such as the economically disadvantaged, the aged and minorities. These units might operate for limited hours and offer only popular materials, with no programming or reference service. Staff would often be recruited from the neighborhood and receive minimal training. Units might be located in bus terminals, enclosed shopping malls and similar high-traffic locations. This trend paralleled the creation of the neighborhood convenience store, offering limited materials but satisfying local demand.

*Determining Service Needs*

The best guide to an administrator faced with the need for more permanent extension service in a neighborhood is to sample the community and study all available demographic statistics. An older community may require a more limited type of agency with popular reading and minimal youth programs. Hours may be shorter because of the reluctance of elderly patrons to travel or walk in the evening hours and their ability to use the facility during normal daytime hours. Conversely, a neighborhood with mostly working parents and many children may require a full range of services and resources, longer hours and a larger professional staff.

Of course, the final major factor is the financial ability of the library system to support additional extension units. No administrator should fall into the trap of overextending the library's services. It is always much more desirable to maintain fewer outlets with a full range of services and resources than to dilute library service with a large number of inadequate agencies. Experience has shown that low-quality service units do not pay their way. Instead, they drain away funds that could be better used to provide attractive facilities, well-balanced collections and trained personnel. While there is a role for the smaller unit, the more common branch constructed today is 10,000 square feet or more, serving 50,000 persons and up.

## Mail Order Service

Mail order extension services have been successful in some communities. In this type of service, an annotated catalog is mailed to the residents of a neighborhood or rural area, and patrons are given the choice of either mailing or telephoning their request to the library. The requested items are mailed book rate to the patron, usually in a padded "jiffy" mailing bag with return label. Often the library offers only popular paperbacks through this service, since they are lighter weight and inexpensive to purchase in the quantity required. The steadily increasing cost of book rate is making this service less attractive and more costly than it once was, but for certain types of communities it provides an attractive alternative to bookmobiles or branches.

Some publishers offer mail-order packages to libraries. These combine a set of several thousand copies of catalogs that may list 100 or more paperback titles, quantities of the books themselves and preprinted order forms for the patron. This method has been used in both urban and rural areas and can increase usage even when the community already has a branch or bookmobile service. Some persons simply prefer the convenience of using the mail to order and return their reading materials.

## Deposit Collections

Deposit collections of books and audiovisual materials are another common method for extending services. In the past several decades this service has been increasingly discouraged because of the tendency of materials to disappear or of deposit collections to stagnate. Bulk loans of children's materials to teachers have been less and less popular because some children's services coordinators feel that this discourages development of school media centers or competes with their existing services. Nonetheless, many libraries still provide collections to nursing homes, hospitals, jails, jury waiting rooms and similar locations. Some believe that this service may promote greater awareness of the library's services and resources. There is no evidence to support this, however.

In the event the administrator believes deposit collections are desirable or finds their use is established practice, it is important to inspect the condition of the deposit collection regularly and not to use any arbitrary formula to increase the library's circulation statistics based on unrealistic estimates of usage. Some libraries place discarded or gift materials in deposit collections. If this is done, some selectivitity should be exercised to ensure the materials do not create a negative image of the library's collections and services.

If possible, deposit collections should be avoided. Other extension methods can be employed if needed by the community. Often a contract can be negotiated with another library for bookmobile service, for example, which may be more efficient. Some state and regional libraries offer this form of service.

### Videotex and Cable Television

Another extension alternative is videotex, which permits the library to use telephone or cable television lines to transfer desired information to the patron. There are two forms of videotex: teletext and viewdata. Both systems require some modification of the patron's television receiver, and not all sets can be modified.

With teletext, the patron can access and read a relatively limited set of files. These might contain information on community events, emergency services or similar data that change frequently. With viewdata, the patron can use either a special terminal or a telephone touch pad to query a computer and display desired information on the home television screen. Local history files, an online encyclopedia or other databases such as a ready reference file could be accessed by the patron.

Some of the references listed at the end of this chapter provide more information on this technology. While American libraries have only experimented with these applications, they hold the promise of extending reference services more efficiently into the community at much lower cost than present methods. A number of libraries throughout the nation already operate broadcast radio stations, and many offer periodic radio, cable television and broadcast television programs. While high-quality productions require considerable effort, they can have a tremendous impact on reaching major portions of the community that do not use traditional services and materials.

### ADMINISTRATION

In the very smallest library, all aspects of administration from bookeeping to security may fall on the shoulders of the librarian. Even in the large public library system, the typical professional librarian is delegated some administrative responsibilities almost immediately. Graduate schools usually focus on "professional" elements, such as cataloging and reference work. Rarely is much time devoted to those mundane responsibilities that in fact occupy most library administrators' time: finance and accounting, public relations, personnel and volunteer services, custodial care and maintenance. These responsibilities are discussed at length in other chapters of this book, but some additional observations on management and a discussion of security are included here.

**Finance and Accounting**

In a smaller library, it is well to contract with one of the many available services for bookkeeping and accounting. Medium-sized libraries can benefit by using data processing equipment owned or leased by the accounting service for better financial reports and analysis. Some cities and counties perform this service for the library.

For larger libraries, or those special districts which are autonomous, a finance or business manager with appropriate training and experience is essential. Often purchasing responsibilities are delegated to this person and his or her staff. It is well to organize this unit so that responsibilities are divided. For example, if one person prepares all checks for issue, someone else should sign them or review accounts prior to mailing. An independent auditor should be retained to review financial procedures on a regular basis. See Chapter 3 for a more extensive discussion of financial management.

**Public Relations**

In the small library, public relations functions are the responsibility of the head librarian. As budgets and staff increase, they are diffused among the staff. Some libraries cooperatively support public relations efforts or contract for special services, such as hiring a part-time person to prepare a newsletter or to design posters. Cooperative agreements are recommended for small libraries. The administrator may be the best representative for the institution before community groups, but the ongoing process of communicating the library's services and resources to the community is very important and requires someone who is trained in those techniques and whose sole responsibility is public relations.

If the library has its own full-time public relations specialist or staff, this department should report directly to the administrator. The public relations specialist should participate in the decisions of the institution and regularly attend the important staff and board meetings to ensure that subsequent actions are throroughly and accurately interpreted for the media and the public.

In libraries with significant PR budgets, there are graphic designers, printing personnel and media specialists. For the bulk of libraries, specialized services are often contracted to permit the most professional product to be produced. More on public relations techniques and procedures is contained in Chapter 8.

## Personnel

The personnel function merits the closest supervision of the administrator. In a small library, the administrator does the recruiting, interviewing, selection, orientation, enrollment and evaluation, and sometimes even maintains the records and administers the fringe benefits program. Libraries that are departments of city or county government may use that jurisdiction's services. Libraries under civil service or merit systems may assume only part of the personnel procedures.

In a typical small library, the librarian's secretary may maintain personnel files, process enrollment and administer the fringe benefits program. In medium and larger libraries, personnel administration may fall to an assistant or deputy director or perhaps the business manager. In large libraries, there is always a personnel department. If payroll is a function of the personnel department, close liaison must exist with the library's finance department.

Consistent recruiting, interviewing and selection procedures that satisfy state and federal laws and regulations and avoid discrimination are important. Arbitrary discharge or selection can result in a lawsuit brought directly against the library board and its director, even when this responsibility has been delegated to others in the organization. (This is another reason for putting this function directly under the supervision of the administrator.)

The library is founded on the realization that education should be continuous, and its staff requires a challenging program to keep up-to-date and growing. Contractual agreements with local academic institutions or with state associations are among the means of accomplishing this. Staff should also be encouraged to become involved in professional organizations and civic activities. Tuition reimbursement programs should be developed to permit staff to increase their training in fields that are beneficial to the library. All of these efforts should be coordinated by the personnel officer. A more complete discussion of personnel administration is given in Chapter 5.

## Volunteers

Volunteer services have rarely received the attention they deserve in public libraries. Some library staff and administrators are reluctant to launch formal volunteer programs for fear that they will encourage public officials to reduce personnel budgets. However, a carefully developed volunteer program is always designed to supplement staff, not to replace them.

Some libraries rely on their Friends organization to manage the volunteer program. Others vest the authority with the personnel officer or the assistant director. If the library cannot afford a paid volunteer coordinator, one alternative is to identify an individual with volunteer experience to serve as a coordinator. Chapter 8 contains a further discussion of the role of volunteers.

## Maintenance

Custodial and maintenance coordination are often ignored in library administrative manuals, yet a clean and well-maintained building contributes significantly to the use of the facilities and to the public's attitude about the management of their tax dollars. In the very small library, the custodian probably reports directly to the librarian, and the administrator soon learns the mysteries of plumbing and electrical systems when the custodian is off duty and the village plumber and electrician are unavailable. Indeed, one of the first responsibilities of an administrator in a new library is to ensure that emergency arrangements exist in case of failures in heating and air conditioning, backed-up plumbing, smashed windows or leaky roofs. Often that requires a service contract to guarantee the availability of a repairman during the extended hours of operation typical in public libraries. The custodian should also be on call to deal with accidents, to aid in setting up meeting rooms for special events, or to cope with heavy snowfall or other inclement weather.

In a larger library, custodial and maintenance functions are often delegated to a business manager or a building engineer. Whatever the organizational position of the function, every administrator should see that maintenance receives careful attention and that it takes advantage of the newer technology and procedures that can save energy and add years to the life of buildings and equipment. Additional discussion of maintenance functions can be found in Chapter 9.

### Security

Maintaining security may be under the direction of the business manager, the personnel officer or the assistant director. Security personnel are responsible for maintenance of order in the facilities and protection of the building and its contents.

Design can play a critical part in reducing the amount of security personnel needed—for example, the use of vandal-resistant surfaces, areas that can be easily monitored from public service desks or strong lighting in parking lots. Nonetheless, a disruptive or abusive patron can create a serious problem, and staff may not have the capability to resolve it. The police can be called, but they may arrive too late. Trained security personnel on the scene can do much to prevent incidents from ever happening.

Some libraries hire off-duty police for this role or contract with private security firms. Others hire and train their own staff. Whatever the practice, every administrator must ensure that there are clear policies and lines of authority to prevent arbitrary actions. A job description and procedures for security staff are essential if the administrator wants to avoid lawsuits. When serious incidents do occur—if property is damaged or individuals are injured or their safety is threatened—the administrator must be prepared to back up the security staff.

### SUMMARY

This chapter has reviewed only the major units and forms of organizations in public libraries. Services to special groups such as the handicapped and aged exist in some libraries, and program specialists may coordinate these services for several departments in a library. Departments may be grouped in a great variety of ways, depending on the administrator's preferences and strengths. It is essential to specialize and delegate authority as the institution grows. In the very largest libraries, the director functions primarily as coordinator and planner, while the role is much broader and less clearly defined in the small public library.

The most basic library functions include circulation, adult, juvenile and young adult services, technical services, audiovisual and extension services, and administration. Whatever level of service a library offers, community analysis and planning are important to ensure that the services continue to evolve to respond to human need.

Whether these functions are handled from a single desk in a small rural or community library or are divided into hundreds of units in a large urban library, there is a need for consistent policies and procedures. The institution should have these written for the benefit of its staff and governing body, as well as the public.

## FOOTNOTES

1. Joseph R. Matthews, "The Automated Circulation System Marketplace: Active and Heating Up," *Library Journal* 107(3):233-235 (February 2, 1982).

2. National Center for Educational Statistics, *Preliminary Report. Library General Information Survey, LIBGIS III: Public Libraries, 1977-78* (Washington, DC: NCES, 1982).

3. Douglas Zweizig and Eleanor Jo Rodger, *Output Measures for Public Libraries: A Manual of Standardized Procedures* (Chicago: American Library Association, 1982).

4. Gary L. Bogart, ed., *Public Library Catalog* (Bronx, NY: H.W. Wilson Co., 1979).

5. Public Library Association, Starter List Committee, *Books for Public Libraries*, 3rd edition (Chicago: American Library Association, 1981).

6. *LIBGIS III*, Table 24.

7. *Ibid*, Table 20.

8. *Ibid*, Table 6.

9. *Ibid*, Table 6.

## SUGGESTIONS FOR FURTHER READING

American Library Association. Library Technology Project. *Development of Performance Standards for Binding Used in Libraries*. Chicago: American Library Association, 1966.

Boss, Richard W. *Automating Library Acquisitions: Issues and Outlook.* White Plains, NY: Knowledge Industry Publications, Inc., 1982.

— — —. *The Library Manager's Guide to Automation,* 2nd edition. White Plains, NY: Knowledge Industry Publications, Inc., 1984.

Brooks, Jean S. and David L. Reich. *The Public Library in Non-Traditional Education.* Homewood, IL: ETC Publications, 1974.

Brown, Eleanor Frances. *Bookmobiles and Bookmobile Service.* Metuchen, NJ: Scarecrow Press, Inc., 1967.

— — —. *Modern Branch Libraries and Libraries in Systems.* Metuchen, NJ: Scarecrow Press, Inc., 1970.

Cockerell, Douglas. *Bookbinding and the Care of Books,* 8th edition. London: Pitman Books, Ltd., 1978.

Cuhna, George David Martin. *Conservation of Library Materials: A Manual and Bibliography on the Care, Repair, and Restoration of Library Materials.* Metuchen, NJ: Scarecrow Press, Inc., 1967.

Dewey, Patrick R. *Public Access Microcomputers: A Handbook for Librarians.* White Plains, NY: Knowledge Industry Publications, Inc., 1984.

Evans, G. Edward. *Developing Library Collections,* Littleton, CO: Libraries Unlimited, Inc., 1979.

Fenwick, Sara Innis. "Library Service to Children and Young People." *Library Trends,* July 1976.

Foster, Donald L. *Managing the Catalog Department,* 2nd edition. Metuchen, NJ: Scarecrow Press, Inc., 1982.

Futas, Elizabeth, ed. *Library Acquisition Policies and Procedures.* Phoenix, AZ: Oryx Press, 1977.

Geddes, Andrew, ed. "Current Trends in Branch Libraries." *Library Trends,* April 1966.

Jones, Clara S., ed. *Public Library Information and Referral Service.* Syracuse, NY: Gaylord Bros., Inc., 1978.

Katz, Bill and Anne Clifford. *Reference and Information Services.* Metuchen, NJ: Scarecrow Press, Inc., 1982.

Kenney, Brigitte L., ed. *Cable for Information Delivery: A Guide for Librarians, Educators and Cable Professionals.* White Plains, NY: Knowledge Industry Publications, Inc., 1983.

Kronus, Carol L. and Linda Crowe, eds. *Libraries and Neighborhood Information Centers.* Urbana, IL: University of Illinois Graduate School of Library Science, 1972.

Ladley, Winifred, ed. "Current Trends in Branch Libraries." *Library Trends,* July 1963.

Lenz, Millicent and Ramona Mahood, eds. *Young Adult Literature: Background and Criticism.* Chicago: American Library Association, 1980.

Morrow, Carolyn Clark. *The Preservation Challenge: A Guide to Conserving Library Materials.* White Plains, NY: Knowledge Industry Publications, Inc., 1983.

Nadler, Myra, ed. *How to Start an Audio-visual Collection.* Metuchen, NJ: Scarecrow Press, Inc., 1978.

Sigel, Efrem, et al. *The Future of Videotext.* White Plains, NY: Knowledge Industry Publications, Inc., 1983.

Stanfield, Jonathan. *Fort Vancouver Regional Library: Electronic Information Systems Feasibility Study. Final Report.* Kirkland, WA: Axon Associates, 1982.

Talarzyk, W. Wayne and Richard E. Widding II. *Introduction to and Issues with Videotex: Implications for Marketing.* Columbus, OH: Ohio State University College of Administrative Science, 1981.

Turick, Dorothy. *Community Information Services in Libraries.* LJ Special Report No. 5. New York: R.R. Bowker Co., 1978.

# 7

# Automation

Few changes in the history of the library profession have had as profound an effect as has the application of computers. Besides releasing staff from many repetitive, labor-intensive tasks, the computer has given access to the holdings of thousands of libraries throughout the world, permitted the rapid transmission of information and interlibrary loan requests, allowed libraries to develop, access and share indexes and files with other information providers, and altered entirely previous concepts regarding the storage, retrieval and delivery of library and information services.

Automation is not an end in itself. It is, rather, an infinitely powerful tool for extending the administrator's and library staff's control over their work, thus making improved quality and a wider range of services available to the public. In this chapter we will review some of the potential applications of automation, to illustrate the value of computers in the library. We will also consider some of the barriers to wider application, as well as ways to overcome them. Other topics include equipment options, methods for estimating the costs of automating, some alternatives for financing, the steps required for planning and selection of systems, and the importance of cooperation with local, state, regional and national networks.

## APPLICATIONS

Virtually every labor-intensive process in the library is a likely candidate for automation, as are quite a few less repetitive and time-consuming routines.

### Circulation

Not surprisingly, automated circulation is the most popular application. Circulation in public libraries is likely to be 10 times greater than in academic libraries of similar size. Registration, charge and discharge, and overdue procedures are so cumbersome in many public libraries that they are a constant source of public dissatisfaction. In addition, the procedures reveal very little information about actual use, and, unless the library elects to tax itself to the limit, it is extremely difficult to determine the actual status of a particular book in the collection.

In contrast, online circulation systems can provide instant information on the status of patrons and materials, can automatically generate overdue notices, and can provide much more detailed management information on use. For this reason, online circulation systems are being used by hundreds of public libraries, and the trend is expected to grow significantly during the 1980s.

### Cataloging

Online cataloging, another popular application, has greatly reduced backlogs in technical processing departments. The typical output for original cataloging by manual methods is three to four books per cataloger per hour. In the case of more specialized items like foreign language and audiovisual materials, the cost of original manual cataloging can exceed the purchase price of the item. Furthermore, original cataloging encourages nonstandard bibliographic practices and allows the perpetuation of unusual classification systems and subject headings.

Manual original cataloging is rare today. Most libraries participate in a major bibliographic network such as OCLC or the Washington Library Network (WLN). The library can locate 95% of the needed bibliographic information online and can automatically order the records. A typical cataloger can process 12 to 15 items per hour using an online terminal, making minor editing changes to conform to local requirements, and still vastly improve the quality of cataloging.

Some libraries elect to use other cataloging methods. Some purchase self-contained systems that rely on Library of Congress MARC tapes. Others purchase their materials preprocessed from a book jobber or centralized processing center. Many of these centers, in turn, derive their cataloging from MARC tapes or a bibliographic utility.

## COM Catalogs

To reduce the need for maintaining individual card catalogs, many public libraries convert their bibliographic records to machine-readable form and provide microform catalogs for public and staff use. These computer output microform (COM) catalogs may be either unit catalogs, containing the records of only that library, or system catalogs, containing the holdings of all libraries participating in the system. COM catalogs vastly expand the resources available to the community. If they are regularly recumulated and reissued, they can be as current as card catalogs and are much more economical.

## Public Access Catalogs

The COM catalog and online cataloging often represent an interim step for many institutions. The eventual goal is conversion to an online public access catalog (PAC), on which both the public and staff can search for materials by author, title or subject or through Boolean search techniques. Because PACs are online, they are always current. They may also provide access either to an individual library or to other cooperating libraries through hierarchical search steps. Thus, the PAC offers even more advantages than the COM catalog. Experience in libraries that offer PACs reveals high acceptance, increased use of the collection and much greater accessibility of local resources.

## Acquisitions

One of the most complex operations in the library is acquisitions. Although it is often a difficult process to automate, the possibility of integrating it with the circulation, accounting or cataloging systems of the library, or all of them, makes acquisitions an application that can benefit several of the library's departments. Typical acquisitions systems provide current budget status reports for selectors and management, generate order forms to jobbers and publishers, provide regular status reports on these orders, and generate payment authorizations to the library's accounting unit.

## Periodicals Control

The periodicals function in a public library can also be improved through automation. Serials control systems can keep track of subscriptions, generate claim notices to publishers for missing numbers, produce current holdings records by title or subject, together with missing numbers, and can even produce labels for shelves and binding notices.

## Online Database Searching

Reference departments are able to access online indexing and abstracting services for both bibliographic and pure text information for patrons, thus greatly expanding their services. Orders for publications cited in these searches can be placed automatically through many of the information brokers. Many public libraries can provide more current information to their patrons through the use of these services and can reduce staff search time in the process.

Increasingly, firms are developing package subscriptions, which allow the library to receive both the traditional hard copy of the index or abstract for general public use and reduced rates for staff searches online of current or more specialized information. These services may seem costly in terms of the computer connect time, telecommunications and the training associated with their use. However, a closer analysis of the amount of information staff can retrieve, its currency and the time it takes to obtain the search results may reveal that online searching is more efficient than traditional reference techniques. Furthermore, most libraries that have implemented online search service find that patrons are more willing to pay all or part of the costs because of the improved quality of the results.

## Interlibrary Loan

Interlibrary loan (ILL) can be expedited and simplified using electronic mail systems. Some of the bibliographic utilities have developed subsystems that automatically cycle ILL requests to a series of libraries if the original institution receiving the request is unable to loan the item. OCLC maintains in its online file not only all the names and addresses of its participating libraries but also their ILL policies, as well as the names and addresses of publishers and other library-related agencies.

## Public Access Microcomputers

An increasingly popular service in public libraries of all sizes is the public access microcomputer. Many community libraries have become involved in this service through a grant from their Friends organization. Others have helped to justify the purchase of a microcomputer for business applications, such as simple accounting, by also making the equipment available for public use. The literature on the experience of libraries has grown enormously during the past several years. The Public Library Association has established a Microcomputer Users Group, and membership has risen dramatically.

Some libraries charge a small fee for the use of the equipment, similar to charges assessed for photocopy machines. Others offer it at no charge. Almost every library has experienced heavy public use, particularly if orientation and training for the public are offered and if a range of popular software, such as word processing and electronic spreadsheets, is available.

### General and Administrative Applications

In addition to applications that are solely library-related, there is a host of general office and administrative applications that can benefit any library. Word processing equipment is now almost as inexpensive as an electronic typewriter and can relieve the workload of clerical or secretarial employees. Board reports, staff manuals, policies and procedures manuals, board bylaws and similar documents that are likely to be frequently revised merit conversion to machine-readable form for ease of maintenance.

Of course, payroll and accounting applications have been automated in many libraries for years. Simple programs such as VisiCalc and other electronic spreadsheets simplify budget preparation and long-range planning and allow administrators to determine with ease the actual costs for services. Even the library public relations department can benefit from the conversion of its mailing lists, which the computer can then automatically sort for special mailings.

## MAINFRAME, MINI OR MICRO?

The automation options facing the administrator are vast. One question is the size of computer that should be used—mainframe, minicomputer or microcomputer. Many applications are available on all three types of computer. Even some circulation systems can run on a microcomputer, and a personal computer equipped with a modem can tap the most powerful bibliographic utility in the world.

## Capacity

Mainframes, minicomputers and microcomputers do, of course, vary significantly in capacity. The size of the computer to be chosen for a particular application depends on the amount of information to be contained in the database and how that information will be handled and stored. For example, the OCLC database contains more than 10 million title records in MARC format. Each of these records contains an average of 502 characters, resulting in a minimum memory requirement of 5,020,000,000 characters. In addition, it is important to organize that information in a fashion that permits retrieval by a variety of means, such as author, title or LC number, to be able to use that same information for acquisitions or interlibrary loan transactions, and to attach holdings symbols.

Further memory requirements exist for the software itself, which instructs the computer on how to control this information. Obviously, no microcomputer has the capacity for this file. Indeed, several large mainframe computers are needed to manage this database and to control access to it by the thousands of participating libraries.

Nonetheless, a microcomputer can access the large databases of a mainframe. Information can be transferred from a mainframe computer, then reprocessed and transferred into another system. For example, many libraries have minicomputer-based circulation systems. The technical services staff may catalog on a major utility such as OCLC and then, through a microcomputer, electronically transfer bibliographic records from OCLC, editing them in the process of transfer into a format suitable for use in the library's minicomputer circulation system. In this type of transaction, the limited storage capacity of the microcomputer is not a problem, for a bibliographic record is brief. If several records are to be transferred at one time, however, a larger capacity computer might be required.

## Defining the Application

In deciding what size computer the library will require, the administrator should carefully define the application required by the institution. If only one application is planned, such as online circulation, then this will simplify the process. Most libraries, however, find that it is desirable to link, or integrate, applications to avoid rekeyboarding records. For example, it would be desirable to link an online circulation system with acquisitions, since staff can determine order status for materials requested by patrons, without having to check another computer.

### Software Selection

The choice of hardware actually depends on the software required for the application. Software is usually written for a specific computer or family of computers and will run only under certain operating systems or languages used by that computer. This holds for even the simplest microcomputer application, such as word processing or accounting. Thus, the administrator should select the software that comes closest to satisfying the library's requirements and then purchase the hardware that will run the software.

The library might also consider developing its own software. However, because software is comparatively expensive to develop, and because packaged software is available for many library applications, it is more common for administrators and libraries to select a system that is already available.

### Size of the Application

Another factor is the size of the application. It should be possible for the administrator, or the administrator in concert with the vendor, to arrive at reasonable estimates of the size of the computer required to handle the application. For example, in estimating the size of computer required for an online circulation system, the vendor or the administrator can multiply the average length of each patron record by the number of registered borrowers in the system to arrive at the capacity requirements of the patron file. The same can be done for the bibliographic record. The number of transactions such as discharges and charges can be determined from the library's circulation records and multiplied by the number of characters required to record these in the computer.

That sum will provide an estimate of the memory requirement for current transactions. However, the administrator should also project growth in registration, bibliographic holdings and circulation, and add these figures to the minimal memory requirement. The vendor can then add the amount of memory required for the software and its operating system. This is only a rough estimate of file and memory requirements, but it represents a start in determining what size computer—micro, mini or mainframe—the application will require. It is a complex process, and if the administrator lacks familiarity with computers, the assistance of a consultant is recommended.

More information on choosing among automation options is given later in this chapter in the sections on Determining Costs and Planning and Selection.

## BARRIERS TO USE OF AUTOMATION

If all of these applications and options exist, the question arises: Why haven't more libraries taken advantage of them? While hundreds have done so, the vast majority have yet to go beyond a standard business application such as payroll. There are several reasons for this resistance. An examination of them should provide the library administrator with a sense of the problems involved in developing automated services.

### Lack of Expertise

The first of these barriers is lack of expertise. While the literature is expanding rapidly and the professional schools are modifying their curriculums to require greater familiarity with computers for their graduates, most public library administrators and professional staff have no knowledge of the field. It may require another generation for this to be corrected.

Every library administrator and board has the option of retaining the assistance of a consultant in assessing automation and its application, but there are many reasons why they fail to do so. Historically, public expenditures for consultants' fees have been suspect, and some administrators and boards are reluctant to risk public criticism for this expense. Some administrators hesitate for fear that a consultant may reveal their own weaknesses on the subject or find fault with the library's management practices. Also, an administrator may have difficulty articulating what is needed and giving sufficient direction for the consultant's skills to be used to the optimum benefit of the library.

There should be no reason for any public official to fear

criticism for contracting with a consultant for necessary information. Most people realize that automation can represent tangible savings, and a well-prepared specification for the consultant will answer any questions about the need for expert information. Aid in preparing specifications for a consultant can be provided by many state library agencies, cooperative library systems or major libraries.

**Staff Resistance**

Another barrier to automation is staff fear or resistance. Many individuals believe that their jobs may be lost or that they may be assigned responsibilities they will be unable to master. An administrator can deal with these concerns by involving staff in the research and decision-making process, and by providing assurances that personnel will not be reduced and that thorough training will be provided in the event of job changes.

Experience has shown that automation does not result in wholesale terminations in libraries. Instead, automation usually permits present staff to cope with increasing usage and work load more effectively. Where reductions do occur, they are generally handled through attrition.

**Conversion**

Another barrier is conversion. Many applications demand rather elaborate steps before the benefits can even begin to occur. For example, in automating the circulation system, a complete inventory of the library's collection is necessary, and all circulating materials must be labeled with a machine-readable tag. For libraries that may have hundreds of thousands or even millions of books and that haven't inventoried the collection since the Great Depression, this can seem an awesome task—particularly if they also have staff shortages.

Converting the card catalog to machine-readable form for COM or PAC purposes can be equally awesome. Decades of cataloging practice may have to be altered and holdings records verified. Many library administrators begin to calculate what conversion will cost, and fall into shock. Nonetheless, this work may eventually have to be done, whether the library automates or not.

*Conversion Options*

The administrator has several options in undertaking conversion to an automated system. Some vendors offer a package price for both the system and conversion. While this is unusual for major projects such as circulation systems, it may be available for smaller, more specialized applications such as accounting or film booking systems.

Some libraries have also found specialty vendors to handle portions of a conversion. For example, several firms can provide matching and merging services for the creation of COM or online catalogs. Library staff need to supply only an LC card number or some other elements of the bibliographic record. The vendor can then match these elements against its machine-readable files to develop full machine-readable records. This saves thousands of hours over constructing the records from scratch.

Some libraries have found it more economical to contract with local service bureaus or other keyboard services to convert cards or patron records into machine-readable form. There are some hazards. For example, the Ohio State University Libraries contracted with a specialty firm in the 1960s to convert its shelflist into computer-readable form. The vendor sent the work to another contractor in the Caribbean, where the wage scale was lower. Unfortunately, the language of the keyboard operators was not English, resulting in significant errors and requiring considerable OSU staff time to correct.

Other vendors have acquired skilled personnel or developed special programs that automatically screen for errors. For example, OCLC maintains a retrospective conversion service for libraries interested in developing machine-readable catalogs.

Another option is the temporary appointment of additional staff for conversion. If proper supervision and training are provided, this might be an efficient method. The use of volunteers is not recommended. While some individuals may have all the dedication and ability required for this task, conversion is a very tedious and exacting process, and the commitment of volunteers may flag. The result is lack of continuity, constant retraining and heavy amounts of supervision.

*Choosing the Best Method*

In deciding on the best method for converting to automation, the administrator will need to consider a number of critical factors: time, degree of accuracy required, the complexity of the application and, of course, cost. If the conversion can be accomplished over an extended period of time and if staff workload permits, it may be possible to complete the task with existing personnel. If the application has various features that allow errors in input to be easily spotted and corrected, this might also dictate the use of existing personnel. However, most applications, such as the construction of a patron or bibliographic database, require a high level of accuracy. If such is the case, the investment in a conversion contract with a specialty vendor may be wise.

The level of complexity in a conversion is also a factor. Flowcharting the steps required may help the administrator decide whether staff has the capability to undertake the task. Finally, if the library has not received sufficient appropriations to contract for conversion, then the cost may be prohibitive. The moral here is: Be sure conversion costs are included in the funds sought for major projects.

**Priorities**

On occasion automation may simply not have high enough priority to fit into the library's plans and budget. Many libraries throughout the nation have, in recent years, faced severe financial constraints, which forced staff reductions or trimmed acquisitions. Their first priorities are to restore service to original levels and correct deterioration in the collections or the facilities.

The administrator must realize that automation can serve these needs. It may, for example, remove the need to fill certain vacancies. And while building the collection is essential to the function of every library, many forms of automation greatly expand access to both local and distant holdings. While nothing can take the place of a modern, well-designed library, some applications of automation may eliminate or reduce space requirements and permit reassignment of existing space. For example, online cataloging should eliminate cataloging backlogs and dependence on large cataloging departments.

## DETERMINING COSTS

Of all the barriers, cost is perhaps the greatest concern to boards and administrators. It is often not the *actual* cost of automation, so much as *uncertainty* about what the total cost will be that presents the problem.

Most administrators are aware that hardware and software

costs do not represent the final expense. There are also the costs for conversion, selection of a system and development of specifications. Then there is the cost of maintaining the system, which involves contracts for both hardware and software maintenance. Operating costs include staff salaries, any necessary supplies and, in some cases, telecommunications costs. Finally, an automated system is not a permanent solution. Eventually the system will have to be replaced as the library outgrows the capacity of the system or as technological advances result in new systems that offer far more efficient use of personnel and databases.

Thus, arriving at the actual cost for automation of any application represents one of the most difficult challenges an administrator can face. Several readings listed at the end of this chapter provide detailed assistance in this task, but there are a number of basic steps that can be applied to analyze the cost of any application.

## Cost of Current Procedures

First, the administrator should determine the actual current costs for the process as it is now being done manually. This can be done by isolating the personnel, fringe benefit, contractual and supply costs for the function to provide a standard for comparison with the costs of automation. Many applications of automation will cost more than existing manual methods because of the need to amortize the equipment and conversion costs. Comparison with present costs will tell the administrator whether the budget will carry that burden.

## System Options

The second cost-related decision is whether to select a turnkey application, modify or adopt some other library's application, or develop original software.

### Turnkey Systems

A turnkey system is a package containing both the hardware and software for a specific function, developed by a private firm for direct sale to the library. Often the package includes conversion, training and maintenance options. The cost for this package may vary depending on the size of the library, its estimated traffic or the amount of conversion required.

In any event, the vendor should be able to supply the administrator with a preliminary estimate of cost for the hardware, software and maintenance once some essential information regarding the library is supplied. Maintenance and operating costs can be verified with other customers of the vendor, assuming that the turnkey system has been sold previously.

The disadvantage of a turnkey system is that it may not possess all of the features desired by the library. Many vendors will alter their systems to satisfy unique requirements. However, that will increase the price of the package, and sometimes that increase cannot be readily determined until formal bidding takes place. For that reason, administrators should consider preliminary quotations with care.

*Software Packages*

Software developed by other libraries or organizations may be offered for purchase or lease for a comparatively modest amount. The library then has the option of going directly to the hardware manufacturer or a local dealer, depending on the policy of the manufacturer, and purchasing the equipment without the turnkey vendor's markup. If the software can be applied without modification or the originating library can supply software support, then this may be an economical approach to automating a function.

However, if modifications are required and support is not readily available, complications and costs could rise. When changes are made, the application may no longer run on the hardware. A larger configuration could also represent a burden on the hardware and software, requiring software specialists to correct the problem.

Estimating the costs for this option may be straightforward if no modifications are necessary and the hardware requirements are well established. The price of the software can be readily determined, and a dealer should be able to furnish a cost estimate for the hardware once an equipment list is developed. The uncertainty will be the conversion and implementation cost. However, if the originating library is anxious to sell the product, it may include conversion and implementation in its price.

*Original Software*

The third option—developing original software—is probably the most difficult for an administrator to calculate. Many libraries have suffered considerable losses in electing to develop their own software and select the hardware for an application.

Sometimes a local firm may approach a library with a proposal to develop or modify software for library use. While this may be a viable alternative for standard business applications, it is not recommended for special library functions. There is a growing effort to standardize data management procedures in many library applications. Even if the local firm is able to produce software, the system may not have the standards required for interconnection with other library systems. For example, online circulation systems should be able to store full bibliographic records in the MARC format. Systems that accept only short records may have to be converted at some future time to permit expansion to a PAC or to allow interface with other systems.

If the library must take this option or feels it necessary to compare the cost of this alternative, the software firm should be required to provide a functional description of what it will produce, together with a firm cost proposal for development, testing and subsequent maintenance. Who will own the software should also be determined. In addition, the software firm should be required to furnish an equipment list sufficient to permit the library to get estimates for required hardware.

## PLANNING AND SELECTION

Any automation project should be consistent with the library's overall long-range plan. There is often a tendency for institutions to segregate goals and strategies for automation from general development, and the result could be conflicting priorities. For example, an objective to modify circulation procedures or extend hours of service in the circulation department will conflict with conversion responsibilities for an online circulation system. Planning for automation should thus begin with a review of the library's long-range plan.

### Setting Priorities

Establishing priorities is essential in marshaling available human resources and setting in process the implementation of any automation project.

Priorities can be best determined by breaking down the steps required to automate each of the desired applications. For example, preparing for online circulation requires inventory of the collection, updating of the bibliographic records, labeling of the circulation materials, training for circulation routines, determination of policy changes, and acquisition and installation of the equipment, among other steps. Conversion to a PAC requires inventory of the collection, correction of the card catalog, development of the machine-readable database, etc.

This process will reveal certain steps that are essential to many of the applications. These should receive first priority. Inventory of the collection and updating bibliographic records may be the logical first steps, even before a system is selected, since it will provide a foundation for all of the applications.

**Participation**

Planning calls for participation by all who hold a stake in the project. As noted previously, participation in research and planning will relieve staff fear and resistance. While it may not be practical or possible to include on a planning team all those staff members who will be affected by the project, it is essential that at least some representation be provided.

The planning team should consist of the administrator, key staff from the affected departments and, depending on the size and nature of the project, representation from the board and the local political jurisdiction (for example, the city data processing department).

The team must be able to obtain adequate information for its decisions. Sites where the application has been used should be visited. Vendors should be interviewed. Facts should be collected to provide greater insight into conversion, training, maintenance and operation, eventual replacement, and any other cost elements. This may be a costly and time-consuming process, but it is better to undertake this preliminary investigation and identify the problems beforehand, rather than to make a commitment and later find that the costs for conversion or operation are too high.

After this research has been concluded, the team should begin to develop specifications and selection criteria for the system. While specifications often call for award to the lowest-bidding qualified contactor, it is possible to design the specifications so that factors that are of importance to the planning team can be given weight in the selection. For example, if the growth potential of an online circulation system is a concern, points can be assigned to this element, giving greater weight to a proposal that promises greater growth flexibility. These selection criteria should be cited in the specifications, so the low bidder who does not end up with the highest score does not sue the library.

### Evaluating Vendors

Among the elements to be considered in evaluating a vendor are financial strength, depth of personnel, relationship with equipment supliers, service, training capabilities, level of communications between the vendor and the vendor's customers, commitment to the market, adherence to standards, and the reputation of the firm with its customers.

### *Financial Strength*

It should be possible to obtain a current credit and performance report on the firm to determine the source of its financing, whether it has experienced any financial difficulties or possesses a poor credit rating. It would be important to determine whether the firm might experience some cash flow problems in completing a major contract. For example, some successful firms with good products have foundered because local governments have delayed appropriation of funds to pay for major public library installations.

### *Personnel and Service*

The depth of the company's personnel is also a critical concern. If 80% of the staff are in sales and marketing, rather than development, some problems are likely to arise. In addition, some of the firm's personnel should have experience in or knowledge of the library market, so they can anticipate problems or needs. There should be enough service personnel to handle normal problems. While some vendors rely solely on the equipment manufacturer to provide service to customers, some technical competency among the vendor's personnel is essential to aid in training, installation and the everyday problems that bedevil even the simplest turnkey application.

Some vendors are authorized dealers for major computer manufacturers. That usually indicates reliability since most manufacturers have rigid standards for authorized dealers, requiring service, sound financing and a minimum level of sales.

## Training

Training support is also an important factor in assessing the quality of the vendor, but all too often an administrator takes this for granted. The vendor should have personnel qualified to introduce the system to the staff. These trainers should be more than salespersons whose major source of income is a commission. They should be familiar with the product and have tested training programs, backed up with manuals and other documentation to support the product. They should also be available for contact later should problems arise.

## Customer Communications

The level of communications between the vendor and the customer is another important factor. If the vendor provides newsletters and its representatives follow up with subsequent visits after the installation, and if the vendor has a user council to recommend revisions to the application, an administrator can have a better basis for assessing the commitment the vendor has to the library market.

## Costs vs. Benefits

Of course, a vendor must make a reasonable profit in order to stay in business, and the administrator should not expect an array of services without some charge. For that reason, cost should not be the sole criterion for judging a vendor's proposal. The best vendor, in terms of depth of service, reliability of product, training and flexibility, may turn out to be the highest bidder. Again, for this reason, it is important to develop selection criteria that reflect the importance of these elements to the library and to weigh them accordingly.

## FINANCING

Libraries may undertake automation individually or cooperatively. In either case, the expense may be great, and every administrator should be aware of the financing alternatives available. Besides using general appropriations, public libraries have financed automation through capital improvement bonds, grants, lease and lease-purchase, and user fees. The application, local and state law and policy, and the needs of the participants determine the method.

Purchasing an automated system through the annual budget presents the fewest complications—assuming that the library can convince budget authorities to approve the expenditure in the first place.

## Leasing

Leasing computerized equipment subjects the library to interest payments, but it does have the advantage of spreading costs over a longer period. An administrator considering leasing should determine the interest rate and the maintenance costs as separate elements of the contract. Since the library is a tax-exempt entity, it should be able to command a lower interest rate, and if the lessor cannot provide that favorable rate, local banks should be approached.

The major disadvantage of leasing is that the library does not build equity in the equipment and software. If the application is anticipated to have a short life and the administrator believes that more efficient and economical equipment may become available in the near future, however, that may not be a concern.

## Lease-purchase

Lease-purchase agreements provide an alternative if the library wants to build an equity in the equipment and software and may elect to purchase it in the future. In lease-purchase agreements, a portion of the lease cost may be applied to the eventual purchase. The administrator must determine how much of the lease cost applies to purchase, whether the maintenance costs are included, and the interest rate. Again, alternative financing might provide a better interest rate.

Some states limit the power of local governmental agencies to lease-purchase, and this should be reviewed with the library's attorney. The vast majority of states, however, realize that this is an important means of equipment purchase and allow it.

## Grants

Grants are another source of funds for equipment purchase. The Library Services and Construction Act has been used by many states to support automation. The Columbus and Franklin County (OH) Public Library received a major grant from the Columbus Foundation to automate its circulation system.

Sometimes a library can piggyback on a grant received by another government agency to automate. For example, for its online circulation system, the Long Beach (CA) Public Library uses a backup minicomputer purchased by the town's police department. Using a special federal grant, the police department acquired the backup unit as protection in the event its main computer system should ever fail. The Long Beach Library has developed procedures that can maintain its own operations in such an emergency.

**User Fees**

While user fees do not seem appropriate for online circulation or cataloging, they can be applied for services such as online database searching. In fact, a majority of public libraries do assess patron charges for computer connect time. If sufficient funds cannot be found for terminal purchase, it may be possible to lease one and set the user fee to cover both its cost and the cost of computer connect time.

## COOPERATION AND NETWORKING

Interlibrary cooperation (to be discussed further in Chapter 10) can play an important role in automation. Not only can the costs and risk be spread among a greater number of participants, but there is a greater likelihood that resources can be better used. Developing a shared application may require more time and some compromises, but the resultant network will be worth the effort.

A great deal of emphasis has been placed in recent years upon the importance of national networks. While they are of critical importance to libraries of all types and sizes, there are roles of equal importance for local, state and regional networks.

**Local Networks**

In its most basic form, the local network may consist of only an electronic mail service or an online circulation system maintained by two or more libraries. The role of this local network, ideally, should be to facilitate access to materials in the immediate geographic area, to share pertinent local databases and to provide for the rapid delivery of resources or information through the local library.

While a national network may be able to provide some of these same services, a locally developed and governed network permits optimum use of local resources, allows greater emphasis on unique local needs and can ensure more rapid delivery. In the formation of local information databases, a local network can ensure more complete coverage and easier retrieval. Because the number of participants is small, response time and uptime should be better than on larger networks. Local networks should be able to interface with state, regional and national networks, and standards to ensure this are rapidly evolving.

## State and Regional Networks

The role of state and regional networks should be to facilitate the development of more local networks, the development and utilization of the state's or region's bibliographic database, the brokering of services offered by the national networks, and liaison between local networks and the national services. Training, consultant assistance and financial assistance in the form of grants would be included in the portfolio of the state and regional network. These networks can also play a role in the establishment of standards to ensure effective resource sharing and interface.

## National Networks

At the national level, networks should focus on those services that require the greatest degree of standardization and on the construction of a national online bibliographic catalog, including the facilitation of interlibrary loan for resources that cannot be supplied locally. National networks should also pursue research and development in newer applications and the pure research that can provide the foundation for standards appropriate for the state, regional and local networks.

Overlapping and interlocking representation between these levels of networks should foster communication and should permit a consensus to be reached on goals and priorities. It should also avoid duplication and ineffective use of the tax dollar, which ultimately fuels the work of all these networks.

# SUMMARY

Automation in libraries can provide greater access to resources and better control of library materials. It can increase staff productivity and relieve staff of repetitive routines. Automation also raises the quality of service and reduces error.

Among the many applications of automation in the public library are online circulation, cataloging and public access catalogs, acquisitions, periodicals control, online reference, interlibrary loan, electronic mail, and office applications that range from payroll and accounting to word processing and budget planning.

Computers are now available in a range of sizes and prices that make it possible for almost any library to consider automation. The size of computer needed will depend on the amount of information it must store and process. Automating circulation usually requires significant computer capacity, and circulation is often linked, or integrated, with other applications such as acquisitions. However, a small microcomputer can be used to access the largest databases. The actual choice of computer hardware will also be determined by the software—the specific applications programs the library wishes to use.

Despite the value of automation, a number of barriers prevent its wider introduction. These include staff resistance, lack of expertise, lengthy and complicated conversion, other priorities and cost. Each must be evaluated when automation is considered. Perhaps the most significant barrier is cost, since it is often difficult to determine exactly what the real cost of automation is. Elements that must be considered include selection and specification development, hardware and software purchase and maintenance, conversion and training, telecommunications, supplies and the eventual need to replace the system.

As with any major decision, the administrator should follow a careful process of planning. Once the decision has been made, a thorough evaluation of vendors should be undertaken. The administrator has several options in financing automation, including general appropriations, the capital improvement budget, grants, lease or lease-purchase, and user fees.

Finally, networks are also important in the use and development of automated systems. Each level—local, state and regional, and national—has an important part to play in using automation to increase patrons' access to library resources.

## SUGGESTIONS FOR FURTHER READING

Boss, Richard W. *The Library Manager's Guide to Automation,* 2nd edition. White Plains, NY: Knowledge Industry Publications, Inc., 1984.

Carter, Ruth C. and Scott Bruntjen. *Data Conversion.* White Plains, NY: Knowledge Industry Publications, Inc., 1983.

Dewey, Patrick R. *Public Access Microcomputers: A Handbook for Librarians.* White Plains, NY: Knowledge Industry Publications, Inc., 1984.

Fayen, Emily Gallup. *The Online Catalog: Improving Public Access to Library Materials.* White Plains, NY: Knowledge Industry Publications, Inc., 1983.

Fosdick, Howard. *Computer Basics for Librarians and Information Specialists.* Arlington, VA: Information Resources Press, 1981.

Grosch, Audrey N. *Minicomputers in Libraries, 1981-82: The Era of Distributed Systems.* White Plains, NY: Knowledge Industry Publications, Inc., 1981.

Lancaster, F. Wilfrid. *Libraries and Librarians in an Age of Electronics.* Arlington, VA: Information Resources Press, 1982.

Sager, Donald J. *A Public Library Administrator's Planning Guide to Automation.* Columbus, OH: Online Computer Library Center, Inc., 1983.

Woods, Lawrence A. and Nolan F. Pope. *The Librarian's Guide to Microcomputer Technology and Applications.* White Plains, NY: Knowledge Industry Publications, Inc., 1983.

# 8

# Public Relations

No public library can expect to gain adequate community support and encourage use of library services without a commitment to effective public relations. Even in the smallest library, it takes staff members some time to master procedures and services. The general public—including frequent or highly educated users—also needs to be educated about many of the library's resources and services.

In fact, most surveys reveal that there is profound ignorance of all but the most common library resources and services. The public knows that a library stocks books but may not know that there are large-print books for the visually handicapped or that the library can obtain books for patrons through interlibrary loan. Some may be aware that children's programs are provided but not realize that educational games and audiovisual materials are also available for this age group.

Many libraries dutifully report that they do have an ongoing public relations program. They will point to posters mounted in the library lobby, brochures distributed from the circulation desk and perhaps some colorful bookmarks that list recommended titles. They can also provide copies of news releases that have been mailed to the local newspaper. Unfortunately, these efforts may be of little value in reaching and informing the community of the library's services and resources.

Effective public relations requires a plan with clear goals, objectives and strategies, based on research into the community's needs and designed to communicate what the library has to offer. This chapter will emphasize research into community needs and the development of strategies toward the satisfaction of those needs. Only through this approach can an administrator be certain that the effort devoted to public relations will be worthwhile.

## MARKETING

Philip Kotler, who pioneered the concept of marketing for public institutions, has defined marketing as

> ...the analysis, planning, implementation and control of carefully formulated programs designed to bring about voluntary exchanges of values with target markets for the purpose of achieving organizational objectives. It relies heavily on designing the organization's offering in terms of the target market's needs and desires, and on using effective pricing, communication and distributing to inform, motivate and service the markets.[1]

Marketing, then, is a process, and Kotler has broken it down into the four components of analysis, planning, implementation and control.

### Analysis

In marketing research, a number of techniques for analysis can be used to determine whether there is a genuine need for a new material or service. For example, a library might be considering a substantial investment in a video tape collection. The library might conduct a survey of a representative sample of users or of the general public to determine the number of video tape players in the community. Another approach would be to draw on industry statistics, which might be regionalized to reveal how many video tape players have been sold in the area. Contacting local stores that deal in this equipment is another possibility.

If the need is established, further research is necessary to determine what the collection should contain. The previous research should also have revealed which video player format, Beta or VHS, is most common in the community. Focused group interviews with representative owners of video tape players might reveal the most popular subjects for the collection. The library might also use census reports on its community and discover a relatively high percentage of families with young children. This would indicate the need for a high percentage of children's titles in the collection. Research by the video tape industry may reveal certain characteristics of video tape purchasers that correlate to the demographics in the community. Other libraries in communities with similar demographic characteristics might be polled to determine their experience with video tape circulation. Surveys and research will also indicate whether competitive suppliers exist and whether the public is being satisfied by them.

The primary methods of conducting research to analyze community needs, therefore, are public surveys and individual interviews based on random sampling, identification of pertinent data from private sector or governmental sources such as the U.S. Census, and the polling of libraries with similar demographic characteristics. More detailed information about these methods can be found in some of the titles cited at the end of this chapter. The critical point, however, is that there is a variety of methods the library can use to assess community need. To avoid duplication and waste, administrators must get into the habit of applying them before new services are initiated.

## Planning

Once a need has been established, the next step in marketing is planning, the development of a well thought-out strategy to reach those people who have that need. For example, research may reveal that job information is desperately needed because of high unemployment. However, mounting a poster in the library lobby or issuing a general news release that the library has resources is not sufficient to reach the people who need the information. Careful planning would indicate that relevant materials should be collected in a prominent location in the library, and posters should be mounted in unemployment compensation bureaus, state employment offices and similar locations where the unemployed are likely to congregate. An advertisement describing the library's services could be placed in the help wanted section of the local newspaper and would probably be far more effective than a news release, which usually gets buried in the social page. Other strategies could include programs highlighting materials on career change and the development of a job club.

## Implementation and Control

Kotler's third and fourth steps are implementation and control. Implementation requires the commitment of sufficient personnel and materials to ensure that the plan works, and control means ongoing evaluation of the results. For example, in the case of providing job information, if use of the job materials is low or programs are poorly attended, the control step may show that the target market was not reached or that research erred, and the need does not exist.

Often a library may start a new service, only to see it fail after a brief flurry of heavy use. This may result either from the failure of the library to commit sufficient resources to the service to satisfy demand, or from overpromotion, that is, promising more than the library can deliver, which creates genuine public relations problems. Either way, this situation reveals poor planning in assessing potential demand or need.

## Pricing

Marketing also involves the pricing of products and services. While public libraries may charge for certain types of services, most are offered free. What the library does seek from its users and the general public is time, and sometimes people would rather spend money than time. Suppose a businessperson is seeking information on a new product. If a commercial service can provide it quickly, without requiring any effort or time from the businessperson, he or she is likely to purchase that service rather than spend time doing the research in the library.

An astute administrator should analyze both current use of the library's services and commercially provided information services to determine whether modifications can make the library easier and less time-consuming to use. The administrator should also consider whether the assessment of a small fee might permit the library to tap newer technology, such as online databases, and so offer vastly improved service.

The community may want programs for children and adults. However, programs that are dull, repetitive and a waste of patrons' time are "priced" too high, and attendance will decline. The library might be wiser to invest in better speakers on more pertinent topics for adults and to offer more creative, exciting programs for younger audiences, even if fewer programs must be offered as a result.

## The Market

Marketing specialists often refer to "target" markets, which are *segments* of the total population. Public libraries have used the opposite approach, designing services and programs to attract as broad and general an audience as possible. As a result, they have been criticized as attempting to do too much for too many people. Administrators have countered by noting that their institutions are supported by the entire public and would be criticized for developing services that served only an elite.

However, nothing should prevent a public library from designing special services targeted to specific groups, such as the aged or the handicapped, so long as the overall range of services is balanced, and no one is prevented from participating in a special program. Targeting an audience permits the library to reach that group more efficiently, to refine materials and services to fit the special needs of that group, and to benefit a segment of the total population that was underutilizing the library.

## The Four Ps

Marketing takes the administrator beyond just knowing the community to applying that knowledge to satisfy whatever community needs the library can serve. E. Jerome McCarthy has specified the factors to consider in developing a marketing plan as the four Ps—product, price, place and promotion.[2] For public libraries, product means services, which should be defined at least in part by research into community needs. Price is not simply the tax dollars that support library service but also the value of time that users must invest to draw on the library's resources and/or services. Place involves comparing the location of the library's services and resources in the community with that of commercial information sources, such as bookstores and information brokers, and alternative libraries, such as academic, school and special. Promotion covers those activities commonly called public relations—publicity releases, posters, brochures and similar techniques.

### BOARD, STAFF AND ADMINISTRATIVE ROLES

The board, the staff and the administrator all have roles to play in public relations programs.

## The Board

The board must establish the broad goals that define the total program—which groups are to be targeted and which services and resources are to be developed. The board is responsible for the control function; it must evaluate the results and provide corrective direction to the administrator. As the representative of the public, the board is accountable for the library's overall public relations program and should require regular surveys to determine whether the public is aware of the institution's services and resources.

## The Staff

Probably the most important public relations work for the library is performed by the library staff in the daily services provided to the public. If service is poor, no amount of promotion will counter that image. By the same token, even if the library has a limited collection, inadequate facilities and a host of other problems, a staff that is motivated and concerned about serving the public to the best of its ability will be deeply appreciated and will provide an impressive foundation for any public relations program.

## The Administrator

The link between the staff and the board is the administrator. For the board, the administrator must provide sound research on which the board can base its policy decisions on marketing the library and making it more responsive to community needs. The administrator is also charged with objectively reporting the results of public relations efforts.

With the staff, the administrator is responsible for developing morale, weeding out ineffective or incompetent personnel, and communicating both the goals of the board and the strategies that can achieve them. Of course, if the administrator uses a participatory management approach, the staff would help select these strategies.

Even if the library has a public relations officer or specialist, the administrator is still the key public relations person for the institution. Both are charged with interpretation of the board's policy and its implementation. The administrator is also responsible for providing feedback from the staff to the board when policies or strategies fail. Thus, although the responsibility for public relations must be shared in all libraries, the administrator must realize the vital link he or she provides in the process.

## COMMUNITY RELATIONS

Allied to the public relations program of the library are its community relations activities. Community relations involves the library in the activities of a community in order to better anticipate changes and needs, and to gather information that will influence library policy and services. Some libraries may have a specialist and staff assigned solely to this effort, while in other libraries this may represent a function of the branch or extension staff.

Critics often view community relations efforts of public institutions as sinister. They argue that such efforts result in manipulation of community leadership and possibly the development of demands for services that are not of real benefit to the community. For example, a small community might be persuaded by the library's community relations specialist to demand construction of a larger and unneeded branch library. Such events may occur, but the normal role of the community relations program is not to influence community goals but to assist the community in the attainment of goals.

Community relations efforts include encouraging library staff to become active in local civic organizations, providing services and resources that contribute to community projects, and communicating needs and concerns to the administration so that appropriate recommendations for new policies or services can be considered by the board. Regular meetings with extension personnel to identify trends and to build effective communication are also important. Where appropriate, staff time may be granted to participate in such efforts, and expenses, such as membership in local civic groups, may be paid by the library.

## EFFECTIVE USE OF THE MEDIA

Most libraries have used news releases to promote public awareness of their services, but few use them effectively. A general news release is a shotgun approach, designed to reach everyone who reads a particular newspaper or listens to a particular radio station. Studies have shown that newspaper readership is declining and that those who subscribe to newspapers may read only one or two sections.

To be effective, the library must target the desired audience.

For a service that benefits the entire community, a general news release may be best. In contrast, the development of a babysitting class for young people is better publicized through the 4-H Club newsletter or Boy and Girl Scout announcements. The local chamber of commerce might be willing to publicize an end-of-year tax planning workshop in its newsletter, and the editor of the local newspaper's financial page might be willing to tuck the announcement in his column, where it could reach the targeted audience better than if the notice went to the city editor.

Just as many libraries develop special mailing lists to reach patrons with unique interests, each library should carefully study the local media from the point of view of an advertiser. Any publication or radio or television station can pinpoint the characteristics of its audience. Radio and television can even refine the audience by hours of the day. Many rural or suburban communities are served by special newspapers geared only for that community. Local units of government, such as park districts, have special newsletters for their clientele. Clubs and civic organizations also have regular newsletters, and every church has a bulletin for the congregation.

On occasion, the library might run a paid advertisement in a key publication or a radio or television time slot, paid for from library funds or by a contribution from a local sponsor. The Chicago Bar Association jointly sponsored the creation of a legal information and referral service with four of the library systems in the Chicago metropolitan area and contributed the cost for full-page advertisements in the major daily newspapers to inform the public of the new service. Increasingly, public institutions are finding it necessary to advertise in order to reach their target market, because the competition for free time or space is so fierce.

## ROLE OF GRAPHIC DESIGN

To catch the public's eye, the library should include professional graphic design in its public relations program. Too many public libraries look like small country stores, with their windows plastered full of library promotions, community events and assorted warnings. Brochures hand-printed by the amateur artist on the staff or posters stenciled by the custodian are probably a waste of time. If something is important enough to have a sign, brochure or poster, then it is important enough to deserve professional design.

A proliferation of signs and announcements in a library can also create visual pollution, which in turn creates a bad public relations image. If the library does not have a professional artist or graphic designer, then it should either contract for this service, enter into a cooperative agreement with other public libraries in the area to share the cost of these services, or attempt to find a professional who will donate his or her services.

Good graphic design requires balance, simplicity and standardization of typeface. Electronic typesetting equipment available today permits professional results to be achieved readily even by a nonartist. Without professional creativity, however, the institution will be left with only a sterile product.

It is particularly important to use professional services to design public relations materials that are used frequently. These include a general brochure describing the library's policies and services, to be given to each new borrower, and the library's annual report. Even small libraries should consider the "image enhancement" of a well-designed logo. Similarly, the library borrower's card should also be attractive, since the individual will carry it all the time.

## LIBRARY PROGRAMS AND EXHIBITS

Exhibits and programs are important components of the library's public relations activity, particularly if they promote greater awareness of existing services or resources. Although the media rarely cover existing services, they will carry announcements of programs and exhibits, which can accomplish the same purpose.

The Columbus and Franklin County (OH) Public Library once sought media publicity for its collection on parenting but had no success. When the library scheduled a series of programs featuring prominent citizens speaking as parents and arranged an exhibit in the window of a local department store, use of the collection increased greatly. Months later the collection continued to be heavily used by parents who could not attend the program but who knew of the collection because they saw the exhibit or the announcement of the program series.

### Display Space

Many libraries do not have an exhibit area or display cases to promote their resources and services. If funds to provide display space are not available, through either donation or the capital budget, library staff should actively seek the use of display areas and windows in other prominent locations in the community. Banks frequently have large lobbies and welcome public service exhibits. A store might also welcome a library exhibit and build its own display around it. Some libraries develop good rapport with local book stores by exhibiting in the library recommended holiday books for gift giving; these displays are duplicated in the book store windows with credit to the library.

If the library does have good exhibit space, it can sometimes develop a reciprocal arrangement with other organizations in the community such as the Scout groups, stamp clubs, civic groups and similar associations. As with printed materials, displays should be professionally done. An amateur display will stand out like a sore thumb and have a negative public relations impact.

### Using Outside Resources

Of course, libraries schedule exhibits and programs for educational and informational purposes in their own right, not just to promote the library's own resources and services. For example, the Smithsonian Institution's Traveling Exhibit Service (SITES) provides outstanding exhibits on the humanities, arts and sciences, at very nominal cost. They are professionally designed and come with descriptive labels, so that almost no effort is required to present an excellent educational exhibition for the community. A program series can often be built around the exhibition to further enhance its value. Major libraries, such as the Folger Shakespeare Library, art galleries and museums, offer similar traveling exhibits, which can be borrowed for nominal rental and shipping costs.

In conjunction with the 300th anniversary of the earliest German immigration to America, the Elmhurst (IL) Public Library borrowed from the Goethe Institute an exhibit of reproductions entitled "America as Seen Through the Eyes of German Immigrant Painters." Because Elmhurst has a large German-American population, a series of programs was arranged to coincide with the exhibit. The programs were very popular and attracted new users to the library. As a result, the library applied for and received a grant from the National Endowment for the Humanities to run a larger program series.

### Programming

Programming is a common activity in many libraries, yet often the staff attitude is extremely negative. Too often, considerable effort is devoted to the development of a program that attracts only a limited audience. Further, sometimes so much effort must be devoted to program preparation that little remains for public service.

In designing a program series, the same fundamentals of marketing must be applied as in the development of any new service. The community should be regularly surveyed to assess program needs, and sufficient resources must be allocated to ensure that offerings are attractive enough to the target audience. Here again, effective use of the media is essential.

## VOLUNTEERS AND FRIENDS

Volunteers and Friends organizations are not often considered as part of the library public relations program, but they represent one of the best public relations tools the administrator has. A volunteer contributes time, which permits the library to offer services that cannot be provided within its budget. In addition, the volunteer develops greater insight to the library's function in the community and can be a spokesperson for the institution wherever she or he goes. Usually, volunteers are active in the community, so the public relations impact is spread widely.

### Effective Use of Volunteers

Making effective use of volunteers takes special attention. Otherwise, the overall impact may be negative. All of the steps essential for good personnel administration are required for the volunteer program. Job descriptions should be prepared and they should provide opportunity for growth and enrichment. Recruitment interviews should be designed to yield enough information to ensure that individuals are placed in suitable activities.

Unfortunately, not all staff welcome volunteers, particularly if they fear they might be replaced by volunteers. All volunteer programs should be based on the understanding that volunteers are only to provide services that complement existing staff and that cannot be provided through public funds. However, some staff dislike working with volunteers, and they should not be required to do so.

Training and evaluation should also be provided for volunteers. Training is, in effect, the price that supervisors must pay for the work of volunteers. It should be thorough and be given in the same spirit it is given to paid staff—an investment in making the most effective use of that individual. In addition, the volunteer program should have a recognition system, with different awards to reflect different levels of contribution to the library.

## The Volunteer Coordinator

The most effective volunteer programs are those that employ full-time coordinators of volunteers. A coordinator can handle the interviewing and placement of volunteers, develop recruiting programs, schedule work shifts, and make sure that important assignments are done. Often the coordinator is recruited from the volunteer staff or from the Friends organization, but formal training may be available. The coordinator's salary will depend on the library's size and resources, but even smaller libraries will usually find that they can justify some funding for this position.

## Friends Organizations

Friends organizations often function as volunteer groups for special projects to supplement library services, such as book sales. More often, however, they are focused on larger social and fund-raising events. The Friends of the Chicago Public Library, for example, periodically manage a giant book sale in Grant Park and run an annual $100-per-plate Literary Arts Ball. The proceeds from these activities and from membership dues help fund special projects developed by the staff of the Chicago Public Library, such as establishment of a computer center in a neighborhood library, program allowances for the children's coordinator and lecture fees paid to authors. The Friends also provide guides for groups wishing tours of the central library.

Some library boards and administrators discourage Friends groups, because they fear the Friends will attempt to dictate policy on library operations. With good liaison and regular communication between the board and the Friends, this should not happen. The library administrator or the assistant administrator should attend the Friends meetings regularly to provide a link between them and the board.

Both board and Friends must have goals and long-range plans. One way to share information and ensure that the roles of both groups remain clear is to have representatives of each group participate in each other's planning sessions. The library board and the Friends of the Chicago Public Library used to meet each spring for a joint luncheon where these plans were shared, and good rapport could be maintained.

Friends organizations also provide another means of spreading information about the library to the community and a channel for communication from the community regarding concerns and needs. In many communities, the training ground of the Friends organization also produces likely candidates for the board of trustees.

## SUMMARY

A successful library is one that serves the needs of the community—and keeps the community well informed of its services and resources. Thus, the library administrator must understand fundamental techniques of marketing and public relations. Although the board and the library staff play important roles in public relations, the major responsibility remains with the administrator.

Basic marketing involves four steps—research and analysis to determine and define the scope of a particular need in the community; development of a plan to reach the target audience for that need; implementation of the service that meets the need; and control, or evaluation, to determine the success or the reasons for failure of the program.

With good public relations, the library will succeed in reaching and informing the community about its services and resources. The library must target the desired audience through effective and selective use of media, including newspapers, radio, television and organizational newsletters.

Public relations goals can also be pursued through less traditional means. Programs and exhibits permit wider dissemination of information about the library, as well as serving as educational or informational tools in their own right. Volunteers and Friends groups are able to share their knowledge of the library with the community.

Public relations is a vast subject, and this chapter has provided only a basic overview. Readers are encouraged to consult the books listed below for more detailed information.

## FOOTNOTES

1. Philip Kotler, *Marketing for Nonprofit Organizations*, second

edition (Englewood Cliffs, NJ: Prentice-Hall, Inc., 1982), p. 6.

2. E. Jerome McCarthy, *Basic Marketing: A Managerial Approach*, sixth edition (Homewood, IL: Richard D. Irwin, Inc., 1978), p. 39.

## SUGGESTIONS FOR FURTHER READING

Dolnick, Sandy, ed. *Friends of Libraries Sourcebook.* Chicago: American Library Association, 1980.

Edsall, Marian S. *Library Promotion Handbook.* Phoenix, AZ: Oryx Press, 1980.

Garvey, Mona. *Library Public Relations.* New York: H.W. Wilson Co., 1980.

Kohn, Rita and K. Teppler. *You Can Do It: A PR Skills Manual for Librarians.* Metuchen, NJ: Scarecrow Press, Inc., 1981.

Leerburger, Benedict A. *Marketing the Library.* White Plains, NY: Knowledge Industry Publications, Inc., 1982.

Sherman, Steve. *ABC's of Library Promotion*, second edition. Metuchen, NJ: Scarecrow Press, Inc., 1980.

# 9

# Construction, Design and Maintenance

As a special function building, a library represents an attractive project for many architects. Every year more creative approaches are taken to designing the model library. Unfortunately, not all these designs satisfy the primary goal of functional effectiveness. Instead, poor design in building and in interior layout may result in unusually high operating expenses, not to mention public relations problems. This chapter will provide the administrator with guidelines for judging needs and expenses for building and remodeling projects—and for avoiding many of the problems.

## THE BUILDING PROGRAM

Before undertaking any new building, expansion or remodeling project, the library should develop a building program. It is not enough to tell the architect that the library needs 10,000 more square feet. The building program should explain space needs by function. It should also provide demographic information on the community and background on the library, including its statement of purpose and relevant goals from the long-range plan. The building program should include policies that apply for use of the new space, the resources or services to be located there, the relationship to an existing facility in the case of expansion, information on the site, exterior features the architect will need to consider, a budget estimate for the project and a summary of all equipment to be included.

Figure 9.1 shows an outline for a typical building program, one that can provide the architect and engineers with exact information they need to design a facility that satisfies the library's requirements.

### Figure 9.1: Outline for a Library Building Program

1. Project title

2. Demographic data on community or service unit

3. Background on the library
   a. History and governance (including statement of purpose)
   b. Services provided
   c. Statistics on total library system activity (circulation, reference, programs, etc.)

4. Details on unit to be constructed or remodeled
   a. Site (requirements, if architect is to help select; if site is known, description should include how building is to be situated, where parking is to be located, etc.)
   b. Function: present and proposed
   c. Staffing: present and proposed
   d. Public service factors (daily and monthly traffic projections)
   e. Resources to be housed in the unit: present and proposed (includes materials, online services, etc.)
   f. Equipment requirements: proposed
   g. Environmental requirements: e.g., lighting, heat, ventilation and air conditioning, electrical and telecommunications outlets)
   h. Present physical facility (if applicable)
   i. Projected space requirements by function
   j. Cost and budget for the project

5. Relation to library's present facilities (other portions of existing building or other agencies of the system)

6. Detailed equipment list (specifications and quantities needed)

7. Space summary (in square feet)

# THE PLANNING TEAM

It is customary to have a planning team for any building project. The members of this team consist of the library board, its administrator, an architect and frequently a building consultant. On occasion an interior designer will also be a member of this team. Each has a specific role; these roles must be clearly understood at the start, or friction will result.

## The Building Consultant

The building consultant, if there is one, will work with the administrator, staff and board in preparing the program's detailed specifications for the architect. During the design phase, the consultant serves as liaison between the architect and the board and the administrator, in order to iron out misunderstandings and ensure that the design conforms to the building program. The consultant often drafts the building program and may remain available throughout the building process to offer advice and mediation.

On occasion a library board may elect to do without a building consultant, particularly if it feels that the administrator has sufficient experience in construction or that the architect has the familiarity with the library's needs to handle this aspect of the work. Usually, however, a consultant's experience and insight will more than justify the cost. A consultant's fee is generally small, usually a flat amount or, on occasion, a small percentage of the total cost of the building project.

Consultants are often library administrators. In selecting a consultant, library boards should follow much the same procedure as in selecting an architect, discussed in the section that follows. Interviews should be held, and selection should be made based on experience and the types of services the individual is prepared to provide to the library and its administrator.

## The Architect

The architect's role is to take the building program and convert it into plans and specifications for a building that can be constructed within the budget set by the board. The architect also often supervises the contractors during construction of the building, although the board may elect not to use this procedure. In some cities, the public works department has staff or contract personnel who supervise such projects. Other institutions have found it more economical to hire specialists to perform this service.

Selection of an architect is often a time-consuming and difficult process, requiring interviews and visits to other facilities designed by the applicant. Some architects specialize in certain types of buildings, including libraries, but the majority have a variety of experience. It then becomes necessary to assess how the architect responded to each individual client's needs.

Selection should also be based on the staff the architect can call upon for assistance. For example, only the larger architectural firms retain their own engineers. Most will contract with individual engineering firms for their technical assistance. It is important to determine what firm the architect will use for this service and what its reputation is.

Another important question is who will be responsible for the design. In large architectural firms, the task may be delegated to a junior member of the firm, rather than to the prominent architect whose name is featured on the letterhead and who may be meeting with the board only for the interview.

The architect's fee is almost always based on a specific percentage of the building cost, ranging from 5% to 10%. Generally, the smaller the project, the higher the percentage. Additional expenses will be charged for additional services, such as supervision of construction. Care should also be taken in defining the basis for the fee. Some architects consider their fee to be based only on a percentage of the construction cost. Others include the cost of equipment, such as shelving, or of all furnishings.

**The Board and the Administrator**

The role of the board is to select the consultant and the architect, to approve the cost of the project, to select the site and to accept the design. In addition, the board must take final acceptance of the building from the contractors.

The administrator serves as liaison among all the members of the team if there is no consultant, assists the consultant, the architect and the board in their various responsibilities, and expedites decisions and action. The administrator must always articulate the library's needs and explain the various functions to be housed in the project. The administrator must also maintain communication with the staff and the public, so they are kept aware of the project as it proceeds.

## PUBLIC LIBRARY CONSTRUCTION

Libraries have evolved in design over the years—and gone through a variety of fads. Originally, most libraries consisted of one room with bookcases around the perimeter. In the center were tables and chairs for the staff and the public. When the shelf space was exhausted, if money permitted, an additional room was constructed, and so the process continued.

### The Alcove Design

At some time, a creative librarian or architect conceived the idea of an alcove, where a table could be surrounded on three sides by shelving. With this arrangement, a very large room or hall could be used effectively and still provide some degree of privacy and convenience; users could seat themselves near the necessary reference materials. The alcove design proved very popular and can still be found in many library buildings today, particularly smaller libraries that prefer a traditional environment.

### Book Stacks

In time, as collections grew, many libraries found the alcove to be restrictive. If sufficient ceiling height existed, mezzanines with additional alcoves could be constructed. Even that solution had its limitations, however, and it became more convenient for large libraries to separate the reader from the book stacks.

In open-shelf libraries, the books were massed in long ranges, at one or both ends of the room, with reading stations in the center. In closed-stack libraries, tiers of book stacks were placed one on top of the other in the central core of the building, and special reading rooms were simply constructed around these gigantic book stacks.

### The Carnegie Library

One of the most prominent designs in public library history is the Carnegie library, which has been both revered and despised by generations of the public and librarians. Folklore has it that communities receiving Carnegie grants for public libraries were required to construct their buildings based on this design. In fact, Carnegie never dictated such a requirement. His secretary did supply copies of a recommended design, however, because of sad early experiences where local architects went to excesses, resulting in dysfunctional buildings.

The typical Carnegie building had a central circulation desk in its "receiving room," where the public entered the building, a large room on either side and frequently a multilevel stack area behind the desk. A lower level would house staff work rooms, an auditorium or meeting room, some storage, rest rooms and a boiler room. The two main rooms were sometimes used to divide the sexes or, when special services and collections for children became accepted, to separate adult and youth services. As collections grew, the lower level was sometimes converted into a children's department.

Carnegie libraries continue to be used today, and many have undergone creative redesign to improve their function.

### Current Design Considerations

Today, standards of design call for large open rooms with as few fixed partitions as possible. Architects generally construct one or more cores, either in the center or on the corners of the building, to house the mechanical equipment, staff rest rooms and work areas, and similar nonpublic service areas. The balance of the space is left open for complete flexibility in layout. Floor load capacity is generally equal throughout the entire building to avoid restrictions on the placement of stacks. Conduit for electrical, telephone and coaxial cable wires is housed in the flooring and has outlets at frequent intervals.

## THE CENTRAL LIBRARY

For those communities that require only one central library, there are a variety of formulas on which to base a determination of space needs. The most commonly recommended formula was developed by Joseph L. Wheeler, based on more than 30 years of experience as a library administrator and building consultant. It is shown in Figure 9.2.

### Space for the Collection

In arriving at the aggregate space requirements for the building, the building consultant and the administrator must consider a number of factors. First is the space required for the

**Figure 9.2: Determining Space Needs for Construction**

| Population Size | Book Stock (Volumes per Capita) | Number of Seats per 1000 Population | Circulation (Volumes per Capita) | Total Square Feet per Capita | First Floor Square Feet per Capita |
|---|---|---|---|---|---|
| Under 10,000 | 3.5-5.0 | 10 | 10 | 0.7-0.8 | 0.5-0.7 |
| 10,000-35,000 | 2.75-3.0 | 5 | 9.5 | 0.6-0.65 | 0.4-0.45 |
| 35,000-100,000 | 2.5-2.75 | 3 | 9 | 0.5-0.6 | 0.25-0.3 |
| 100,000-200,000 | 1.75-2.0 | 2 | 8 | 0.4-0.5 | 0.15-0.2 |
| 200,000-500,000 | 1.5 | 1.25 | 7 | 0.35-0.4 | 0.1-0.125 |
| 500,000 | 1.0-1.25 | 1 | 6.5 | 0.3 | 0.06-0.08 |

Source: Table 7 (page 405) from *Wheeler and Goldhor's Practical Administration of Public Libraries,* revised edition, by Carlton Rochell. Copyright© 1981 by Carlton C. Rochell. Reprinted by permission of Harper & Row, Publishers, Inc.

collections. Estimating space for shelving of books is comparatively easy. There is an average of 7 books per linear foot, 50 books per linear foot of standard 84-inch high stacks and 100 books per linear foot of standard 84-inch double face stacks. (The exact number will vary from one section of the library to another—for example, children's books are generally slimmer than reference books.) Calculating storage space for audiovisual materials is another matter, and the best recourse is to employ sampling techniques to arrive at the right figure.

One element that is frequently forgotten in calculating space requirements is the percentage of the collection that is in circulation at any time. This can be deducted from the total collection size estimate—except, of course, in noncirculating portions of the collection.

**Space for Users**

Another factor in space estimates is seating for the public. For the past 20 years the formula has been 30 square feet per adult and

20 square feet per child. Despite the best efforts of hundreds of diet book authors, that formula still holds true today. Some variations are needed, however, to allow for lounge seating and study carrels. Increasing use of microform, audiovisual hardware and computer terminals requires a comparable increase in the size of individual study stations and, consequently, additional floor space (as well as wiring access).

### Space for Staff

A third factor is staff work space. The standard formula is 100 to 150 square feet per person, depending upon the level and nature of the person's assignment. Some space is also required for storage of coats and other personal belongings, rest rooms and lounge areas. There is considerable variation in space allowances for these. A central library will have a technical processing department, where materials are processed and cataloged for the entire system. There may also be a data processing department, with special requirements for environmental controls and electrical and telephone access.

The relative space allotment for all of these work areas must be judged according to the importance of each to the public service functions of the institution. For example, the most flexible design for a public library is a room with no fixed partitions. Nonetheless, some work rooms are necessary to support such key public services as circulation and reference. Each work area has office equipment that could disturb public service, and therefore these areas should be closed. That usually dictates fixed partitions.

### Space for Meeting Rooms

A fourth element in space planning is meeting rooms. Today no library should be designed without space for holding programs and public events. Some libraries may be able to justify only a general multipurpose room. Others find that an auditorium with a raised stage and projection booths is required for the level of programming undertaken both by the library and by community groups. Another factor may be local codes that specify requirements for emergency exits and limit the number of people allowed to occupy a given floor space.

The best guide for the building consultant or administrator in estimating these space requirements is to review past programming and future plans, and to develop the building program based on estimated audience sizes. Certainly a great deal of flexibility is desirable to permit the library to handle a variety of different sized programs. These spaces should also be designed so that they can be easily sealed off from the rest of the building when programs run past normal library hours.

## Space for Mechanical Functions

Sufficient area must also be provided for mechanical functions such as heating and air conditioning, custodial closets, public rest rooms, electrical and telephone access, etc. These are usually dictated by local building codes and by engineering requirements, and it is not likely that the consultant or the administrator will need to get involved in assigning this space.

Mechanical functions may consume between 20% and 25% of the total floor space for the library; depending upon the architect's design, it could be much more. For example, the main lobbies and entrances of many major public buildings consume enormous amounts of space, which the architect may charge off as mechanical or design-related, but they contribute nothing to the function of the building. The architect's proposal should be carefully evaluated to determine how much of the floor space will be devoted to satisfying the building program. It could spell the difference between a costly project and an economical one.

## Space and Budget Limitations

In the event that costs for the desired space exceed the amount budgeted, the committee must decide whether to reduce the planned space, and if so, which space to reduce. Some libraries choose to cut back on the amount of equipment that will be included. Others proceed with the plans for the original amount of space but leave some of it unfinished. The remaining areas can be finished later, when funds permit and needs expand.

## NEIGHBORHOOD OR REGIONAL LIBRARIES

Most of the same design criteria apply for neighborhood branch libraries. Exceptions include large work areas, since public relations and technical processing functions are usually performed in the central library. Large storage and closed stack areas are also unusual in a neighborhood library.

The regional library building is a hybrid, combining certain elements of both the neighborhood and the central library. Regional libraries are common in larger urban library systems or in rural areas where one facility is expected to serve a comparatively large population. They may have special collections pertinent to their local neighborhoods and cataloging personnel assigned for maintenance of those collections. Regional libraries may also have large administrative staffs including subject coordinators and closed stack areas to accommodate larger reference collections.

The basic starting point in determining the space requirements for both neighborhood and regional libraries is determining the service area. Particularly for regional libraries, this is not as simple as drawing lines on a map and arbitrarily determining that the agency will serve that portion of the city or the county. Geographic features such as rivers or interstate highways may interfere. Racial or ethnic barriers may exist. Main traffic thoroughfares and public transportation have to be considered.

In an existing facility, some indication of the service area may be estimated by sampling user addresses. City, county and regional planning agencies should be able to lend assistance in arriving at the population of the potential service area. It will then be possible to apply the formulas given in Figure 9.2 to arrive at an estimate of the space needed.

## GENERAL DESIGN CONSIDERATIONS

Some common design factors should be part of every building program, whether it is for a large central library or a small neighborhood branch.

• A single main entrance will help control losses from the collection and reduce staffing requirements. There should be as few floors as possible with as much floor space as possible. No small neighborhood library should be constructed with more than one floor; the more floors there are, the greater the staffing requirements. As few fixed partitions as possible should be employed, to grant the library as much flexibility as possible to reorganize space in the future.

• Floor load capacity should be equal throughout the entire building. This means reinforced floors capable of supporting book stacks, which adds to the cost of the building, but the resulting flexibility will pay a dividend in the future.

• Bay sizes should be standard throughout the building and should be large enough to accommodate a full range of library stacks. Adequate ductwork for power and communications lines should be located throughout the building to allow for future needs.

• The building should be designed to accommodate collection growth and increased public usage for the next 20 years.

## INTERIOR DESIGN

An interior design consultant may be a member of the project planning team. In that case, he or she can influence choices of interior finishes and can develop specifications for equipment at an early enough stage to ensure that everything is available when construction is completed. Most library equipment must be special ordered. Steel stacks, for example, may require a lead time of up to a year, and many a library has had to wait for shelving before it could open. Beyond those elements, however, the interior designer's role will vary considerably, depending upon the needs of the library. In some instances the architect may assume responsibility for interior design.

Generally, the interior designer should work with the building consultant, the board and the administrator in developing the equipment layout based on the functions of the various areas of the building. The interior designer will then propose paint, carpeting, wood or metal finishes, technical equipment such as card catalog cabinets, general and lounge seating and tables. After committee approval, formal specifications will be prepared by the consultant, who is responsible for following up on manufacture, delivery and installation. The interior designer is paid either a flat fee or a percentage of the total equipment contract.

### Furnishings

Whether the library employs an interior designer or an architect or relies on the administrator's recommendations, it is important that library-quality equipment be selected. Many architects or designers specify custom items, which may complement their design but which lack the heavy-duty quality to withstand public use. Tables and chairs designed for library use represent a standard that is difficult to beat. While they may not offer the range of finishes or styles desired by the architect or designer, the library administrator should insist upon their use.

Lounge furniture is another problem area in library interior design. Once again, library equipment manufacturers offer lines that may not appear as attractive to the designer, although most can be upholstered in a variety of fabrics. A satisfactory alternative is hotel-quality lounge furniture. Both library- and hotel-quality products command a premium price, but they will pay for themselves many times over by their longevity.

Wood finishes are universally preferred for their warmth. As a rule, however, wood finishes will not hold up under daily public use. Study tables, doors, countertops and similar surfaces are much better covered with a wood grain formica to match other wood finishes in the library.

While leather and fabric are attractive, they are also very susceptible to wear and vandalism. Loose fabrics will require frequent haircuts. The best upholstered finish is vinyl, preferably in a dark color which does not show graffiti.

## Shelving

Steel shelving is the most flexible equipment to use in the public library. While wood shelving is attractive, it is susceptible to more damage and is less interchangeable than steel. Shelving should always be purchased from established library manufacturers to ensure that standard widths and heights are acquired. While many office supply houses sell this equipment at lower cost, it may not be the standard 36-inch wide shelf or have the load capacity and stability required for heavy library bindings.

## Lighting

Lighting requirements in public libraries have changed radically during the past 20 years. At one time, consultants recommended 150 foot candles of illumination for work and study areas. Subsequent studies and the energy crisis have brought that recommendation down to 70 foot candles. There are many types of lighting that can be used, offering some alternatives to the traditional incandescent bulb and the fluorescent tube.

The most important factor is to ensure that lighting will not have to be altered if stacks and public seating aras are shifted. In many public libraries, lighting runs parallel to stack aisles. Any attempt to decrease aisle space or shift the stacks will create large dark sections in the stacks. Similarly, lighting arranged for public seating areas may not be sufficient if stacks are relocated to that section.

Ease of maintenance is another important factor. Some architecturally stunning fixtures are impossible to relamp without bringing in an electrician and a fire truck and ladder. The administrator should also consider possible energy savings from the use of low-energy ballasts and fluorescent tubes. In reviewing the lighting requirements with the building consultant and the architect, the administrator should seek technical information on power consumption for these alternatives, to use as a factor in estimating future energy costs.

**Signs**

Selecting signs for the library generally falls either to the architect or to the interior designer. It is important enough, however, to merit the attention of the administrator. Many designers and architects tend to select sign systems that blend perfectly with the building or the interior design. Indeed, they may blend in so well that no one sees them. That can burden the staff with unnecessary requests for directional assistance. Such signs are usually replaced—at significant expense.

The best signs are those that have contrasting letters and background. Letters should be simple, standard and large enough to be read from a distance. Language should be nontechnical and brief. Many sign systems employ pictographs. While these may be useful, it should be realized that standard pictographs have not been developed for many library services.

## SPECIFICATIONS AND CONTRACT ADMINISTRATION

The architect and engineers are responsible for the preparation of the building plans and specifications and for development of the contracts. However, it is important for the administrator to understand these documents. Most experienced architects and engineers simply assemble specifications like boiler plate, bolting on sections for electrical work, plumbing and heating. These contain the appropriate standards and guidance on meeting local and state codes. The only things that may vary from one project to another will be specific equipment unique to those projects.

## Equipment Specifications

Specifications that cite a specific manufacturer and model number plus the words "or equal" are called comparative. When a long, detailed description of an item is given, complete with input and output characteristics, the specifications are called functional. In that case, the contractor must supply equipment that satisfies the functions and meets the detailed requirements described in the documents, but he is not limited in the choice of manufacturers or models.

The architect or engineer chooses between these two options based on experience with the equipment, research or recommendation by someone familiar with the field. If the administrator has any concern about critical equipment contained in the specifications, the architect or engineer should identify a similar installation that the administrator can visit to verify performance.

## Awarding the Contract

Contracts for almost all construction work today are awarded through competitive bidding. Part of the architect's job is to ensure that qualified contractors are notified and are encouraged to submit a bid. Public advertisements are also almost always required for public library construction, so that almost anyone may submit a bid. It is customary to require a bid bond, usually 5% of the total bid, as discussed in Chapter 3. This may weed out some of the less qualified firms.

The architect then studies the proposals. If the low bid is submitted by a contractor whom the architect does not know, some investigation must be made of other projects done by that contractor. Following this, the architect can meet with the board and the administrator and make a recommendation. It is then up to the board and the administrator either to accept the recommendation or to conduct an investigation to provide assurance of the contractor's ability to perform the work.

While almost all construction contracts require the contractors to provide a performance bond equal to the size of the contract, rarely will this fully compensate the library if the contractor goes bankrupt or if other problems arise in completing the job. The best protection the library has is the experience and reputation of the firm. If the contractor has been in the business a number of years, has handled projects of similar magnitude or complexity, and has a good credit rating with little or no history of lawsuits with clients or subcontractors, then the firm will probably be satisfactory.

On occasion the low bid may be submitted by a firm without any experience or with a bad history. It is advisable to include in the bid documents a clause allowing the rejection of the low bid if it appears that the low bidder does not have the necessary qualifications. Without such a clause, the library could be involved in a lawsuit.

Sometimes a contractor will submit an alternate proposal, which lists a number of exceptions to the specifications. The architects and engineers must review these alternates and provide their recommendation, but it is then up to the board and the administrator either to accept the recommendation or to conduct their own investigation.

**Contract Administration**

Once the contract is awarded, a rather strict procedure is adhered to by the participants. Both starting and completion dates are specified in the agreement. The contract may contain a penalty clause, which will result in a reduction of the contract price for each day of delay, unless extenuating circumstances arise. Provision for progress payments is also customary, unless the job is very small. If the architect is supervising the construction, he will notify the administrator when the contractor is at 25% or 50% completion and authorize release of a specified payment.

The architect should also arrange regular site inspections and meetings with the contractors, which the administrator should attend. At these meetings, deficiencies in work or problems in interpreting plans and specifications are reviewed. The library board should be informed of the results of these meetings in order to keep the members advised of the progress.

On occasion the contractor may ask for a change order because some additional work not originally contained in the plans or specifications becomes necessary. This is particularly common in remodeling or renovation work, where the architect may not have been able to gain access to complete plans to a building. As another example, bad soil conditions may dictate unexpected additional foundation work.

It is never desirable to have a large number of change orders for a project, since this will increase the cost of the project beyond the original budget. It may also reveal poor design or inadequate testing by the architect and engineers. Each of these change orders comes to the administrator and the board for approval, and sometimes there is no choice on the matter. For that reason, it is well for any construction project to have contingency funds set aside. Otherwise, the cost is usually covered by reductions in the equipment contracts, which are usually awarded after the construction gets under way.

## MAINTENANCE AND CUSTODIAL CARE

Proper maintenance and custodial care of the library are the responsibility of the administrator and require careful selection of equipment, building design and competent personnel. The rule of thumb is one custodial person for every 15,000 square feet of space. However, this varies, depending upon the age of the building and the quality of design.

Carpeting is considered easier to maintain than other floor surfaces, which require periodic stripping, waxing, polishing and mopping. Extensive glass surfaces could also increase custodial costs. If the library is divided into a number of small rooms that cannot be supervised and if it contains many surfaces that are easily vandalized, this could also increase costs.

### Contractual Services

Some libraries operate entirely with contract custodial services. This may be a matter of board policy, or a review of the specifications, performance and costs may reveal that contracting is more economical than hiring a person for these responsibilities.

The administrator must determine who will be responsible for what maintenance functions. Normal maintenance functions in a library include replacement of lights, replacement of filters and adjustment of heating and air conditioning, minor repair of furniture and office equipment, snow removal, lawn care and the variety of odd jobs essential to any building. It is common to contract for ongoing maintenance of major equipment such as the heating and air conditioning system. In a city or county library, contractual arrangements may be possible with the city or county public works department. If the library does not have someone on call for odd jobs, it is essential that the administrator have a current list of skilled and reliable tradespeople who can be called for emergency repairs.

## Custodial Employees

Judging by the statistics gathered by the National Center for Educational Statistics, the vast majority of libraries employ their own custodian/maintenance person. This individual must be kept current on changes and plans and must be made to feel a part of the library. Care should also be taken to keep wages competitive with similar positions in the community. The custodian is frequently the forgotten person on the library staff when pay adjustments or recognition are given. This is unfortunate, for this individual can make a valuable contribution to the attractiveness and safety of the facility.

# INSURANCE

There are several forms of insurance related to the library building. Every library should be covered by building and contents insurance, liability insurance, workmen's compensation and unemployment insurance, and errors and omissions insurance.

## Buildings and Contents

The library is probably among the most valuable buildings in the community, particularly when its contents are considered. Risks include fire, flood, explosion and the particular perils (e.g., earthquakes) common to the geographic region. For this reason every administrator should see that the facilities are fully insured, so that the building can be replaced in the event of total destruction, or adequately repaired in the event of partial disaster. Coverage may be based on the original cost less depreciation, or on replacement cost. The latter is desirable, and an annual adjustment in property valuation is required to ensure that the library receives sufficient coverage.

There are various methods of estimating contents. A professional appraisal firm can be employed, or the library can calculate the value of its contents based on costs less depreciation or on cost of replacement. Again, the latter is recommended, since it will provide a more realistic basis for replacement of the collection.

The usual formula for calculating the cost of collection replacement is based on the annual average cost for new books by category contained in the annual statistical issue of *Publishers Weekly*. These current figures are then multiplied by the total number of books contained in the library's collections. Some libraries deduct the average discount they receive from this figure. Others do not, since they believe the discount will partially compensate for the cataloging and processing of the material. Whichever method the library employs, it should be documented for the insurance company, and there should be annual updates in the collection valuation.

The building and contents policy should be "all-risk" and should cover equipment as well as building and collection. Some insurance policies exclude boiler protection. If so, an additional policy should be acquired for this portion of the building, since it is also highly susceptible to loss. All-risk coverage may include an option for interim operational expenses. Should the library suffer total or partial loss, it may have to relocate until repair is made. This option will provide funds for moving, temporary rental and other expenses, and it is highly recommended.

## Liability Insurance

Liability protection is also essential, given the increasing number of lawsuits against public services today. In the event someone falls on the front steps, slips in the lobby, is struck by a falling light fixture or experiences some similar calamity, liability insurance will provide for medical care, legal expenses in the event of a suit and any claims in the event the court rules that the library was negligent. The amount of coverage is up to the board and administrator, but claims of $1 million or more are not uncommon. Any contractors for the library should be required to carry liability insurance and provide proof of coverage, as an added precaution for the library.

## Workmen's Compensation and Unemployment Insurance

Many states automatically require that every organization carry workmen's compensation and unemployment insurance, but some exclude governmental entities. Every library should carry this protection. Workmen's compensation reimburses library employees for any medical expenses, long-term disability or lost wages during recovery. Contractors for the library should also be required to carry workmen's compensation for their employees, to ensure that the library isn't sued in the event of an accident.

Unemployment insurance continues an employee's income for a specified period in the event the library must temporarily or permanently reduce its staff. These are perils that libraries regularly face, and the administrator should prepare for them.

## Errors and Omissions

Errors and omissions insurance supplements liability coverage, which often excludes protection for certain types of error made by the board, administrator or staff. Errors may include loss of funds, discrimination suits, taxpayer suits and similar cases that might be brought by an irate staff member or citizen against the board, the administrator or the staff. The errors and omission coverage pays for legal fees and for any awards that might be made by the court. Intentional illegal acts such as fraud are not covered by this insurance.

## SUMMARY

This chapter has provided a brief introduction to library design, construction and maintenance. Any undertaking must begin with a building program that includes information on the community and on the library's programs, policies and purpose, as well as the details of the current project.

It is customary to appoint a planning team, consisting of a building consultant, the architect, the board and the administrator. The building consultant oversees the development of the details of the building program and acts as liaison between the architect and the board and the administrator during the design stage. The architect converts the building program into a building design that meets the requirements and the budget of the library. The board and the administrator must select the building consultant and the architect, set the budget, choose the site, approve the design and oversee the construction.

Library design has changed as libraries have grown in size and complexity. Contemporary standards call for large open rooms that allow the maximum flexibility for layout. However, staff work areas, public meeting space and mechanical equipment areas are generally isolated from public use areas. In larger libraries, the book stacks may also be closed. Formulas for calculating the size of library and the space needed for certain functions, as well as general design considerations, were included in this chapter.

The administrator may need to watch carefully that both architectural and interior design remain functional and appropriate for library use. Special requirements include equal floor capacity throughout the library, library-quality furnishings and equipment, and adequate and flexible lighting. The administrator must also be familiar with the contracts and the contracting process, although the architect will probably be directly responsible for this stage of the building process.

The administrator has two other responsibilities relating to the library building. The first is to provide for proper maintenance and custodial care, whether by contracting for services or by hiring custodial staff. The second is to ensure that the library has adequate insurance protection. Coverage that will pay for the full cost of replacing the building or the collection, or any part of it, is recommended. The library should also have liability insurance, workmen's compensation and unemployment insurance, and errors and omissions coverage.

## SUGGESTIONS FOR FURTHER READING

Bahr, Alice Harrison. *Book Theft and Library Security Systems, 1981-82.* White Plains, NY: Knowledge Industry Publications, Inc., 1981.

Cohen, Aaron and Elaine Cohen. *Designing and Space Planning for Libraries: A Behavioral Guide.* New York: R.R. Bowker Co., 1979.

Lushington, Nolan and Willis N. Mills Jr. *Libraries Designed for Users.* Hamden, CT: Shoe String Press, Inc., 1980.

Mallery, Mary S. and Ralph E. DeVore. *A Sign System for Libraries.* Chicago: American Library Association, 1982.

Mason, Ellsworth. *Mason on Library Buildings.* Metuchen, NJ: Scarecrow Press, Inc., 1980.

Pierce, William S. *Furnishing the Library Interior.* New York: Marcel Dekker, Inc., 1980.

# 10

# Interlibrary Cooperation

The past 20 years have seen the emergence of a rich variety of cooperative library efforts. Cooperation has been fostered by federal and state grants and reinforced by a number of other factors. These include increasing demands for services and materials, which small and medium-sized libraries could not provide solely on a local basis, the impact of new technology and a growing realization in the public library profession that no library can afford to be everything to everyone.

Interlibrary cooperation has been defined in many ways. In its simplest terms it is sharing a common need and assuming a mutual responsibility. For example, in the late 1940s a number of public libraries wanted to provide 16mm films for organizations and individuals in their communities. With grants and a great deal of local commitment, these libraries agreed to purchase these resources jointly and to rotate them in small collections each month. Each library assumed the responsiblity for repairing and booking these films and for promoting their use locally. Each agreed to contribute a specified sum to expand the collections and to pay for shipment each month to the next library. Many of these early "film circuits" are long gone, but they provided useful experience in interlibrary cooperation.

Today there are more formalized structures and procedures for interlibrary cooperation. It is important for every administrator to understand their operation and their disadvantages as well as their advantages. This brief chapter will discuss cooperative systems, primarily as they exist within states. Networks—a special form of cooperative system, generally emphasizing computerized services over a broad geographic area—were discussed in Chapter 7.

## COOPERATIVE SYSTEMS

Some states call them cooperative systems. Others call them federations. Whatever the name, almost every state has a formal structure for the support of library cooperation. Under state laws, these systems are thus legal entities, which permits public funds to be contributed or contracted in return for certain specified services provided by or delivered to the participating member libraries. Stoffel and Gregory have defined these systems as "the combining of the talents and the resources of a group of independent libraries, within a reasonable geographic radius, for the purpose of attaining excellence in service and resources for the benefit of the actual and potential users of all the member libraries."[1]

### Organization

A cooperative system may consist of a headquarters with an executive and staff, supported by state and/or federal funds or by fees assessed the members in return for cooperative services. More simply, it may be a contractual agreement by which one of the libraries extends some existing services to the residents of another political jurisdiction.

### Services

Wherever two or more libraries discover they have a common need, some form of cooperation can be proposed to satisfy it. Among the services offered by cooperative systems are:

- interagency delivery

- provision of consultant services

- centralized cataloging and processing

- audiovisual services

- backup reference services

- storage of infrequently used materials

- automation (such as online circulation)

- bookmobile operation

- direct management of small libraries

- training

- interlibrary loan coordination

- accounting and payroll

- administration of cooperative fringe benefit programs

## The Administrator and Cooperative Systems

The administrator must, of course, understand the governance and responsibilities of cooperative systems, which are usually set forth in the state's library laws. Systems may offer new administrators orientation in the activities and services they provide, as well as the obligations that the member library has to the system. The administrator should also determine the degree of authority the system exercises over the local libraries. For example, some systems administer grants of state or federal funds to be distributed to member libraries. As a condition for receipt, the system may impose certain requirements, such as honoring other member library cards on a reciprocal basis or participating in a local interlibrary loan procedure.

While all cooperative systems are built on the foundation of local autonomy, member libraries may have to make compromises in order to gain full benefit from some of the system's projects and services. For example, participation in an online circulation system may require the library to change its policy regarding delinquencies in order to conform to the practices of other libraries.

It is also important to determine what the system's plan of service will be in the future—i.e., what its goals and priorities are, and what role the member library has in this process. Just as every library should have a long-range plan, every good system should have a document that represents a consensus among its members about the services that will be provided. This serves as a guide for any increasing obligations that will be placed upon the member libraries in the future. If the intention is to develop additional automated cooperative activities and services funded by member contributions, then this is important for future budget planning.

## Voluntary Membership

Interlibrary cooperation is based on voluntary membership. No library is required to participate, and there are usually provisions in state law or local bylaws that permit members to resign from membership if they disagree with the system's operations, services or plan of service. The fact that this so rarely happens in the U.S. indicates the responsiveness of these systems to member needs and concerns.

## Governance

The governance of the system should provide for representation from the member libraries, often through trustees or citizen representatives from the communities being served. An administrators council is also customary. This may or may not be representative, depending upon the number of participating libraries. Through the administrators council or the board representatives, each library should have a voice in influencing the service program and plan of service for the cooperative system.

## Participation

In most systems, the degree of local member participation is directly related to the amount of local funds that go to the system. For example, the system may receive state funds to maintain a headquarters building, coordinate interlibrary cooperation, and provide interagency delivery and one or two other services. These may be state mandated, thereby giving the local system board little voice in their operation.

However, the same system may also operate a printing operation, a technical processing center, joint purchasing plans and a central computer facility, all of which are supported through member fees and contributions. These services will be under the full review of the local system board, and there may be advisory committees, consisting of member libraries, providing policy decisions on how they will be operated.

## COOPERATIVE CONTRACTS

While cooperative library systems are extremely helpful in facilitating interlibrary cooperation, individual libraries still may find it advantageous to contract directly with one another for simple or more specialized services. All state laws grant libraries this right, and the procedure does not demand elaborate steps. A contract is simply a statement of what the participants intend to do, a summary of the obligations and services to be provided by the participants individually and mutually, and information on costs, starting and ending dates. The procedure in the event that one of the parties elects to drop out of the agreement is also defined.

Administrators should consider developing a contract whenever a service or resource might be shared with another library. In any joint venture among libraries, it is wise to rely on more than a handshake, by stating responsibilities and expectations clearly and in writing. It is also desirable for the library's attorney to review any contract; for a project involving major expenditures, this is mandatory.

Contracts between libraries may provide for one library to offer a service to the others or for two or more libraries to share equally in providing a service that none can offer alone. For example, a large library may determine that its computer facilities are underutilized and may elect to offer this service to neighboring libraries at a cost sufficient to recover overhead and additional expenses. Such a service may be welcomed by a smaller library that could never afford to undertake automation by itself. Two libraries anxious to offer video tapes to their communities, but unable individually to afford a basic collection, may elect to contract with one another for the joint purchase of a collection. Rotating the collection between them will provide both libraries with access to the full selection of tapes.

## BENEFITS OF INTERLIBRARY COOPERATION

Interlibrary cooperation has grown because it offers libraries a number of significant benefits.

## Cost Savings

The primary benefit of cooperation is potential cost savings. Economies of scale occur whenever a larger quantity of equipment or supplies can be ordered. Also, expensive equipment becomes affordable when more than one library participates in its purchase. The cost of new technology (and of conversion to it) is steadily rising. At the same time, acquisition of more sophisticated resources is no longer a luxury but mandatory if libraries are to maintain their effectiveness in society. As a result, interlibrary cooperation may become the predominant method for library development.

## Increased Resources

Increased resources are another benefit of cooperation. The classic example is automated cataloging. A library can establish its own system, converting its cataloging to machine-readable form and centrally storing it for use by its public and staff. However, the majority of libraries have found that it is infinitely more desirable (and less costly) to cooperate in an online cataloging system. There is a great likelihood that the library's books have been cataloged and that those records can be borrowed for use, as an alternative to original cataloging.

The same situation exists with online circulation. An individual library may find it is economical and efficient to purchase a circulation system for its own use. However, a jointly owned system offers the benefit of knowing the holdings and loan status of materials in other neighboring libraries.

Another resource of a cooperative system is the wealth of personal expertise that can be shared for training and consultant purposes. Large city and county systems have long been attractive to beginning professional staff because of the growth opportunities these systems provided. Today, any group of libraries can offer this benefit through exchanges, joint training programs, frequent staff conferences, participation in decision making on system objectives and similar techniques.

## Improved Quality of Service

Improved quality of service, though often unstated, may be the benefit that should be of greatest value to the administrator. If 40 or 50 libraries work together, their services and collections will far exceed what any individual library can offer. It is no accident that those parts of the nation with the most sophisticated forms of interlibrary cooperation have the reputation for the highest level of local library service.

## DISADVANTAGES OF COOPERATION

There is another side of the coin, of course. Every administrator should also consider the problems that cooperation may cause.

### Costs

First of all, there are some costs associated with interlibrary cooperation. The main cost may be the additional time that must be devoted to working out agreements and assessing and assigning equitable shares in the cost of cooperative services. That can be a burden for any library, especially a smaller one. Conferences and meetings also represent time that the administrator and staff must spend away from local library service.

There will also be actual cash contributions required for any cooperative venture. Despite probable aggregate and long-term savings, the cooperative project may force the library to make allocations it never anticipated. For example, a cooperative printing operation may be large enough to require the purchase of folding equipment, a printing press, composers and similar equipment.

### Loss of Autonomy

Some loss of autonomy is also certain to occur. While it may be possible to develop an agreement or service that requires no compromise for a local library, eventually there will be pressures to standardize in order to further reduce or control the costs associated with the service. Policies or practices that the board and community have accepted may have to be scrapped in order to continue a service on which the library has become reliant.

While most cooperative services permit one of the participants to drop out, this usually results in the loss of any equity the library has built up in the service. It may not be possible to get that investment out of the service without dissolving the activity, and there would be great pressures from the other participants against that step.

## Political and Financial Repercussions

There could also be political and financial repercussions from cooperative services. For example, reciprocity is often a requirement of participation in a local cooperative system. Residents of a community that supports its library at a relatively low level could then draw upon the better services and resources of a neighboring library, supported at a higher level by its community. The result can be a great deal of resentment among those who have willingly let themselves be more heavily taxed.

In such situations, there would be less incentive for communities to increase support for poorer libraries and less willingness for the residents of wealthier communities to maintain the excellence of their institutions. These concerns are sometimes advanced as reasons for not joining a cooperative system.

# EVALUATING INTERLIBRARY COOPERATION

The administrator and board must evaluate the extent of interlibrary cooperation that is desirable or affordable. There may be additional advantages and disadvantages besides the ones noted in this chapter. Local animosity toward a neighoring community may make cooperative agreements impossible. The policies of local political jurisdictions or legal opinions may prevent them. The library may have sufficient support so that it does not need to consider sharing the cost of various projects.

More likely, however, major improvements in service will require cooperation. In each project the administrator must be careful not to be so involved with the procedures that the original purpose for cooperation is lost. Each project should specify the time for development and implementation. The cost for an individual library to provide the service should be determined, to be used for comparison as the cooperative understanding unfolds. The terms of the participants' responsibilities should be carefully prepared and put in writing, to avoid misunderstandings regarding ownership and long-term financial commitment. These terms should be carefully reviewed with the library board and local city or county officials, so that all parties are aware of local obligations, as well as benefits.

If these steps are followed, there should be far fewer fears and problems resulting from interlibrary cooperation. Not every service is suited to a cooperative approach, but a good administrator will consider cooperation in automation, collection development, staff development, business applications or any application where he or she may lack adequate finances.

## MULTITYPE COOPERATION

This book deals with public library service, and this chapter has focused on cooperation among public libraries. Current trends, however, are toward the involvement of all types of libraries in cooperative agreements. For example, if public libraries can benefit from sharing their resources, why can't these benefits be further increased through the involvement of academic, school and special libraries? Many states have changed library laws to permit the conversion of public library cooperative systems to multitype systems.

Some problems exist in these conversions. For example, a special library serving a private company is not likely to share proprietary resources. Some concern exists as to whether cooperative systems supported by tax funds can legally extend services to benefit privately supported colleges and business libraries. Public libraries that have been receiving services from public library cooperative systems wonder whether the level of support will be decreased if the system must also extend these services to school, academic and special libraries. College libraries fear that research collections designed to support the curriculum and faculty might suffer serious losses if they are accessible to the general population.

Despite these concerns, early evidence from states with multitype cooperation, such as Illinois and New York, indicates that the benefits far outweigh the problems. No library is compelled to lend every item it possesses, and reasonable constraints can be placed by participating libraries. The benefits of multitype cooperation—greatly increased access to the collections of all the participating libraries, increased human resources, the capacity to refer users to special libraries in the geographic area and the increased scale of library service—should be sufficient motivation for this trend to continue.

## SUMMARY

More and more public libraries are becoming involved in cooperative systems, in which libraries that share a common need assume a mutual responsibility to meet that need. Cooperative systems provide a wide variety of services and range from sizable organizations to simple contractual arrangements between two libraries.

The administrator of a library that belongs to a cooperative system must become well acquainted with the system's services, future plans and governance. He or she must also understand the responsibilities and obligations of the member library. When cooperation is based on a direct agreement between two libraries, the administrator should consider a contract to ensure that obligations and services are clearly defined.

The administrator should also be aware of the advantages and disadvantages of cooperation. Benefits include cost savings through economies of scale, increased resources and improved quality of service. Among the hazards of interlibrary cooperation are hidden costs (such as time required to develop agreements and procedures), loss of autonomy, and possible political and financial repercussions.

In evaluating interlibrary cooperation, the administrator should consider the development of clear objectives, a cost comparison with individual implementation of the same service, and written commitments.

The most recent development in interlibrary cooperation is the multitype system, including academic, school and special libraries as well as public libraries. Despite concerns about equal access, levels of support and protection of collections, experience with multitype systems suggests that the benefits are far greater than the problems.

## FOOTNOTE

1. Ruth W. Gregory and Lester L. Stoffel, *Public Libraries in Cooperative Systems* (Chicago: American Library Association, 1971), p. vii.

## SUGGESTIONS FOR FURTHER READING

Markuson, Barbara and Blanche Woolls, eds. *Networks for Networkers: Critical Issues in Cooperative Library Development.* New York: Neal-Schuman Publishers, Inc., 1980.

Martin, Susan K. *Library Networks, 1981-82.* White Plains, NY: Knowledge Industry Publications, Inc., 1980.

Nelson Associates. *Public Library Systems in the United States: A Survey of Multijurisdictional Systems.* Chicago: American Library Association, 1969.

# 11

# Renewal and Growth

At the foundation of public library service is the belief that the institution will enhance the life of the individual and contribute to society as a whole. Indeed, the formal education system has as an established goal the preparation of the individual for a meaningful role in society. The public library is one of the institutions that should participate in this process. It can do so in many ways.

## GOALS AND OPPORTUNITIES

The average adult will change careers at least once, and the needs of the workplace are changing so rapidly that the skills mastered in school, college and graduate school soon become obsolete. Providing tools for continuing professional learning and growth is one role for the public library.

Information is growing at an exponential rate and is becoming the principal "product" of the United States and other nations. Organization and retrieval of this resource is of national importance if our civilization and democracy are to survive in the world. Again, it would seem logical that the public library should play some part in the preservation, utilization and extension of this resource.

This nation has been blessed with a rich cultural heritage, based on the great diversity of our population. In turn, we have created a culture that is influencing all corners of the world. While relatively few communities contain a museum, a gallery or a legitimate theater, most support a public library. The library can not only build an audience for the achievements of the past and present, but can provide the tools to foster creativity and new growth.

Rather than being threatened by new technology, the public library should flourish because of the opportunity technology provides. Computers allow libraries to improve access to information, increase storage capacity, speed information retrieval, and reduce or eliminate routine procedures that have burdened libraries for centuries. New communications technologies, plus the spread of microcomputers, can extend the library's reach into the home, school and workplace economically and conveniently.

## FAILURE FACTORS

Nonetheless, the public library often fails to meet even traditional expectations. There are those who look at decreasing local appropriations and predict the institution's demise. This final chapter examines some of the reasons why public libraries have not achieved their potential and what can be done about it.

### Lack of Financial Support

The most apparent reason for failure is lack of financial support. (Unfortunately, there is also no evidence of a correlation between a high level of financial support and excellence.) At one time the Public Library Association recommended a minimum level of support, as part of its responsibility for setting national standards. That was dropped, along with other quantitative standards, when it became evident that communities differed considerably in their needs and their ability to support library service.

While it is unlikely that a community library receiving $1 per capita will achieve excellence, there are a great many public libraries that possess small collections, limited staff and antiquated facilities, yet deliver outstanding service to their community. Some very large, well-supported institutions provide terrible service.

### Poor Governance

One factor that surely contributes to failure is poor governance. There is a general belief that library trustees should serve short terms so that new blood can be recruited. Length of service, however, is immaterial. It is the commitment a trustee has to the institution that matters. Boards that have difficulty gaining quorums and that conclude their business in 30 minutes are unlikely to have much insight into the quality of service provided by their institution.

## Poor Administration

Certainly the administrator should share the blame for lack of excellence. It is the administrator's job to develop goals and policies and to educate the board, the staff and the community. Too many administrators achieve their position at middle age, undertake a flurry of activity and then retire from active involvement, even though they may continue in that post for another 20 years.

## Staff Problems

The staff cannot be held blameless. Some people enter the library field because they believe it does not represent a challenge. They may fear change, and the library may seem to be the most changeless entity of all.

The career ladder may contribute to staff problems. A creative individual, anxious to specialize in an area of service, may be unable to advance without leaving behind the chosen specialty. Children's service is an example. In the typical public library system, the bottom rung on the ladder is service as a children's librarian in a branch. It may be possible, after 30 years or 20 moves, to advance to a children's coordinator position, but, more likely, advancement opportunities will come in areas other than children's service.

Despite the presumed commitment of libraries to continuing education, the majority of libraries devote almost no money to it. Staff members must pay for additional training out of their own poor salaries or risk becoming obsolete.

A related concern is professional isolation. Because professional conferences are considered junkets by many boards and local budgeting authorities, they are automatically cut from the budget. Since so many librarians work in small, isolated units, they rarely have the chance to gain from meeting with colleagues the breadth of experience and knowledge of trends that would keep them vital and creative.

Then there is the work load. While it may be true that some libraries have ample staff and time for those responsibilities that textbooks say should be performed, statistics reveal steadily increasing levels of reference services, collections, circulation and programming, but almost stagnant staffing levels—sometimes actual decreases. Automation of many of these procedures will certainly contribute to productivity, and some procedures probably ought to be eliminated. (There is a procedural emphasis in the library field which is smothering.) Nonetheless, the staff work load can become so oppressive that genuine burnout occurs.

## Inappropriate Demands from the Public

The public also plays a part in the failure of libraries. While every library should remain responsive to community needs, many institutions are manipulated by community leaders and civic groups into providing services or maintaining facilities that are beyond the capacity of the institution and do not merit the allocation. Examples include providing branches in neighborhoods that are too small and that do not use the facility and the host of special collections, deposited by well-meaning civic groups, that drain personnel, space and other resources sorely needed to satisfy real needs.

## RENEWAL FACTORS

A number of other factors contribute to the inability of many public libraries to reach their potential, but it might be better to examine instead ways to renew the public library.

## Improved Governance

The first of these steps is improved governance. The public library board must be committed to quality services, and the starting point may be the appointing official. If the mayor or county executive uses library board appointments to reward friends or ensure that only sycophants are placed in policy-making positions, then the administrator must convince that official of the role of the library trustee and its importance. If the administrator cannot achieve this directly, then he or she must find someone else who can reach the official.

Once a concerned and committed board exists, the administrator must educate and inform its members. The board will need goals, priorities and clearly understood policies regarding critical services. It must begin to ask questions, and it must gain a sense of mission. Board members should be encouraged to attend trustee conferences and to visit other libraries. The administrator should also publicize their contributions to the library and the community.

## Staff Development

A critical factor in renewal is staff development. The administrator must fight to get increased appropriations for training and conference attendance. Civil service regulations must be stretched to permit staff exchanges and educational leave. Every employee should be assessed in terms of his or her personal career goals and potential. A commitment should then be made to see that those individuals who demonstrate promise get the opportunities to pursue and achieve their goals.

Employees should get recognition for civic and professional achievement. Funds and time should be granted to permit staff to become more active in the community. Supervisory staff should have progressively more advanced managerial training, arranged in concert with local academic institutions. Periodic retreats should be arranged to plan, implement and review programs and service.

Job descriptions, fringe benefits and salary plans should be revised to reflect increasing responsibilities and productivity. Merit increases should not be granted solely for time served but should be based on contributions made to improved services. The library should strive to offer not merely comparable fringe benefits and salaries, but superior levels of compensation based on the excellence of the staff. Personnel policies will require similar overhaul to reflect the increasing responsibility of the staff. For example, expenses for travel associated with improvement of skills should be reimbursable.

Evaluation of personnel and supervisory staff should be based not only on the job description but also on personal work-related goals and objectives that are linked to departmental goals and the library's overall long-range plan. Participation in the critical decisions of the institution should be fostered, with authority for implementation of decisions delegated to those responsible for implementation. Communications with the staff, to discuss board goals and policies and to identify individual staff and unit achievements, should be frequent.

### Experimentation

Experimentation should be fostered. Funds should be sought, either individually by the library or in concert with other libraries and community agencies, to test new services, different formats in the collection and policy changes. The decisions on how such innovations should be implemented and evaluated should be delegated to the staff of the affected units. When the results are shared with the community and the profession, staff members should be recognized for their efforts.

## Improved Community Involvement

In working with the community, the administrator should make better use of the Friends organization and other library-related groups. Besides maintaining strong liaison and communication, the administrator should see that these groups adopt plans, goals and projects that relate to the library's own long-range plan. Representatives from these groups should be involved in the pertinent decisions affecting public service and library development.

The mission of the Friends should be clarified so the group realizes its role in informing the community of the library's services and understands the importance of links with other community and civic groups to broadcast the word further. Staff and Friends should be encouraged to share information about the library with local community groups to which they belong. As a result, the library may become involved in the attainment of local goals.

Individual complaints and suggestions from users should be studied and should receive a prompt response. If policy changes are required, they should be communicated to the administrator and board.

Regular surveys of users and citizens should be undertaken to assess community reaction to changes and to identify needs that are unmet. Often a library will conduct a survey and implement some changes based on community input. However, there is frequently no followup survey to determine the effectiveness of changes after they have been in effect for a reasonable time. Better use should also be made of city, county and regional planning agencies to identify shifts in demographics, planned community developments, and analytical tools that may aid the library in assessing community change.

## ADMINISTRATIVE BURNOUT

A great volume of literature exists today on the hazards of employee burnout. The renewal factors mentioned in the preceding section—improved staff development, exchange programs, merit pay plans, innovation, better employee evaluation programs and long-range planning—as well as more effective use of automation, can counter this problem. Burnout is also a hazard for administrators. While many of the same remedies apply, there are additional alternatives that administrators and boards may wish to consider.

The traditional solution to burnout taken by many administrators is relocation. The opportunity provided by a new setting with different challenges can keep an administrator fresh. Unfortunately, not everyone has the opportunity or the flexibility to adopt this alternative. Moreover, some larger institutions may be so complex, or so troubled, that it would require years before the administrator could cope with the problems effectively.

Many administrators are also "workaholics" and are reluctant to take the same opportunities for self-development that they prescribe for their staff. To preserve their effectiveness, all administrators should have the self-discipline to set aside the time to keep current with the literature and to take advantage of continuing education opportunities. They should also consider exchange and travel as important means of advancing their knowledge of administration. Involvement with professional associations and civic groups, acceptance of consulting assignments, and teaching are additional avenues that will keep a good administrator from going stale.

Library boards play a critical role in ensuring that burnout does not occur, and their regular evaluation of the director's performance should be an opportunity for setting new goals and encouraging the director to further his or her skills.

## THE EVOLVING ROLE OF THE LIBRARY

The primary role of the public library as a provider of resources for education, information and cultural enrichment is likely to remain. Indeed, change and innovation as discussed in this chapter can enhance this role. The library has too great an investment in this function, and this traditional role is too ingrained in the public's consciousness, for change to occur readily. However, the way libraries organize, retrieve and deliver these resources may change.

### Meeting Specialized Needs

Another thing that will not change is the problem of balance between satisfaction of public demand and service to the specialized user. Charles Robinson, the director of the Baltimore County (MD) Public Library, has written and lectured widely about the importance of satisfying the public's demand for current and relevant fiction and nonfiction. Certainly this is important, and a library that does not meet this demand will soon lose much of its clientele. Yet even Robinson acknowledges the importance of satisfying the more specialized needs that will arise in every community and notes that his system has been able to balance its service by drawing upon the extensive research holdings of the Enoch Pratt Free Library in Baltimore.

The needs of the handicapped, the gifted, the scholar, the businessperson and countless others must be satisfied if the entire community is to be well served. If the community is too small or its library too poorly supported to afford this, then these resources can be provided through a cooperative agreement. In many instances even the well-supported library may elect this method, if a special demand is limited.

### Early Childhood/Parenting Centers

Another library role that deserves strengthening, particularly in light of recent concern about the deficiencies of the American educational system, is as an early childhood/parenting center. Public libraries have long served as a starting point in the education of many children. Their attendance at preschool story hours, the individual guidance given by children's librarians and the assistance extended to parents have facilitated the education of millions of young people.

Unfortunately, that has not benefited as many children as it should. Single-parent families and households where both parents work are increasingly common and are likely to increase in the future. As a result, parents have less time to take children to their local library. Busing in many cities also breaks the contact with the neighborhood library that children's librarians can foster through class visits. To counter that, more public libraries must develop "magnet" centers, which, like the concept of the magnet school, are designed to attract children and their parents by focusing on service to families. Extension to day care centers and home day care providers will also have to be made.

### Continuing Education

Better partnership among schools, colleges and libraries should permit more effective continuing education services to adults. Such cooperation is being fostered by the National Endowments for the Arts and the Humanities, as well as state and local agencies. Libraries can perform an invaluable service by introducing adults to a range of information that may lead them on to formal training or degree-based programs. As the pace of change continues in American society, it is likely that the public library will play a growing role in continuing education.

Some cities have witnessed the growth of independent learning programs and educational brokerages, with the library as a key partner and frequently the foundation for the service. Through independent learning exchanges, teachers are placed in contact with individuals seeking tutorial assistance or individual training, and the public library is a logical center for this exchange to take place. Educational brokerages provide individual counseling for adults considering career change or planning to reenter the job market. Libraries can house these centers, provide resources for career exploration and tap online databases containing current information on employment and educational opportunities. Referral to appropriate formal training opportunities can then be made by the brokerage.

**Cultural Opportunities**

As the demands on public funds continue to grow, it will become increasingly difficult for many communities to develop the cultural opportunities common to larger cities. Thus a community's ability to support museums and performing arts groups will lessen at the same time leisure time opportunities and educational levels are increasing. The public library, particularly in the small and medium-sized city, will probably play an important role as a cultural center. In fact, the origins of many museums, art institutes and music associations are linked with the public libraries of many major American cities.

While many large public libraries have long sponsored a variety of cultural programs, there may be greater opportunity for partnership with leading cultural institutions in the future. These organizations are facing severe financial problems and need to develop methods of reaching a larger audience and building support. For example, major city orchestras regularly tour smaller communities in their state; the public library can offer performing space to these groups for chamber music presentations. A similar approach can be applied in theater, art and dance. Public libraries will also play a growing role in the introduction of new cultural formats to the community, such as video art.

**The Library as Information Utility**

The library's role as an information utility in the community should also increase. Reference service is growing at a prodigious rate, and public libraries will need to employ newer technologies such as videotex to permit faster and more comprehensive service. By harnessing the computer and telephone or cable television technology, the public library should be able to build databases pertinent to local needs and draw upon national databases for more specialized information.

Some believe that the explosion of sales for home micro-computers and the ready availability of specialized databases will result in the bypassing of the public library, as individuals go directly to the online services. Experience has shown, however, that using any database requires training in search techniques. While the frequent user with a personal computer may well bypass the public library, the average citizen is likely to seek the assistance of a trained professional.

The emergence of the public library is as an information utility at the local level, linked to a national network, raises the strong possibility that more and more of the library's services may be fee-based. Certainly to fuel the development of these more efficient services, some additional major venture capital will have to be obtained at the local level. Since it is not likely to come from public funds, user fees may play an important part.

## LOCAL, STATE AND FEDERAL ROLES

While it is certain that local taxes will continue to be the major source of local public library revenues in the foreseeable future, state and federal partnership in supporting library services will increase. There are many parallels between libraries and other educational institutions. Already the federal and state governments provide major portions of the support for local public schools. If national policy continues to stress education as the ultimate solution to many of the nation's problems, there may be growth in state and federal support for the local library.

Even today, despite the efforts of several administrations, the federal government remains very much involved in the improvement of local public libraries. The Library Services and Construction Act continues to be a major source of funds for research and innovation. The trend toward multitype cooperation will mean that increasing federal funds will have to be channeled through LSCA to foster resource sharing. As the national economy becomes more and more information-based, this should also encourage the development of special programs on research, use of newer technology and manpower training.

## A State Role for Major Urban Libraries

Major urban public libraries are likely to become state entities. Many states already provide grants to such institutions—including the Detroit Public Library, the Chicago Public Library, the Free Library of Philadelphia and the Enoch Pratt Free Library (Baltimore)—to support wider access for reference and research. Many cities could not support the excellence of their central library collections without state subsidy and reimbursement for the backup service they provide. While the neighborhood libraries of these cities are likely to remain locally supported, the central libraries will increasingly function as members of a state network of resource centers open to everyone in that state.

## Statewide Access

One of the goals of many state library agencies is statewide access to local public libraries. To encourage this, state grants are being made directly to local libraries. State grants are also fueling interlibrary loan services and automated networks essential for the sharing of these resources. It is likely that these efforts will accelerate in the coming years to permit everyone in a state to gain access to information, regardless of the level of local support for the community library.

## Local Control

Growing support from states and the federal government will impose more controls and requirements upon the local public library, creating some problems for governance and administration. However, the evolving partnership will still leave the community with majority control over its public library. The concept of local control of this institution is too deeply ingrained to be easily and rapidly altered.

## PUBLIC EXPECTATIONS

There has long been a correlation between educational levels and library usage. It is likely that public library usage will continue to grow as long as our society continues to place high value upon education. The younger generation is also likely to have higher expectations of service from their public library.

Many children are now taught computer science in elementary school. They will attend colleges and universities that use interactive computer-assisted instruction and draw upon rich and highly specialized collections to prepare students for new careers. Upon graduation, they will enter fields that will be very information-conscious. When they visit their local public library, they will expect something more than a rack of bestsellers and *Popular Mechanics*.

At the same time, a growing portion of the population is information-poor. Unable to compete for the best jobs, they will still be seeking a way out of ghetto existence and underemployment. They will demand assistance from governmental agencies, and it will become increasingly important that public libraries provide the bridge over the handicaps of illiteracy and poverty.

Some changes will have to be made in traditional forms of library service if public libraries are to be effective in serving this part of the community. Much of the impetus of the 1970s has been lost as national priorities have shifted. Society cannot afford to neglect any portion of the population without eventually paying a terrible price.

## IMPORTANCE OF LEADERSHIP

In the recent bestseller *In Search of Excellence: Lessons from America's Best-Run Companies,*[1] the authors identified eight factors that their research led them to believe were common to the success of a number of major corporations. These were:

• bias for action;

• maintenance of close ties to customers;

• enhancement of productivity by emphasis upon respect for the individual employee;

• granting sufficient autonomy among employees to foster entrepreneurship;

• chief executives who keep their hands in the daily operations of the organization;

• sticking to the business the company knows best;

• keeping the organizational form simple and the staff lean; and

• decentralized decision making on local policies and centralized control over corporation issues.

In the authors' research, however, the one element that surfaces most often is the leadership exercised by the chief executive officer. A truly great administrator is one whose influence fosters leadership throughout the organization. No one person has the ability to control all aspects of an institution, particularly one as complex as a public library. Achieving excellence requires a variety of skills and opinions from many people, but all must reach consensus and commitment on the important goals.

The public library field has known many great individuals who have brought innovation, focused attention upon the critical issues and built rich collections to the benefit of subsequent generations, but the greatest have been those who have nurtured leadership among all those with whom they worked.

This book has emphasized staff development, effective relationships with governance and public officials, building community support, and mastering the techniques of finance and personnel administration. The value of innovation and the adoption of newer technology have also been stressed. But even more important than these is the quality of leadership that each administrator must develop. Individuals are not simply born with leadership capacity. Rather, it comes from the experience an individual gains in his or her career. It comes from the lessons learned from people that the administrator works with. It comes from the pain that is felt when plans fail, when projects collapse. It is gained when the risk succeeds and when the goal is reached.

Leadership is earned by those who are willing to take risks and to commit their time and talent, and who have the courage to fail. If a library administrator has that capacity, the library will succeed and fulfill its promise.

## SUMMARY

The public library is based on a capacity to renew the community it serves. It has the potential to facilitate continuing education, foster cultural development and draw upon newer technology to achieve those ends. The library often fails in its mission because of a number of factors, which include disinterested governance, moribund management and a staff that may be overworked, undertrained and stagnating. The public may place unreasonable demands upon the institution, and there may be inadequate support to permit the library to develop new services and resources.

Ways of correcting these problems include the education and development of a more commited governance and intensive staff development. More effective use of community organizations and better community assessment will also aid in renewing the organization.

The role of the public library is evolving. It continues to provide resources to satisfy both general demand and special needs. It can also become an early childhood/parenting center, a continuing education agency, a cultural center and an information utility. Partnerships among local, state, and federal governments are evolving to support and develop the local library. Public expectations about library services are also rising as educational levels increase. Above all, the success of the library will depend on the administrator's leadership in marshaling the resources of the institution.

## FOOTNOTE

1. Thomas J. Peters and Robert H. Waterman Jr., *In Search of Excellence: Lessons from America's Best-Run Companies* (New York: Harper & Row, Publishers, Inc., 1982), p. 13.

## SUGGESTIONS FOR FURTHER READING

*The ALA Yearbook 1982: A Review of Library Events.* Chicago: American Library Association, 1982.

*Bowker Annual of Library and Book Trade Information 1983,* 28th edition. New York: R.R. Bowker Co., 1983.

Riggs, Donald E. *Library Leadership: Visualizing the Future.* Phoenix, AZ: Oryx Press, 1982.

# Selected Bibliography

*The ALA Yearbook 1982: A Review of Library Events.* Chicago: American Library Association, 1982.

Alley, Brian and Jennifer Cargill. *Keeping Track of What You Spend: The Librarian's Guide to Simple Bookkeeping.* Phoenix, AZ: Oryx Press, 1982.

Altman, Ellen, ed. *Local Public Library Administration,* second edition. Chicago: American Library Association, 1980.

American Library Association. *The Personnel Manual.* Chicago: American Library Association, 1977.

——. *Personnel Organization and Procedure: A Manual Suggested for Use in Public Libraries,* second edition. Chicago: American Library Association, 1968.

——. Library Technology Project. *Development of Performance Standards for Binding Used in Libraries.* Chicago: American Library Association, 1966.

*American Library Directory.* New York: R.R. Bowker Co./Jacques Cattell Press, annual.

Bahr, Alice Harrison. *Book Theft and Library Security Systems, 1981-82.* White Plains, NY: Knowledge Industry Publications, Inc., 1981.

Bobinski, George S. *Carnegie Libraries: Their History and Impact on American Public Library Development.* Chicago: American Library Association, 1969.

Bogart, Gary L., ed. *Public Library Catalog.* Bronx, NY: H.W. Wilson Co., 1979.

Bommer, Michael R. and Ronald W. Chorba. *Decision Making for Library Management.* White Plains, NY: Knowledge Industry Publications, Inc., 1982.

Boss, Richard W. *Automating Library Acquisitions: Issues and Outlook.* White Plains, NY: Knowledge Industry Publications, Inc., 1982.

— — —. *Grant Money and How to Get It: A Handbook for Librarians.* New York: R.R. Bowker Co., 1980.

— — —. *The Library Manager's Guide to Automation,* 2nd edition. White Plains, NY: Knowledge Industry Publications, Inc., 1984.

*Bowker Annual of Library and Book Trade Information 1983,* 28th edition New York: R.R. Bowker Co., 1983.

Bowler, Roberta, ed. *Local Public Library Administration.* Chicago: American Library Association, 1964.

Breivik, Patricia and E. Burr Gibson. *Funding Alternatives for Libraries.* Chicago: American Library Association, 1979.

Brooks, Jean S. and David L. Reich. *The Public Library in Non-Traditional Education.* Homewood, IL: ETC Publications, 1974.

Brown, Eleanor Frances. *Bookmobiles and Bookmobile Service.* Metuchen, NJ: Scarecrow Press, Inc., 1967.

— — —. *Modern Branch Libraries and Libraries in Systems.* Metuchen, NJ: Scarecrow Press, Inc., 1970.

Carter, Ruth C. and Scott Bruntjen. *Data Conversion.* White Plains, NY: Knowledge Industry Publications, Inc., 1983.

Chen, Ching-Chih. *Zero-Base Budgeting in Library Management: A Manual for Librarians.* Phoenix, AZ: Oryx Press, 1980.

Cockerell, Douglas. *Bookbinding and the Care of Books,* 8th edition. London: Pitman Books, Ltd., 1978.

Cohen, Aaron and Elaine Cohen. *Designing and Space Planning for Libraries: A Behavioral Guide.* New York: R.R. Bowker Co., 1979.

Corry, Emmett. *Grants for Libraries: A Guide to Public and Private Funding Programs and Proposal Writing Techniques.* Littleton, CO: Libraries Unlimited, Inc., 1982.

Creth, Sheila and Frederick Duda. *Personnel Administration in Libraries.* New York: Neal-Schuman Publishers, Inc., 1981.

Cunha, George David Martin. *Conservation of Library Materials: A Manual and Bibliography on the Care, Repair, and Restoration of Library Materials.* Metuchen, NJ: Scarecrow Press, Inc., 1967.

Dewey, Patrick R. *Public Access Microcomputers: A Handbook for Librarians.* White Plains, NY: Knowledge Industry Publications, Inc., 1984.

Dolnick, Sandy, ed. *Friends of Libraries Sourcebook.* Chicago: American Library Association, 1980.

Drott, M. Carl. "Random Sampling: A Tool for Research." *College & Research Libraries,* March 1969.

Edsall, Marian S. *Library Promotion Handbook.* Phoenix, AZ: Oryx Press, 1980.

Evans, G. Edward. *Developing Library Collections.* Littleton, CO: Libraries Unlimited, Inc., 1979.

*Fact Book of the American Public Library,* compiled by Herbert Goldhor. Occasional Papers No. 150. Urbana, IL: University of Illinois Graduate School of Library Science, 1981.

Fayen, Emily Gallup. *The Online Catalog: Improving Public Access to Library Materials.* White Plains, NY: Knowledge Industry Publications, Inc., 1983.

Fenwick, Sara Innis. "Library Service to Children and Young People." *Library Trends,* July 1976.

Fosdick, Howard. *Computer Basics for Librarians and Information Specialists.* Arlington, VA: Information Resources Press, 1981.

Foster, Donald L. *Managing the Catalog Department,* 2nd edition. Metuchen, NJ: Scarecrow Press, Inc., 1982.

Futas, Elizabeth, ed. *Library Acquisition Policies and Procedures.* Phoenix, AZ: Oryx Press, 1977.

Garvey, Mona. *Library Public Relations.* New York: H.W. Wilson Co., 1980.

Gaudy, Frank W. "General Revenue Sharing and Public Libraries, an Estimate of Fiscal Impact." *Library Quarterly,* January 1982.

Geddes, Andrew, ed. "Current Trends in Branch Libraries." *Library Trends,* April 1966.

Getz, Malcolm. *Public Libraries: An Economic View.* Baltimore, MD: The Johns Hopkins University Press, 1980.

Gregory, Ruth W. and Lester L. Stoffel. *Public Libraries in Cooperative Systems.* Chicago: American Library Association, 1971.

Grosch, Audrey N. *Minicomputers in Libraries, 1981-82: The Era of Distributed Systems.* White Plains, NY: Knowledge Industry Publications, Inc., 1981.

Johnson, Elmer. *A History of Libraries in the Western World,* 2nd edition. Metuchen, NJ: Scarecrow Press, Inc., 1970.

Jones, Clara S., ed. *Public Library Information and Referral Service.* Syracuse, NY: Gaylord Bros., Inc., 1978.

Josey, E.J., ed. *Libraries in the Political Process.* Phoenix, AZ: Oryx Press, 1980.

Katz, Bill and Anne Clifford. *Reference and Information Services.* Metuchen, NJ: Scarecrow Press, Inc., 1982.

Kenney, Brigitte L., ed. *Cable for Information Delivery: A Guide for Librarians, Educators and Cable Professionals.* White Plains, NY: Knowledge Industry Publications, Inc., 1983.

Kohn, Rita and K. Teppler. *You Can Do It: A PR Skills Manual for Librarians.* Metuchen, NJ: Scarecrow Press, Inc., 1981.

Kotler, Philip. *Marketing for Nonprofit Organizations,* second edition. Englewood Cliffs, NJ: Prentice-Hall, Inc., 1982.

Kronus, Carol L. and Linda Crowe, eds. *Libraries and Neighborhood Information Centers.* Urbana, IL: University of Illinois Graduate School of Library Science, 1972.

Ladenson, Alex. *Library Laws and Legislation in the United States.* Metuchen, NJ: Scarecrow Press, Inc., 1982.

Ladley, Winifred, ed. "Current Trends in Branch Libraries." *Library Trends,* July 1963.

Lancaster, F. Wilfrid. *Libraries and Librarians in an Age of Electronics.* Arlington, VA: Information Resources Press, 1982.

Leerburger, Benedict A. *Marketing the Library.* White Plains, NY: Knowledge Industry Publications, Inc., 1982.

Lenz, Millicent and Ramona Mahood, eds. *Young Adult Literature: Background and Criticism.* Chicago: American Library Association, 1980.

Lushington, Nolan and Willis N. Mills Jr. *Libraries Designed for Users.* Hamden, CT: Shoe String Press, Inc., 1980.

Lynch, Mary Jo. *Financing Online Search Services in Publicly Supported Libraries: The Report of an ALA Survey.* Chicago: American Library Association, 1981.

Mallery, Mary S. and Ralph E. DeVore. *A Sign System for Libraries.* Chicago: American Library Association, 1982.

Markuson, Barbara and Blanche Woolls, eds. *Networks for Networkers: Critical Issues in Cooperative Library Development.* New York: Neal-Schuman Publishers, Inc., 1980.

Marshall, John David, ed. *American Library History Reader.* Hamden, CT: Shoe String Press, Inc., 1961.

Martin, Allie Beth, coord. *A Strategy for Public Library Change.* Chicago: American Library Association, 1972.

Martin, Murray S. *Issues in Personnel Management.* Greenwich, CT: JAI Press, Inc. 1981.

Martin, Susan K. *Library Networks, 1981-82.* White Plains, NY: Knowledge Industry Publications, Inc., 1980.

Mason, Ellsworth. *Mason on Library Buildings.* Metuchen, NJ: Scarecrow Press, Inc., 1980.

Mason, Marilyn Gell. *The Federal Role in Library and Information Services.* White Plains, NY: Knowledge Industry Publications, Inc., 1983.

Matthews, Joseph R. "The Automated Circulation System Marketplace: Active and Heating Up." *Library Journal* 107(3):233-235 (February 2, 1984).

McCarthy, E. Jerome. *Basic Marketing: A Managerial Approach,* sixth edition. Homewood, IL: Richard D. Irwin, Inc., 1978.

McClure, Charles R. and A.R. Samuels, eds. *Strategies for Library Administration: Concepts and Approaches.* Littleton, CO: Libraries Unlimited, Inc., 1982.

Morrow, Carolyn Clark. *The Preservation Challenge: A Guide to Conserving Library Materials.* White Plains, NY: Knowledge Industry Publications, Inc., 1983.

Nadler, Myra, ed. *How to Start an Audio-visual Collection.* Metuchen, NJ: Scarecrow Press, Inc., 1978.

National Center for Educational Statistics. *Preliminary Report. Library General Information Survey. LIBGIS III: Public Libraries, 1977-78.* Washington, DC: NCES, 1982.

National Center for Educational Statistics. *Statistics of Public Libraries, 1974 (LIBGIS I).* Washington, DC: Government Printing Office, 1978.

Nelson Associates. *Public Library Systems in the United States: A Survey of Multijurisdictional Systems.* Chicago: American Library Association, 1969.

O'Reilly, Robert C. and Marjorie I. *Librarians and Labor Relations: Employment Under Union Contracts.* Westport, CT: Greenwood Press, 1981.

Palmour, Vernon E. *A Planning Process for Public Libraries.* Chicago: American Library Association, 1980.

Peters, Thomas J. and Robert H. Waterman, Jr. *In Search of Excellence: Lessons from America's Best-Run Companies.* New York: Harper and Row Publishers, Inc., 1982.

Pierce, William S. *Furnishing the Library Interior.* New York: Marcel Dekker, Inc., 1980.

Public Library Association, Principles Task Force. *The Public Library: Democracy's Resource. A Statement of Principles* Chicago: Public Library Association, 1982.

Public Library Association, Starter List Committee. *Books for Public Libraries,* 3rd edition. Chicago: American Library Association, 1982.

Riggs, Donald E. *Library Leadership: Visualizing the Future.* Phoenix, AZ: Oryx Press, 1982.

Rizzo, John. *Management for Librarians.* Westport, CT: Greenwood Press, 1980.

Rochell, Carlton, ed. *Wheeler and Goldhor's Practical Administration of Public Libraries,* revised edition. New York: Harper & Row, Publishers, Inc., 1981.

Sager, Donald J. *The American Public Library.* Columbus, OH: Online Computer Library Center, 1982.

— — —. *Participatory Management in Libraries.* Metuchen, NJ: Scarecrow Press, Inc., 1982.

— — —. *A Public Library Administrator's Planning Guide to Automation.* Columbus, OH: Online Computer Library Center, Inc., 1983.

Shera, Jesse H. *Foundations of the Public Library: The Origins of the Public Library Movement in New England, 1629-1855.* Chicago: University of Chicago Press, 1949.

Sherman, Steve. *ABC's of Library Promotion,* second edition. Metuchen, NJ: Scarecrow Press, Inc., 1980.

Sigel, Efrem, et al. *The Future of Videotext.* White Plains, NY: Knowledge Industry Publications, Inc., 1983.

Stanfield, Jonathan. *Fort Vancouver Regional Library: Electronic Information Systems Feasibility Study. Final Report.* Kirkland, WA: Axon Associates, 1982.

Talarzyk, W. Wayne and Richard E. Widding II. *Introduction to and Issues with Videotex: Implications for Marketing.* Columbus, OH: Ohio State University College of Administrative Science, 1981.

Turick, Dorothy. *Community Information Services in Libraries.* LJ Special Report No. 5. New York: R.R. Bowker Co., 1978.

U.S. Department of the Interior, Bureau of Education. *Public Libraries in the United States of America; Their History, Condition and Management: Special Report, Part I.* Washington, DC: Government Printing Office, 1876.

U.S. Office of Management and Budget. *Catalog of Federal Domestic Assistance,* 17th edition. Washington, DC: Government Printing Office, 1983.

U.S. White House Conference on Library and Information Services. *Summary* (of Proceedings). Washington, DC: U.S. Government Printing Office, 1980.

Van Zant, Nancy, ed. *Personnel Policies and Procedures in Libraries.* New York: Neal-Schuman Publishers, Inc., 1980.

Wilkins, Barratt. *Survey of State Library Agencies, 1977.* Occasional Papers No. 142. Urbana, IL: University of Illinois Graduate School of Library Science, 1976.

Woods, Lawrence A. and Nolan F. Pope. *The Librarian's Guide to Microcomputer Technology and Applications.* White Plains, NY: Knowledge Industry Publications, Inc., 1983.

Young, Virginia G. *The Library Trustee: A Practical Guidebook,* third edition. New York: R.R. Bowker Co., 1978.

Zweizig, Douglas and Eleanor Jo Rodger. *Output Measures for Public Libraries: A Manual of Standardized Procedures.* Chicago: American Library Association, 1982.

# Index

## ABOUT THE AUTHOR

Donald J. Sager is director of the Milwaukee Public Library and the Milwaukee County Federated Library System. His long and varied career as a public library administrator includes positions as Commissioner of the Chicago Public Library and director of the Elmhurst (IL), Columbus and Franklin County (OH) and Mobile (AL) Public Libraries. He was a Distinguished Visiting Scholar at OCLC in 1982 and president of the Public Library Association in 1982-83.

Mr. Sager is the author of *A Public Library Administrator's Planning Guide to Automation* and *Participatory Management in Libraries,* among other books. He has published more than 50 articles in professional journals and is active as a speaker and consultant. He holds a B.S. in English and an M.S. in Library Science from the University of Wisconsin.